WIRING

WIRING

BASIC REPAIRS
ADVANCED PROJECTS

MORT SCHULTZ

CREATIVE HOMEOWNER PRESS®

A DIVISION OF FEDERAL MARKETING CORPORATION,
24 PARK WAY, UPPER SADDLE RIVER, NEW JERSEY 07458

Manufactured in United States of America

Current Printing (last digit)
17 16 15 14 13

Editorial Director: Shirley M. Horowitz
Editor: Gail N. Kummings
Art Direction and Design: Léone Lewensohn
Illustrator: Norman Nuding

Technical Review and Assistance: Kenneth
Rademacher, Electrical Engineer; Orval Bequest,
Master Electrician, Milwaukee Area Technical
College

ISBN: 0-932944-38-8 (paperback)
ISBN: 0-932944-37-X (hardcover)
LC: 81-67293

CREATIVE HOMEOWNER PRESS®
BOOK SERIES
A DIVISION OF FEDERAL
MARKETING CORPORATION
24 PARK WAY,
UPPER SADDLE RIVER, NJ 07458

FOREWORD

Many do-it-yourselfers do not give a second thought to doing repairs or projects around their homes, until it comes to electricity. Then, confidence ceases and professionals are called to do the work. More is the pity, because many homeowners are as capable as many professional electricians. Perhaps the home do-it-yourselfer shies away from electricity because he or she feels uncomfortable dealing with something that cannot be seen, especially when that something is an element that can injure or kill.

It is not that replacing a switch or wiring a lamp is more difficult than, say, replacing a sink or paneling a room. Surprisingly, the opposite is true. Electrical repairs and electrical projects can be as easy to do as anything else—in many cases, much easier. In fact, the most difficult aspects have nothing to do with electricity. They involve opening and closing up walls before and after doing advanced projects.

This book provides simple step-by-step instructions for electrical repairs and projects. The first four chapters cover most common repairs and projects you may attempt in your home. Chapters 5 through 8 cover basic electrical projects that work with the system of switches, outlets, fixtures and circuits in your home. Chapters 9 through 12 introduce projects that usually require extending the existing circuits in your home. When browing through Chapters 9 through 12, you will finds suggestions for interesting projects. After using the book to make basic repairs, you might be anxious to try your skills with something more advanced.

Interspersed throughout the chapters you will find discussions of electrical terms and principles. These are presented as aids to a basic understanding of your electrical system and of the safety recommendations made in every chapter. Even a novice needs to know what all those abbreviations mean so that he or she can protect against shock, fire and damaged appliances. However, this book is not intended to make you a professional electrician. Therefore, you will find notations every so often that indicate the need to consult a professional for certain procedures. In some areas of the country, local codes require that you have advanced work inspected by a professional once a project is complete.

As easy as this work can be, don't forget that electricity is dangerous and must be treated with respect. Respecting electricity involves turning off a switch or unscrewing a fuse, and testing to make sure the circuit is dead. Use quality materials that bear a UL label and are appropriate for your project. Then, after doing a job, check your work carefully against the information in this book before restoring electrical power to the circuit.

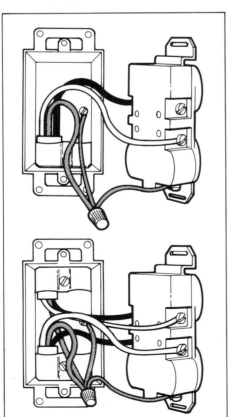

CONTENTS

SIMPLE WIRING REPAIRS

BASIC WIRING PROJECTS

ADVANCED WIRING PROJECTS

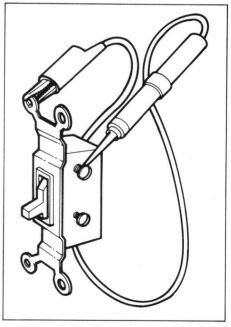

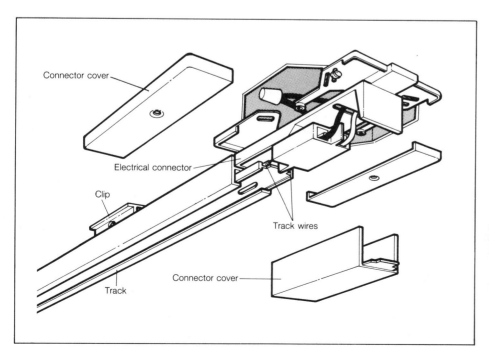

Connector cover

Electrical connector

Clip

Track wires

Connector cover

Track

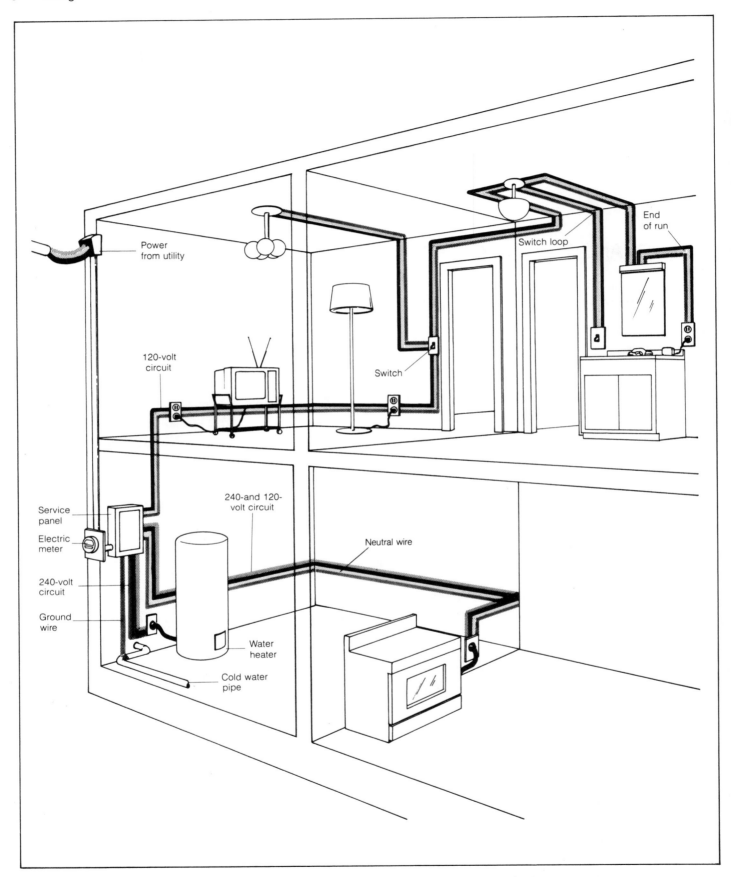

Power from utility

120-volt circuit

Switch

Switch loop

End of run

Service panel

Electric meter

240-volt circuit

Ground wire

240- and 120-volt circuit

Neutral wire

Water heater

Cold water pipe

This simplification of a house wiring system shows how power from the utility company is split into 240- and 120-volt circuits at the service panel. In the circuit wiring, black (or red) wires are "hot," or power-carrying, wires. White wire is neutral. The ground wire is bare or green. All switches and outlets are grounded to their junction boxes, and the service panel is grounded to a cold water pipe. In case of a short circuit, the circuit ground wire carries excess current to the service panel; from there the current passes out of the house.

There are any number of reasons for the reluctance of a homeowner do-it-yourselfer to work with electricity. One is an element of fear. Electricity is dangerous—even deadly—if not properly handled. The safety rules necessary to electrical work cannot be ignored. Another barrier is terminology. The scientific "jargon" is unfamiliar to us, so we shy away from this type of work. The result is that electricity seems mysterious to most of us.

However, the cost of a professional electrician is just the spur most of us need in order to learn more about this "mysterious" element. In addition, the more you know about electricity, the safer you will be. Knowledge is the best way to make electricity "unmagical."

RULES AND REGULATIONS
Local Building Codes
When anyone does electrical work, procedures and materials are governed by local building codes. Codes vary from one locality to the next. Building departments may prohibit the use of a certain type of electrical cable or require a particular size wiring or a minimum number of circuits. Contact your municipal building inspector to determine the wiring requirements that the town places on professional electricians. You also may be required to have an official inspect your work after it has been completed, to be sure it conforms to specifications.

The Purpose of the National Electrical Code
Anyone planning to do more than superficial electrical repairs in a house or condominium should be acquainted with the National Electrical Code (NEC), which spells out safe, functional electrical pro-

cedures to follow. The Code, which is updated every three years, specifies as its purpose, "The safeguarding of persons and of buildings and their contents from hazards arising from the use of electricity for light, heat, power, radio, signaling, and other purposes."

The NEC does not, in itself, carry the weight of law. However, most states and municipalities conform to the specifications laid down by the Code or add to them. The NEC does not provide step-by-step instructions on how to do electrical work. Instead, it states approved methods for doing electric wiring and indicates proper materials.

If you expect to do advanced electrical work, become familiar with those sections of the National Electrical Code that apply to your projects. To do so obtain a copy of the Code by writing the National Fire Protection Association, 470 Atlantic Ave., Boston, MA 02210. There is a fee. In Canada, the Canada Electrical Code serves the same purpose as the National Electrical Code in the United States.

UL Ratings
Electrical parts that you purchase for any project should bear the "UL" symbol. "UL" refers to the Underwriters' Laboratories, which is an independent non-profit organization that acts as a watchdog over electric equipment. Manufacturers of electric products and components submit their devices to UL for testing. When a product or component passes tests, indicating it meets minimum safety standards when used for the purposes for which it is intended, the manufacturer can then use the UL symbol on the item. If there is a question in your mind as to whether a device you are going to use has been listed

by the Underwriters' Laboratories, ask the Public Information Office, Underwriters' Laboratories, Inc., 207 East Ohio Street, Chicago, Illinois 60611.

THE COMPLETE CIRCUIT
Electric Company Service
A circuit is defined as a closed path over which electricity moves from the source of supply, to outlets, and back again to the source of supply, and on, and on, and on. Electricity reaches your home through a service entrance by means of overhead or underground conductors. A conductor is a wire (it may also be a bar or strip of metal) that offers minimum resistance to the flow of electricity. If service entrance conductors are buried, they are encased in metal pipe called conduit, which protects conductors from moisture.

Electricity flows from the service entrance through conductors to the electric meter, and from there to the fuse or circuit breaker box inside the house. The fuse or circuit breaker box is also called the service box or service panel.

The utility company is responsible for everything from the power-plant up to the point where the wires touch the house, and for the meter. You are responsible for the remaining wiring.

Two-Wire vs. Three-Wire Systems
Two-wire systems. Most homes built before World War II had, and may still have, two-conductor service. One conductor carries 120 volts of electricity, while the other is a neutral conductor having zero voltage. With this service, the home is limited in the number and type of electrical appliances that can be used. Even if the electric company increased the amount of service by running in a third

power line to the home, antiquated wiring in the home itself still would not allow use of many modern-day electrical conveniences. The only way to change this situation is to tear out the old wiring and install wiring that is able to handle a greater load.

Three-wire service. Since World War II, most homes have been wired to meet the demands of modern electrical living. Typically, three-conductor service is provided. Two of the conductors are live, or "hot," and the third is the neutral conductor. There are 120 volts between the hot conductors and the neutral conductor, and 240 volts between the two hot conductors. This provides a home with sufficient electrical capability to operate lights and small appliances, which generally require only 120-volt service, and also to operate major appliances, which need 240-volt service.

The neutral wire. The neutral wire in three-wire service serves the same purpose as in two-conductor service. The neutral conductor from the utility is connected at the fuse or circuit breaker box to what is called a neutral bus bar. Attached to the bus bar is a ground wire, which attaches to a cold water pipe or metal rod buried in the earth. This neutral bus then provides a common connection for the neutral conductors in the home wiring, to allow current to complete its circuit without interruption.

In summary electricity involves the flow of electricity from the power plant into the

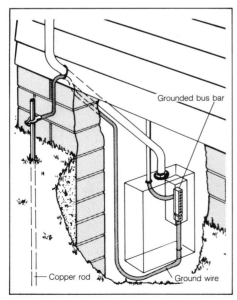

The wiring in some homes connects the ground system to a steel or copper rod driven in a minimum of 8 ft. into the earth.

home to the fuse or circuit breaker box. At the fuse or circuit breaker box, electricity branches off to outlets throughout the home, where it does its job of making electric lights and appliances work.

Electricity, after completing its travel through the hot wires, returns through neutral wires of each branch circuit to the service entrance neutral conductor, and then returns to the power plant where once again it begins its circuitous route. The neutral wire is not intended to carry live current.

Electrical Terms
An understanding of several terms will permit you to speak the same language as those who supply electrical equipment needed for many of the projects. The terms primarily refer to measurements of electrical energy. Knowing the meanings of terms will also allow you to interpret technical data printed on components such as switches or receptacles. Most importantly, applying the knowledge attained through an understanding of these terms will enable you to make safe installations of electrical equipment. The three basic terms are voltage, ohm and ampere. All three are interrelated.

Voltage, volt. Voltage, or volt, is the unit of measurement that expresses the amount of electromotive force, or pressure, that starts electric current moving and keeps it moving. One volt equals the amount of pressure required to move one ampere through a wire that possesses a resistance of one ohm.

The voltage in most of the outlets in your home is maintained at between 110 and 120 volts, with the exception of special outlets for a major appliance such as an electric stove or a clothes dryer. Outlets for such appliances are wired to deliver 220 to 240 volts. As a safety measure, these outlets are designed to accept only specially shaped plugs. Unless you have a problem in the home's circuitry, the voltage level remains consistent at every outlet. When your lights dim or brighten, the decrease or increase in voltage is due to an unusual circumstance, such as a storm.

Although the service supplied to most homes by the electric company is 120/240 volts, not all homes utilize the 240 volt availability. If you are uncertain about the level of your service, call your electric company. The larger service is highly recommended, given the electrical demands

of most households. However, do not attempt to increase the service yourself. This work requires the services of a professional electrician.

Ohm, ohmage, resistance. An ohm, which is commonly referred to as *resistance* and less commonly as *ohmage,* is a measurement of a conductor's resistance to current, or electrical flow. Every conductor offers resistance that impedes current, to a greater or lesser degree. There is no known conductor that is perfect (has zero resistance to current). The degree of conductor's resistance depends upon such factors as its length, its diameter and the material from which it is made. Wood, for instance, offers a great deal more resistance to electrical flow than metal. Some metals offer more resistance than others.

The electrical resistance of the wiring in your house depends upon the thickness and length of each wire. Thick wires offer less resistance; thin wires offer more. A long wire offers more resistance than a short one. However, the resistance of the wiring itself is only a small fraction of the total resistance built into a circuit, for the appliances and lights attached to the circuit also offer resistance to the flow of electrical current.

The resistance of a light or an appliance determines how much current will flow through it and, consequently, through the circuit wiring. Since the voltage in the wire remains constant, as you turn on more lights and appliances, the resistance lessens and more current will flow. In other words, decreased resistance results in an increase in current.

Ampere, amperage, amp. An ampere, amperage, or amp is a unit of measurement that defines the rate of electrical flow. Amperes are measured in terms of the number of electrons flowing through a given point in a conductor in one second when electrons are under a pressure of one volt and the conductor has a resistance of one ohm. A conductor is rated according to how much amperage can flow through it in one second, much the same as a pipe is rated according to how many gallons of water can flow through it in one minute.

Household circuits are described in terms of the number of amps—15, 20, 30 or more—that they can safely handle. Some appliances, although not all, are described in terms of the number of amps of current they require to operate correctly. Homes with 120/240 service typically have up to 200 amps of power available to them.

Wattage, watts. Wattage can be discussed in two ways. All appliances are rated in terms of the number of watts they use per hour. The information is included on a metal plate on all appliances, or is printed on lights and fixtures in some manner. A 100-watt light bulb consumes 100-watts of energy per hour, converting the energy to heat and light. A freezer consumes between 300 and 588 watts of energy per hour.

Use these figures to help you determine how much wattage is being used on a given circuit. If you multiply the volts times the amps in a circuit, you will find out how many watts are available for use in that circuit. This is important if you wish to add appliances, outlets or switches to a circuit.

WORKING WITH THE SERVICE PANEL

No matter how simple or advanced your project, you need to know how to handle your service panel. The service panel is also called the fuse box or circuit breaker box. Delivering electricity from the outside to the inside of the home, the service entrance cable from the electric meter terminates here. The electricity is then parceled out to the different areas of the house by means of branch circuits.

Circuit Breakers and Fuses

As previously described, a circuit is a path

This panel's circuits are protected by conventional fuses. The size of the fuse is dictated in part by the size of the circuit wiring.

that electric current follows as it flows from a source to components that use electricity, and then back to the source. Your home has fuses or circuit breakers, or maybe both, as circuit protectors. Fuses and circuit breakers act as safety devices to shut off electrical service when a circuit is overloaded or there is a short circuit.

In most homes, circuit breakers usually protect all circuits of the house, while fuses give added protection to major current-drawing equipment such as a well pump or a clothes dryer. In other words, a given circuit may be protected by both a circuit breaker and a fuse. Such a circuit is said to have redundant protective features. This redundancy is often necessary, since there is a chance of major damage to equipment if a circuit breaker or fuse fails to interrupt current during an emergency. Since fuses and circuit breakers have different response times, if one protective device doesn't respond quickly enough, there is a backup to protect the equipment.

Special cartridge fuses protect the service panel itself. These fuses carry a much higher voltage level than ordinary fuses.

Main circuit protection. In addition to the individual protection built into every circuit in your home, the main circuit bringing electricity into the house is also equipped with a protective device, in the form of a main fuse or main circuit breaker. When deactivated, this device shuts off electrical power in the entire house.

Recurring circuit interruption. Fuses or circuit breakers interrupt current flow in a circuit when a condition arises that could start a fire or that presents the danger of shock. Before replacing a fuse or resetting

a circuit breaker, determine and repair the cause of the power failure. If you replace a fuse or reset a circuit breaker without remedying the cause, the failure will recur.

Caution: If the power failure was recent and occurred as a piece of equipment was in use, do not touch the metal end of the fuse. It may be hot. Let the fuse cool before testing.

Types of Fuses

There are two main types of fuses: plug and cartridge. Plug fuses are more common, so let's discuss them first.

Plug fuses. Plug fuses contain a small wire that melts or disintegrates when a circuit is overloaded or a short circuit occurs. There are three types of plug fuses: standard, Type S, and time-delay.

Fuses come in two styles. Ordinary fuses look like light bulbs. Compare the shape with the Type S fuse sitting on the box ledge.

A standard fuse. A standard fuse has a base shaped similarly to the base of a light bulb. The fuse screws into a socket in the fuse box, in the same way that a bulb screws into a lamp socket.

A Type S fuse. This fuse is the same as a standard fuse, except for one notable difference. A Type S fuse consists of two parts, the fuse itself and a socket adapter. The adapter screws into and becomes part of the socket in the fuse box. Do not remove the adapter unless it shows signs of being defective, such as cracking or discoloration. The other part, the fuse itself,

A Type S fuse comes in two parts. The specially shaped shank of the fuse fits into a special adapter in the service panel.

screws into the adapter. Threads of a particular size (ampere) Type S fuse are designed to be screwed into threads of the same size adapter and no other. For example, a 15-ampere Type S fuse fits only a 15-ampere Type S fuse adapter; a 20-amp Type S fuse cannot be substituted for a 15-amp one. A fuse of varying size will not fit. A Type S fuse assembly, therefore, prevents someone from replacing one size fuse with an incorrect size, either by accident or on purpose.

A time delay fuse. This fuse, which is also called a time lag fuse, allows temporary circuit overloading. In homes, time delay fuses are used in circuits that accommodate heavy appliances, such as air conditioners, that cause a temporary surge in power when they are turned on. The time delay fuse is made with a spring-loaded metal strip (link) that attaches to a plug of solder. As the power surge takes place, the fuse doesn't blow immediately, as would happen with a standard or Type S fuse. Instead, the solder begins to melt. It must melt through completely before the fuse will blow. The delay allows for a limited period of power surge. However, if the overload continues beyond a certain point, the solder melts completely and the spring pulls the link free. The fuse then blows and interrupts the circuit.

Cartridge fuses. Two types of cartridge fuses are used in homes. One type, having round ends and a capacity of 10 to 60 amperes, is used to protect a circuit on which there is a major electricity-drawing appliance, such as a kitchen range, clothes dryer or air conditioner. Each circuit serving a large appliance may be protected by a cartridge fuse. The other type of cartridge fuse is usually used to protect the main power circuits. This fuse has knife-blade contacts on each end and is rated at a capacity of 60 to 600 amperes.

It is rare for a cartridge fuses to fail, but if there is no other explanation for an inoperative appliance or for a power failure, it may be due to the particular cartridge fuse. The main reasons for cartridge fuse failure are the same as reasons for plug fuse failure—that is, overload on the circuit or a short circuit. A cartridge fuse also may fail because of old age.

Major appliance fuses. In a typical fuse box, fuses that protect major electrical-drawing equipment requiring 240 volts are set off by themselves in separate compartments. These normally are cartridge fuses. To deactivate the circuit, pull the separate compartment out of the fuse panel. Each of the other circuits, requiring 120 volts, is protected by an individual conventional window-type fuse.

Warning: Do not change fuse size in a circuit. If your system has been plagued by burned fuses because of overloaded circuits, do not solve the problem by substituting a larger fuse for a smaller one. Such action seriously jeopardizes the safety of your home. The wire in a 15-amp circuit has more resistance than wire in a 20 amp circuit. When a wire resists current, energy is dissipated in the form of heat, which in turn can cause a fire. The resistance level of the metal strip in a fuse should match the resistance level of its wire. Normally the wire and the fuse strip don't heat up because they carry no more current than they can handle. If, however, you replace a 15-amp fuse with a 20-amp fuse, your system is in trouble. Once the current goes over 15 amps, the wire begins to heat. However, the 20-amp fuse, which responds only to an amperage level of over 20 amps, does not respond at all. Because of the difference between the fuse and the wire sizes, there is too much current in the circuit and you have created the potential for an electrical fire.

Circuit Breakers

Homes that do not have fuses rely on circuit breakers. Circuit breakers, which have the same amperage capacities as fuses, are protective switches that automatically flip off when there is an overload or short circuit. Resetting a circuit breaker is done by pushing the switch to the ON or RESET position.

The main power switch in a circuit breaker setup is a large toggle switch. In some instances, there are two main switches. It is not necessary to turn the main switch off when resetting a tripped circuit breaker.

Major appliance circuit breakers. In a typical circuit breaker box, single breakers serve 120-volt circuits. Linked breakers (two breakers tied together) serve heavy-drawing electrical equipment that requires 240 volts. Such equipment might be kitchen ranges, central air conditioning systems or clothes dryers. To serve this equipment,

Time-delay fuses protect circuits subject to temporary power surges from major appliances. After a short surge, the breaker trips.

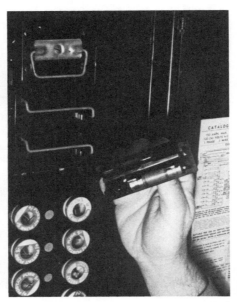

Cartridge fuses often protect circuits of air conditioner/heating units or other appliances. Remove the cartridge to break the circuit.

a hot wire runs from both circuit breakers of the linked unit to the component. If a fault develops in either line, both circuit breakers trip.

HOW TO MAP A CIRCUIT

Most circuits in a home are 120-volt circuits. These are designed to meet the needs of light fixtures and most appliances, such as toasters, clocks or vacuum cleaners. Because the demands upon any 120 circuit are not high, it serves several fixtures. Often the fixtures are located in several rooms. Typically, the area usually ranges between 375 and 500 square feet per circuit. This is governed by the potential con-

The alternative circuit protector is a circuit breaker. Here the toggles are labeled and color-coded according to amperage level.

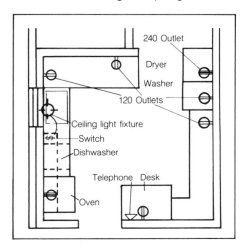

A circuit map of your home is an aid when a circuit develops trouble or when the existing wattage load on the circuit is unknown.

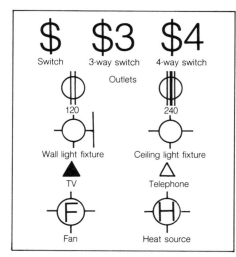

The featured symbols are used to indicate electrical items. Label switches, outlets or fixtures; indicate the circuit controlling each.

nected load, the size of the wire and of the fuse or circuit breaker.

Since the area governed by a given circuit is never obvious, any homeowner should map out the routes of all circuits in a house. The map will prevent the occurence of overloads, which can be an all-too-common event in many homes. It is helpful to know that the iron you plug into a kitchen circuit is going to affect the size of the television picture in the living room.

For safety's sake, you must turn off the circuit with which you will be working before you attempt even fairly simple repairs, such as replacing a receptacle or a light switch. To do this quickly and efficiently, it is best to have a map of your system. Once the map is complete, you can compute the amount of power each circuit carries.

Safety Precautions

Do not take unnecessary chances when you work at the fuse box. Stand on a dry surface. If the floor is damp, stand on a plank of dry wood. Be sure your hands are dry, and keep one hand at your side or in your pocket, so you don't accidentally touch any metal object as you disconnect and reconnect main power.

Circuit-Testing Procedures

The simplest way to map out your circuits is to work with a helper. One person works at the service box; the other person tests the switches, outlets and appliances. To make the circuit map, take the following steps.

Step one: the working sketch. Draw a rough floor plan of each room. Note every

receptacle, switch, and light fixture. Also sketch heavy electricity-drawing equipment that taps directly into the service panel, such as a well pump, a hot-water tank or heating system. Although this type of equipment is normally served by its own individual circuit, you still should be able to distinguish which circuit breaker or fuse controls each unit.

Step two: numbering the circuits. At the service panel, number each circuit breaker or fuse with a glue-backed label.

Step three: setting up the test. Work on one room at a time. To determine which circuit breaker or fuse powers what, turn on all lights and small appliances. Plug lamps into every unused receptacle in the room and turn them on, too. In a duplex receptacle (one holding two outlets), be sure to plug lamps into each receptacle. Do not take it for granted that both receptacles are connected to the same circuit; such is not always the case. Do not turn on heavy electricity-drawing equipment. Their circuits will be identified later.

On the service panel door, write in the area controlled by each circuit. This information is important when you plan advanced projects.

Step four: recording the first circuit in the room. The person at the service panel now deactivates a circuit breaker or fuse (preferably Circuit No. 1.) On the floor plan, the other person records the number of the circuit or fuse and notes each affected switch, light fixture and receptacle.

Step five: identifying the remaining circuits. Reactivate the first circuit breaker or fuse and turn off the next one. Continue the recording procedure until every switch,

Use convenient and easy-to-read self-sticking labels to indicate circuits controlling major appliances. These circuits must never provide power to other fixtures or appliances.

light fixture and receptacle in the room has been labeled with its circuit.

Repeat the procedure in every room of the house. If you find any light, switch or outlet that you cannot turn off, contact an electrician; you probably have a defect in the service box, which should be repaired immediately.

Step six: accounting for the heavy appliances. When the circuits governing all switches, receptacles and light fixtures have been identified, determine the circuits serving the heavy appliances. This is very important. If you attempt advanced electrical projects, such as those discussed in later chapters, always make sure that each circuit governing an individual piece of heavy-drawing equipment remains the province of that equipment alone and that no other electrical device is tapped into it. Otherwise, you could cause a dangerous overload.

PREVENTING OVERLOADS

Once you complete a circuitry map, you can compute the wattage available in each circuit. This is useful information, for it can help you prevent overloads arising from two major causes.

Too Many Appliances

The usual cause for an overloaded circuit is an overabundance of demands made upon it. This situation is often common in the kitchens of older homes. Their circuit capacity is not high enough to supply the needs of the growing number of appliances. The circuitry map can help you determine which circuit can safely tolerate

the added load of a new toaster oven or food processor, and which cannot.

Overextending the Circuit

The second cause of overloads is an overextension of the circuit, which in turn leads to too great a demand for current. Many advanced projects involve extending an existing circuit to add a new receptacle or fixture. This can overload a circuit. To prevent a potential overload, use the circuitry map of the service panel to calculate the unused capacity of existing circuits. You will then know which circuit, or circuits, is safe to tap for power. Most of the time, ample capacity is available with existing circuits. However, if every circuit is being used to full capacity, you will have to add a new circuit. This involves working inside the service panel, a job outside the province of this book. Hire a professional electrician to open the service box and add new circuits.

Calculating Circuit Wattage and Demands

Calculating wattage. It is easy to determine the wattage available in a circuit. Take the map to the service box, and note down the amperage level of each numbered circuit. Then follow this formula: Watts=Volts x Amps. Simply multiply the amperage level by 120, the number of volts usually present in household circuits. To determine heavy-duty circuits, multiply by 240 volts. Thus a 15-amp circuit carrying 120 volts (120x15) carries 1,800 watts; a 20-amp circuit carries 2,400 watts.

Calculating demands. Figure the present wattage load on each circuit by totalling the wattage of all lights, fixtures and appliances presently on the circuit. Then determine the unused capacity of each circuit by subtracting the present circuit wattage from the maximum circuit wattage. If you intend to add a new appliance to the circuit, deduct a safety margin of 15 percent from the final figure. Here are several examples that will help guide you.

Example A. Circuit No. 1 has an 1,800-watt capacity. You wish to add a new ceiling fixture that will accommodate three bulbs. The fixture's maximum load will be 450 watts. The circuit presently carries a maximum load of 750 watts.

Total wattage available	1800
Present load	750
Total wattage reserve	1050
Anticipated wattage for fixture	450
Reserve	600

There is more than ample wattage here. Go ahead and install the new ceiling fixture.

Example B. Circuit No. 3 has a 2400-watt capacity. You want to determine if you can safely use a room heater rated at 1600 watts. At present, the circuit carries a maximum load of 750 watts.

Total wattage available	2400
Present load	750
Total wattage reserve	1650
Anticipated wattage for heater	1600
Reserve	50

There is very little reserve on this circuit. You are pushing it. If you do use the heater, be careful not to add anything else to the circuit.

Wattage Ratings. The table below provides a list of wattage ratings for the most commonly used appliances in a home. It can be used for a number of purposes: to determine when an appliance can be added to a circuit, to help you decide how to more evenly distribute the electrical load in the home from circuit to circuit, and to determine how much of a load you can place on new circuits.

Use wattage ratings for estimating only. If the estimate falls close to a circuit's maximum load, determine the exact wattage of the load by totaling the exact figures given the information plates on the appliances and fixtures.

Converting amps to watts. On rare occasions, the appliance information plate will list only the amps required, not the watts. To figure out this appliance's wattage, use the same formula, Volts x Amps = Watts. Thus, a typewriter requiring 1.2 amps uses 144 watts (120 x 1.2 = 144).

Converting horsepower to watts. With certain electric components, such as some power tools, information plates give only motor horsepower (HP) ratings. Figure that one horsepower is equivalent to approximately 1000 watts. Thus, ¼ horsepower equals about 250 watts.

Kilowatts and Electrical Costs

The terms kilowatt (KW) and kilowatt hours (KWH) have significance primarily when it comes to reading an electric meter. A kilowatt is 1,000 watts. Hence, 10 kilowatts would be 10,000 watts.

A kilowatt hour (literally, one kilowatt consumed in one hour) is a measurement of the total amount of electricity used in a home over a given period of time. Your electric bill is computed on the basis of so many kilowatt hours for a given period of time multiplied by the rate per kilowatt hour charged by the electric company. Let's take an example.

Suppose you used 520 kilowatt hours of electricity last month, and suppose the price charged by the electric company were 0.0407 cent per kilowatt hour. The amount you owe for the use of electricity is, therefore, $21.16. As you probably know, there are charges reflected on electric bills other than actual electricity usage—for example, tax and energy cost adjustments for each KWH used.

APPROXIMATE WATTAGE RATINGS OF HOME APPLIANCES

Appliances	Wattage Ratings
Air conditioner (room size)	800-1500
Air conditioner (240-volt control)	5000
Blanket (single control)	150-200
Blanket (dual control)	450-500
Blender	200-400
Broiler (rotisserie)	1400-1500
Can opener	150
Clock	13
Clothes dryer (240 volt)	4000-5000
Clothes iron (hand)	700-1000
Coffee maker	600-750
Crock pot (two quart)	100
Dehumidifier	500
Dishwasher	1100
Drill (hand)	200-400
Drill press	500
Fan (attic)	400
Fan (exhaust)	75
Fan (pedestal type)	500
Fan (portable)	50-150
Floor polisher	300
Food mixer	150-250
Food freezer	300-600
Food processor	1800
Fryer (deep fat)	1200-1600
Frying pan	1000-1200
Furnace (gas)	800
Furnace (oil)	600-1200
Garbage disposer	500-1000
Hair dryer	400
Heater (permanent, built in)	1000-2300
Heater (portable)	1000-1500
Heating pad	50-75
Hot plate	600-1000 per burner
Hot water heater (electric, 140 volt)	2500-5000
Microwave oven	650
Radio	10
Range	5000 per burner
Range oven	4500
Razor	8-12
Refrigerator	150-300
Roaster	1200-1650
Saw (radial)	1500
Saw (table)	600
Sewing machine	60-90
Stereo	250-500
Sun lamp (ultraviolet)	200-400
Television (black and white)	50-100
Television (color)	200-4500
Toaster	250-1000
Toaster/oven	1500
Trash compactor	500-1000
Vacuum cleaner	300-600
Waffle iron	700-1100
Washing machine	600-900

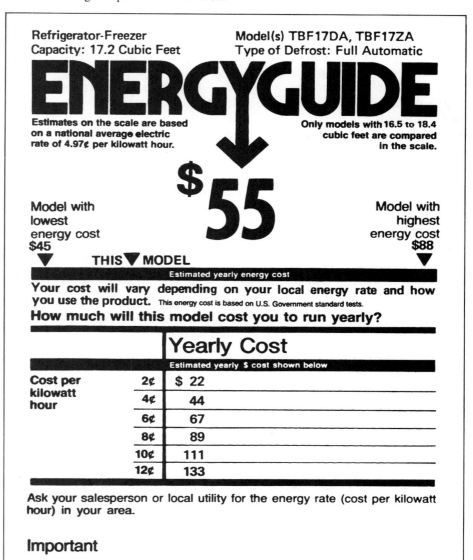

The amount of energy a particular appliance consumes is now spelled out for the consumer. An Energy Efficiency Rating label must include an estimate of the cost of the appliance's annual energy consumption. The cost of running the appliance is given for a number of unspecified brand names and for a range of energy rates. At the time that this particular label was printed, national rates were running between two and twelve cents per kilowatt hour.

There are many electrical problems that you can remedy simply and quickly. However, their causes are more numerous than many people realize. It is easy to change a light bulb, but if you replace the bulb in the same lamp time after time, it may be that the lamp requires repairs rather than another replacement bulb. For safety's sake, you can't replace fuse after fuse in a troublesome circuit, while neglecting to locate the reason for the continuous power failure.

BLOWN FUSES AND CIRCUIT BREAKERS
Determining the Cause of a Blown Fuse

Frequently, examination of the small window of the fuse will reveal whether a short circuit or an overload has caused a blown fuse.

Overload. An overload occurs when too many appliances and lights on a circuit demand more current than the circuit is able to deliver safely. In such an instance, the small wire in the fuse will break without heating excessively. The window will be clean, and you should be able to see the broken wire.

Short circuits. A short circuit occurs when a bare wire carrying electricity touches another bare wire carrying electricity or touches the metal case of an appliance. The rate of the flow of the current quickly becomes excessive. This in turn produces heat, which destroys the fuse wire. The fuse wire vaporizes and sprays the fuse window with discoloring material.

Discovering Cause for an Opened Circuit Breaker

There are no outward signs to explain why a circuit breaker has tripped open. In some cases, the appearance of a fuse also gives no indication of the reasons for its failure. In either case, you must determine if an overload exists by calculating the circuit's load. Make a list of the lights and appliances that were operating on the circuit when the fuse blew. Find the total of the items to see how much power you were pulling at the time of the power failure.

If the wattage exceeds the capacity of the circuit that is marked on the failed fuse, there was an overload. Before installing a new fuse, switch some of the appliances on the circuit to a circuit that can handle the load. Otherwise, the circuit will continue to disconnect.

Finding Causes of a Short Circuit

If a fuse has failed because of a short cir-

cuit, find the faulty unit and disconnect it before installing a new fuse. Follow these steps. Remember to follow safety procedures when you work at the service panel.

Procedures:
1. Disconnect all lamps, overhead fixture light bulbs, and appliances served by the failed circuit.
2. Examine all plugs and power cords.
3. If a plug is cracked, melted or has broken prongs, or if a power cord is frayed or twisted, do not reconnect the lamp or appliance until you repair the damage.
4. With all equipment on the circuit disconnected, replace the blown fuse.
5. Wait a few seconds. If the new fuse blows, the short circuit is located in the house wiring. Leave the blown fuse in place until the wiring has been repaired. This helps you keep track of which circuit is troublesome. In addition, if you leave the fuse socket open, the exposed contact point at the base of the socket poses a serious shock hazard.
6. If the new fuse doesn't blow, the house wiring is all right. Now remove the fuse.
7. Reconnect one of the disconnected devices; then replace the fuse. If the fuse does not blow, this device is not the source of the problem. Repeat this process with each device.

Do not plug in any device that you suspect might be faulty while the circuit is fully operational. There is too great a possibility of shock. Always remove the fuse, plug in the device and then replace the fuse. The device with the short circuit will blow the fuse. Repair that device before replacing the fuse again.

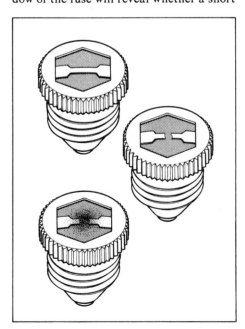

The metal strip in a good (nonblown) fuse is whole. A cleanly broken strip indicates a circuit overload. If the fuse has a discolored window, the cause is a short circuit.

Some service panels are controlled by a lever along the outside edge of the panel. This shuts off all power to the house.

Sometimes a cartridge fuse can cause problems in a circuit. To remove the fuse, pull it from its spring clips with a plastic fuse puller. Then, test the fuse with a continuity tester.

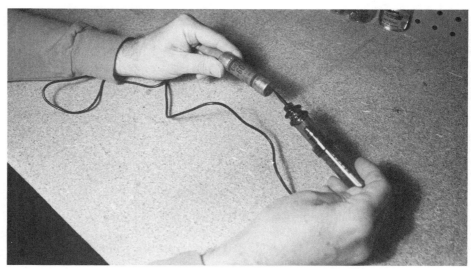

The continuity tester houses a small battery. Press one end of the tester against the fuse, the probe against the other. If the fuse is working, the tester bulb will light.

REPLACING FUSES
How to Replace Plug Fuses

The first step is to turn off all lights and appliances on the circuit controlled by the fuse. Then turn off the main power. In newer houses, the main power is controlled by two boxes that are equipped with cartridge fuses. To shut off the main power so you can safely remove the blow fuse, grasp the handles of the cartridge boxes, one at a time, and pull the boxes from place. In older houses, the main power is controlled by a lever-type switch on the side of the fuse box. To cut the power, pull this switch downward.

Actual fuse replacement is simple:
(1) select a fuse rated for the same amperage as the one you are replacing;
(2) turn the blown fuse counterclockwise to remove it from the box;
(3) install the new fuse by screwing clockwise into the socket;
(4) replace the main fuse boxes or turn the main power switch on.
Use care when working at the panel.

How to Replace Faulty Cartridge Fuses

Using a continuity tester. Testing a cartridge fuse requires two tools: a plastic fuse puller and a continuity tester. The continuity tester is designed to test the ability of electricity to flow from a power source to an end point. The simplest kind of tester is an assembly consisting of a light, a tester housing, and two probes. A small battery in the housing sends current through a circuit to establish whether current is reaching its destination. Continuity testers are also available in a meter design. However, this kind of tester is not required for home electrical work unless you are going to test and repair appliances.

Continuity tester: caution. A word of caution about using a continuity tester: although it is a simple device, you cannot be lax when you use it. Always hold the insulated section of the wires of the tester, rather than the metal probes. If you don't, you will be the item that the current passes through. Even if you firmly believe that a circuit is off and the outlet you are testing should not be carrying current, you may be mistaken. Remember that while you use the tester, if your hands come in contact with a metal box, or metal staples in a carpet, you can provide a path to ground for the current. The rule here is the same as at any time when you are working with electricity: be alert and be careful.

Procedure. To determine if a cartridge fuse has failed, proceed as follows:
(1) turn off the main power (see above);
(2) open or pull out the box or boxes holding the cartridge fuse or fuses;
(3) using the fuse puller, grasp the middle of the fuse and pull it from between the spring clips that hold it in place;
(4) touch one probe of the continuity tester to one end of the fuse and the other probe to the other end—if the continuity tester bulb lights, the fuse is okay, and you can reinstall the fuse;
(5) if the tester does not light, replace the fuse;
(6) to install the old (or new) fuse, push it into the spring clips by hand;
(7) turn on the current; if a new fuse now fails, the problem is due to the circuit wiring or a short in the appliance.

SIMPLE TESTS FOR INCANDESCENT LAMPS

An incandescent lamp produces light by passing electric current through a thin wire called a filament. This is usually made of tungsten. As the wire heats, it produces a white glow referred to as "incandescence."

Problems and Solutions

There are several indications that an incandescent lamp is not working properly. When the lamp is turned on, the bulb won't light, the bulb flickers, or the lamp blows a fuse or trips the circuit breaker. Each of these problems has certain defined causes. Always check the simplest trouble sources before you assume the worst.

Bulb doesn't light. Here are some places to begin your investigation and suggestions for repairs.

1. The plug has been pulled from the wall outlet. Push the plug back into the outlet.
2. The bulb is loose and isn't making contact with the socket. Tighten the bulb.
3. The bulb is burned out. Replace the bulb.
4. The line cord is damaged. Replace the line cord.
5. The switch is defective. Replace the switch.

Bulb flickers. Examine the lamp for these signs.

1. The bulb is loose and barely makes contact with the socket. Tighten the bulb.
2. There is a loose wire at the socket terminal. Turn off the power to the circuit or unplug the lamp; then secure the wire.
3. The switch is defective. Replace the switch.

The lamp blows a fuse or trips the circuit breaker. After checking the service box for overloads or short circuits (above), check these areas.

1. There is a short in the line cord. Replace the line cord.
2. The plug is defective. Replace the plug.
3. The socket is defective. Replace the socket.

Spotting Symptoms

Visible signs. How can you tell if any of the above problems apply in your case? Usually, there are signs to let you know if a plug, switch, or line cord is faulty. A defective plug normally has visible damage, such as cracks in the plug housing or loose, broken or bent prongs. A bad switch usually feels "sloppy" (loose) as you turn it on and off, or the bulb may flicker as

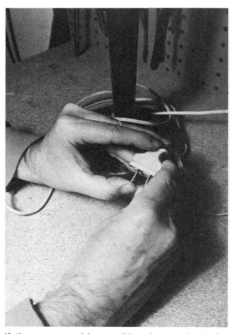

If there are problems with a lamp, check for obvious damage before you begin your repairs. Loose plug prongs indicate a faulty plug.

the switch is jiggled. A damaged line cord often looks frayed.

Tests for a broken wire. *Caution:* Do not do this test if the cord is frayed or a bare wire is exposed. A broken wire inside the line cord can cause the lamp to malfunction. Follow these steps to see if a broken wire exists.

1. Plug the lamp into the wall outlet and turn on the lamp switch.
2. Flex the line cord back and forth over its entire length. If the bulb flickers, a wire in the cord is broken. By flexing the cord you have opened and closed the two ends of the broken wire. When

If the bulb flickers or goes out when you flex a lamp's line cord, the cord has a broken wire. Replace all the cord, for safety's sake.

a faulty plug, switch, or line cord has been located, replace the bad part, as explained below.

BASIC WIRE-HANDLING TECHNIQUES

Before you can undertake nearly any repair, several basic procedures must be mastered. For example, although repairing an incandescent lamp is not hard, the work involves several techniques that are used in more advanced electrical work. The instructions in this chapter for attaching wires will be useful whether you are replacing a lamp line cord or rewiring a room.

Cutting Wires

Whenever you cut electrical wires or strip the insulation from a wire, you must use a combination wire cutter-wire stripper. *Do not* use a knife. A knife may nick the wire, which could create an electrical problem. To use the combination tool, insert the wire in the tool opening that accommodates its size. In the case of lamp wire, this is either hole No. 18 (corresponding to No. 18 wire) or hole No. 16 (corresponding to No. 16 wire). Close the tool and twist it back and forth until the insulation is stripped off.

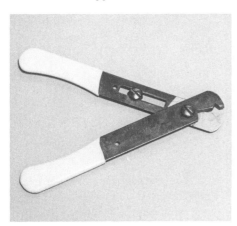

This wire-cutter-stripper is simple and reliable. Close the notches firmly on the wire; set the nut; then pull off the insulating coat.

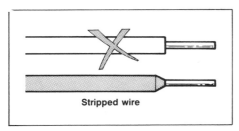

Stripped wire

Use a wire stripper rather than a knife. The stripper's cutting edges will create a beveled edge along the insulation for a better seal.

The amount of insulation you should strip off a wire depends on what you plan to do with the ends of wires. If you are going to attach them to screw terminals, strip off only enough insulation to wrap the bare ends three-quarters of the way around the screws. If you are going to insert bare ends into push-in terminals, lay wires across the strip gauge found on this type of receptacle.

How to Splice Wires

Whether you replace a faulty switch in the base of a lamp or add to an existing house circuit, you will have to splice wire ends together. When splicing, do not just twist the ends together and cover the splice with electrician's tape. This method does not meet today's codes. Instead, you must use what is called a wire nut, which is a plastic cap lined with threaded metal.

Types of wires. The method used for splicing wire depends upon the type of wire involved. Appliances usually use stranded wire. Each "wire" is actually a number of fine wires wound together and encased in an insulating sleeve. House wiring, the kind found attached to ceiling fixtures or outlets, is solid wire; inside the insulation sleeve is a single solid wire.

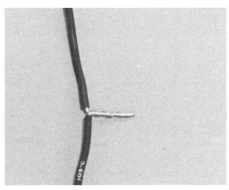

To splice stranded wires together, first twist each wire so that the wire strands are tightly packed. Then twist the wires together.

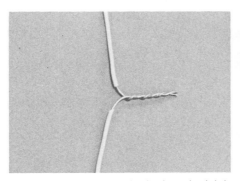

To splice solid wires, twist both ends tightly around each other. You may have to use a pliers to get a good, tight splice.

Splicing procedures. Strip off about ¾ of an inch of insulation. Then follow the appropriate procedure.

1. If the wires are stranded, twist the end of each individual wire very tightly together. Then hold the ends together, facing the same direction, and twist all the wires together.
2. If the wires are solid, keep wire ends pointing in the same direction, and twist them around each other with a pair of pliers.
3. If there are both solid and stranded wires, strip off about one-half inch of insulation from the end of the stranded wire in addition to the one inch already removed (you will now have 1½ inches of stripped wire). Twist it so it is packed as solidly as possible; then wind it around the solid wire in a spiral pattern.
4. Turning it clockwise, screw a wire nut over the splice. When the wire nut is tight, no bare wire should show. If bare wire does show, remove the wire nut and snip off enough wire so no bare area will be exposed. When you attach

To splice stranded and solid wire, twist the stranded wire around the solid one; then hook the remaining solid wire over the splice.

Covering a wire splice with electrician's tape (left) is no longer up to local codes. Instead, cap the splice with a wire nut.

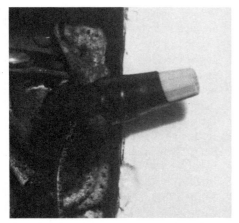

Use electrician's tape to secure the wire nut in place. The resulting splice is far more reliable and safe than the old method.

wire nuts, wrap electrician's tape around them and the wires to keep the wire nuts in place.

REPLACING A PLUG

Pull the plug from the wall outlet before making repairs. The procedure outlined here is used to replace plugs of appliances as well as lamps.

Plug Types

Lamps use a standard or clamp-type plug. Either can be used as a replacement, regardless of the type of plug presently on the lamp.

If a standard plug is used as a replacement, wires of the line cord, stripped of insulation, are attached to terminal screws of the plug. If a clamp-type plug is used as a replacement, wires of the line cord, *not* stripped, are pushed into the plug where prongs pierce through the insulation to establish contact between the wires and

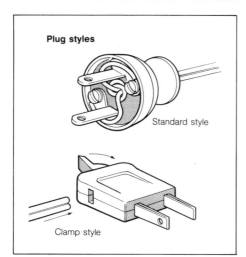

Plug styles

Standard style

Clamp style

If you rarely unplug a lamp or appliance, a clamp-style plug is fine. If you need a durable installation, select a standard plug.

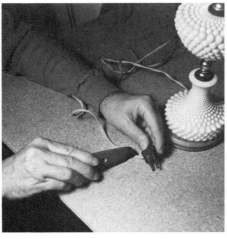

1 To remove an old clamp-style plug, cut through the line cord with a razor knife.

6 Pull the ends tightly to secure the knot. It should rest at the base of the prong.

plug. Obviously, clamp-type plugs require less work to replace than standard plugs. However, this should not be the reason for selecting one over the other. The reason for selecting one or the other is the need (or lack of need) for durability.

Selecting the plugs. Wires attached to a standard plug are tied into an Underwriter's knot (see below) and secured by screws to provide a strong installation. A clamp-type plug holds wires only by prongs, providing a relatively weak installation. For this reason, if you will plug and unplug the lamp often, replace a bad plug with a new standard plug. If the lamp is going to remain stationary, you may prefer the ease of installation that a clamp-type plug offers.

Replacement Procedures

Replacing a clamp with a standard plug. To remove a damaged clamp-type plug and install a new standard plug in its place, proceed as follows:

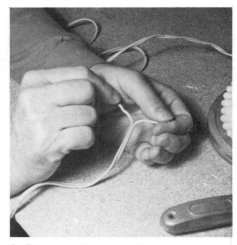

2 Zip cord splits in two without damaging the wires inside. Separate about 1½ to 2 inches.

7 Pull the wires around the terminals at the base of the prongs to create an "S" pattern.

1. Cut the plug from the line cord.
2. The cord used for lamps is called zip cord, because the two wires of the cord can be separated. Pull apart the two wires making up the line cord, until the split measures about 1½ inches.
3. Strip about 1½ inches of insulation from the ends of each wire, using a combination wire cutter and stripper.
4. An Underwriter's knot secures line cord to a standard plug. Slip the plug on the line cord and form the ends of both wires into loops. One end crosses in back of the wire, the other in front. Slip the ends through the loops, as shown, and pull the knot tight. In making the Underwriter's knot, it may be necessary to pull apart the zip cord to provide more length with which to work.
5. Fit the looped wire ends clockwise around the plug screw terminals, so the wire ends follow the direction that the screws turn when they are tightened.

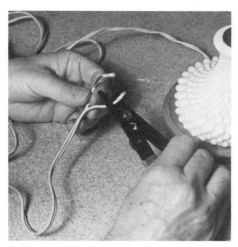

3 Use a wire stripper to strip 1½ inches of insulation from each of the wires.

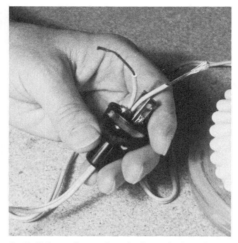

4 Pull the split cord ends through the plug so that the insulation is inside the plug.

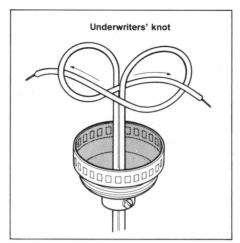

5 Secure the cord with an Underwriters' knot. This will hold the cord firmly in place.

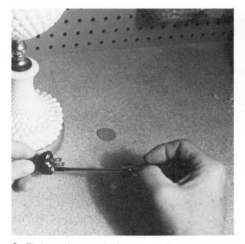

8 Tighten the terminal screws; do not squeeze the wires from under the terminals.

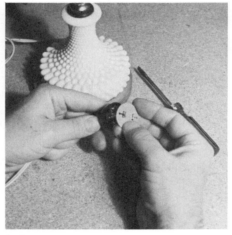

9 Finish off the plug with its cardboard insulator. This protects against short circuit.

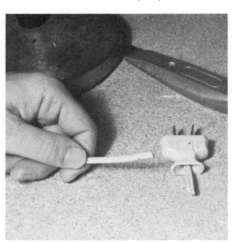

To install a clamp-style plug, do not split the zip cord after the old plug is removed.

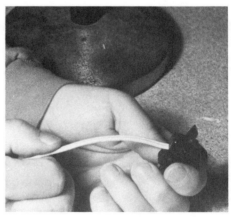

When the clamp mechanism closes, it bites through insulation to contact the wires.

If loops are placed in a counterclockwise direction, the connections may come apart as the screws are tightened.
6. When you finish making the connections, place the cardboard insulator over the plug.

Replacing a standard with a standard plug. To remove a standard plug that has failed, remove the insulator, loosen screws, detach wires, and slide the line cord off the plug. Attach a new standard plug as explained above. Don't forget to cover the plug with the insulator.

Installing a clamp plug. To install a clamp-type plug, detach the old plug and cut away bare or pierced wires. Do not separate the zip cord. Release plug clamps so you can slide the line cord into the new plug. The releasing device is normally a lever. In other styles, one of the prongs acts as the releasing device. When purchasing the plug, ask the salesperson to show you how to release and tighten clamps.

Push the cord into the plug; snap the lever in place. This allows plug teeth to pierce line cord insulation, so that the plug terminals make contact with bare wire.

REPLACING A LAMP SWITCH
Be certain the lamp is unplugged before you attempt this repair.

Types of Switches
Lamps use one of two general kinds of switches. The most common type is incorporated in the socket. The switch itself may be one that rotates, pushes in and out, or operates by a pull chain. When an in-the-socket switch goes bad, the entire socket, except the housing, has to be replaced.

The other kind of switch, found in some lamps, is not part of the socket. Instead, the switch is a rotary one that is located in the lamp base or somewhere on the housing. This switch can be replaced without replacing the socket.

Procedure: Replacing an In-socket Switch
Removing the harp. To remove a socket containing a switch, unplug the lamp and remove the shade and bulb. If a harp holds the lamp shade, examine the harp for fasteners, such as finger nuts. Remove them to remove the harp. Most harps, however,

To remove the harp, slide up the small finger nuts; squeeze the harp and lift it off.

Pull off the cap and the insulating sleeve. Detach wires from the socket terminal screws.

Inspect the wires. If they are in good condition, install the new socket.

are not held by fasteners. They fit into arms of the harp seat. To remove this type of harp, pull the harp from its seat.

The socket structure. A socket containing a switch has an outer brass or aluminum casing. Beneath the casing is a cardboard insulating sleeve that covers the socket itself. The bottom of the socket fits into a cap, which has an insulating liner. The cap may be screwed to the lamp.

Replacing the socket. To replace a socket, follow this procedure.

1. Press in on the base of the outer socket casing and pull it off the cap.
2. Remove the cardboard insulating sleeve, exposing the socket-and-switch assembly terminal screws to which the line cord is attached. It may be necessary to pull the socket out of the cap to reach the terminal screws.
3. Loosen the terminal screws and unhook the line cord.
4. Examine the cap. If it is dented or corroded, untie the Underwriter's knot, loosen the setscrew holding the cap to the lamp, and remove the cap. Replace the cap with a new one. Be sure to retie the Underwriter's knot. If the old cap is not damaged, let it stay in place.
5. Install the new socket-and-switch assembly in the reverse order of disassembly. Be sure to attach the line cord to terminal screws in a clockwise direction, the same direction that the terminal screws are tightened.

Procedure: Replacing a Switch Not in a Socket

To replace a separate switch, follow these steps.

1. Disconnect the lamp from the wall outlet.
2. If the switch is mounted in the base of the lamp, turn the lamp upside down and peel back the cover. In most lamps, this cover is made of felt material that is glued to the base.
3. With the base opened, notice that the line cord is attached to wires emanating from the switch. Usually, the splice is made using wire nuts. Remove any electrical tape, unscrew the wire nuts, and untwist wires to separate them.
4. Unscrew the knob outside the lamp base; then unscrew the switch locknut. Pull the switch from the lamp.
5. Install a new switch using a procedure that is the reverse of the disassembly procedure. Twist the wires securely to-

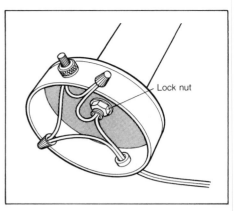

Lock nut

If the switch and the socket are separate, loosen the wires. Remove the switch by releasing the locknut holding the switch in place.

gether, and be sure that wire nuts are tight. Reinstall the felt cover with an adhesive that won't damage felt. This is available in hardware stores.

Replacing a Lamp Line Cord

If your tests reveal that the line cord is damaged, select UL-approved cord containing appliance wire that is the same size as the cord already in use. This probably will be No. 18 lamp wire, which may also be used for electric clocks and other small appliances that draw less than 7 amps. This type of cord is often referred to as zip cord. Replace the entire cord, even if only a small section is damaged. It is not wise to splice an old, damaged line cord. Many fires have started because of faulty splicing or because of a line cord that has outlived its usefulness. A new line cord, which is not expensive, is a worthwhile investment. To find out how much you need, measure the old cord plus the length of the lamp; then puchase at least one foot more than the total.

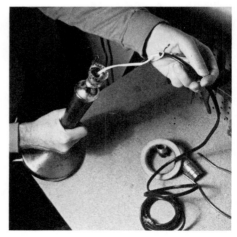

Once you remove the socket and the plug from the old cord, tape the old and new cord together; pull the new cord through the lamp.

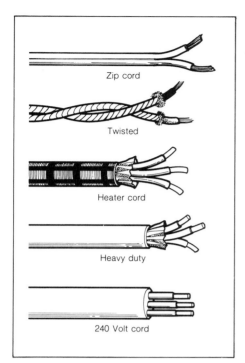

Zip cord

Twisted

Heater cord

Heavy duty

240 Volt cord

1 Replace the line cord from any lamp or appliance when the cord shows signs of wear and tear. Always select the same type of cord.

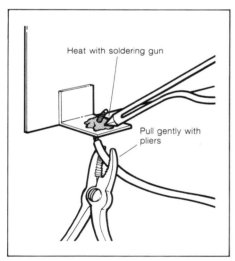

Heat with soldering gun

Pull gently with pliers

2 To release a soldered connection, heat the terminal; pull wire free. Heat new wire and connection; touch with new solder to secure.

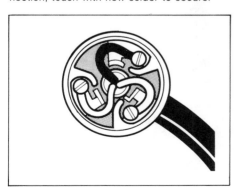

3 This illustrates a plug for a heavy-duty appliance using 240 volts of power. Release the terminals; pull the cord out the back.

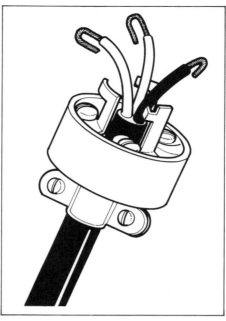

4 Nest the new wires into the plug. Screw black and red wires to the brass terminals, white wires to the silver terminals.

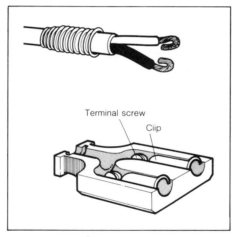

Terminal screw

Clip

5 Do not throw an old appliance away because of a worn cord. Unscrew the plug's cover; release the cord from the terminal screws.

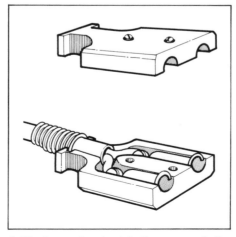

6 Slip the cord spring into the grooves in the plug base. This protects the cord connection. Screw the plug cover in place.

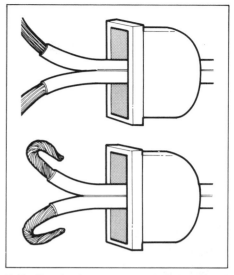

7 If a flat plug has screw terminals instead of clamps, remove the insulator, pull the plug out of the housing and release the wires.

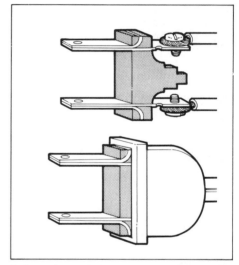

8 Draw the cord through the housing and separate. Fasten the stranded wires to the terminals; seat the assembly in the housing.

9 Once the plug is installed, tie an Underwriter's knot at the base of the socket. Fasten the zip cord wires to the terminal screws.

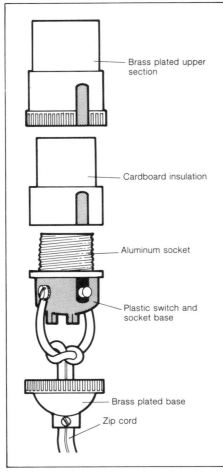

1 This blow-up shows the structure of a common socket connection on a lamp in which the switch is included in the socket.

Brass plated upper section

Cardboard insulation

Aluminum socket

Plastic switch and socket base

Brass plated base

Zip cord

2 With a razor knife, split the insulation in half between the two "ridges." Do not cut through the insulation and sever the wires.

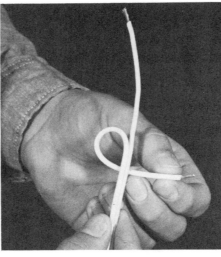

3 To tie an Underwriter's knot, first form a fairly large loop with one of the wires. Big loops will be easier to work with.

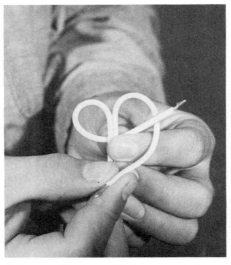

4 Form another loop with the second wire, so that this second loop is behind the end of the first wire. The placement is important.

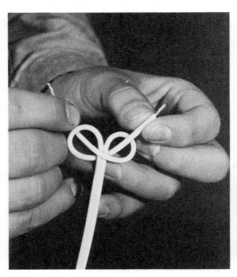

5 Insert the end of the second loop back through the first loop. The wire from the first loop then goes back through the second loop.

6 Pull the knot tight. It should be large enough so that it cannot pull through the hole in the plug yet small enough to fit snugly.

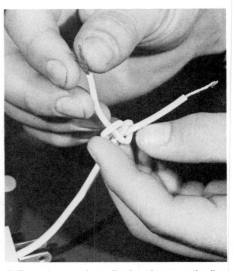

7 To replace a plug, slip the plug over the line cord, strip ½ inch of insulation from each wire, and tie an Underwriter's knot.

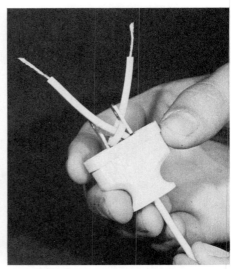

8 Pull the knot to seat it solidly in the base of the plug. Then connect the wires to the terminal screws and replace the insulator.

To replace the faulty line cord of a one-socket lamp, proceed as follows.

1. Unplug the lamp from the wall outlet.
2. Remove the plug from the old line cord (see above).
3. Remove the socket and untie the Underwriter's knot in the socket cap (see above).
4. Attach the new line cord to the socket end of the old line cord by wrapping a wide strip of masking tape around the two.
5. Now pull the old cord out the base of the lamp. As you do so, the new line cord will be pulled into place.
6. When the new cord emerges from the base, strip off the masking tape and discard the old wire.
7. Make an Underwriter's knot in the bottom end of the new line cord. Be certain there is sufficient length at both ends of the lamp. Attach the plug to the bottom end of the cord.
8. As before, tie an Underwriter's knot in the line cord at the socket cap. Attach the socket to the line cord at this end.

Repairing Multi-switch and Multi-socket Lamps

Lamps come in a variety of forms. There are two-socket lamps that have one on-off switch for each socket. Three-socket lamps also can have individual switches or a single on-off switch. There also are other variations. Whatever kind of lamp

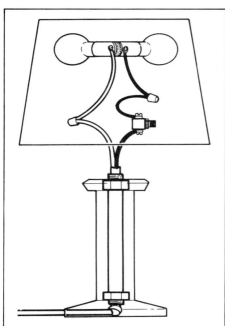

To replace a soldered double socket, remove wire nuts and release the splices. Then rewire. Follow all color coding.

you have, follow the basic repairs explained in this chapter. To connect wires between sockets and switches, follow the procedure accompanying the four illustrations show.

Two-socket lamps. One type of two-socket lamp has sockets that are molded together. Wire connections run internally between the sockets. The switch turns both sockets on or off at the same time. If one socket goes bad, both have to be replaced. If the switch goes bad, undo the wire nuts holding the switch and the power wires together, and detach the switch wires from the power wires. Discard the old switch, and connect the wires of the new switch to the power wires.

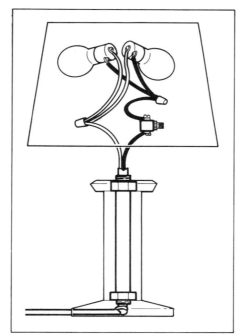

If the lights work independently, you can replace either socket separately. Release the wire nuts; install the new socket.

In the other type of two-socket lamp, the sockets are wired separately and can be replaced individually. As with a lamp using molded sockets, the switch turns both bulbs on or off at the same time. The wiring arrangement, therefore, is more complex than that of a molded two-socket arrangement, because jumper wires (shown here as wires No. 1 and No. 2) perform the function of the internal wires in molded sockets. Wih the exception of these two jumper wires, the arrangement is the same as for a lamp using sockets that are molded together.

Three-socket lamps. A three-socket lamp in which each socket has its own switch has the wiring arrangement shown here.

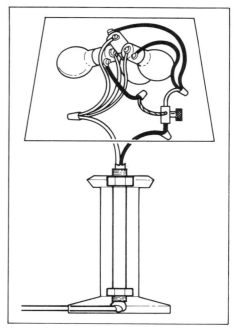

To replace a single-switch, multi-socket fixture, attach a white wire to each socket; then attach a color-coded hot wire to each socket.

If each socket has its own switch, each can be replaced separately. Again, you do not need to bother with the complex wiring.

Each socket can be replaced without affecting the others. Remove the wires from the socket's terminal screws, withdraw the old socket and reattach the wires to the terminal screws of the new socket. Notice that all three sockets receive current through a single power cord. Therefore, the arrangement requires jumper wires from the line cord to the terminal screws of each socket.

The most complex wiring arrangement

is used by a three-socket lamp having one switch. This switch is a four-way switch. The first position turns on the bulb in socket No. 1 only; the second position turns on the bulbs in sockets No. 2 and No. 3; and the third position turns on the bulbs in all the sockets. Notice that the switch utilizes three wires. A black wire connects the switch to the line cord, a blue wire connects the switch to socket No. 3, and a red wire connects the switch to socket No. 1.

REPAIRING FLUORESCENT FIXTURES
Structure of a Fluorescent Fixture
The three main parts of a fluorescent fixture are a fluorescent tube, which may be straight or circular, a starter and a ballast. These components cause most of the problems associated with fluorescent fixtures.

The fluorescent tube. Inside a fluorescent tube, electric current jumps (arcs) from an electrode (cathode) at one end of the tube to an electrode (anode) in the other end of the tube. The center of the tube contains a combination of mercury and argon gasses. As the electric arc passes through the gasses, it emits invisible ultraviolet light. To make this light visible, the inside of the tube is coated with a phosphor powder that glows (fluoresces) when struck by the ultraviolet light.

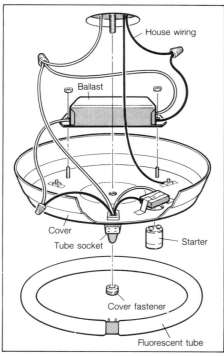

A circular fluorescent is called a circline fixture. The wiring arrangement is simple, especially if starter and ballast are separate.

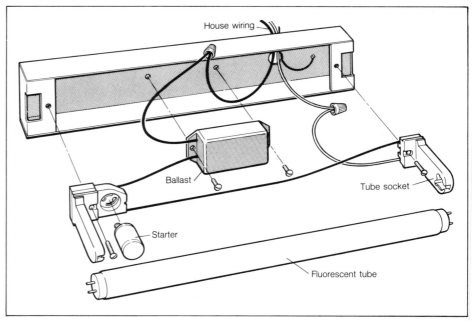

This is a standard straight-tube fluorescent. It, too, has the simple wiring of a fixture with a separate ballast.

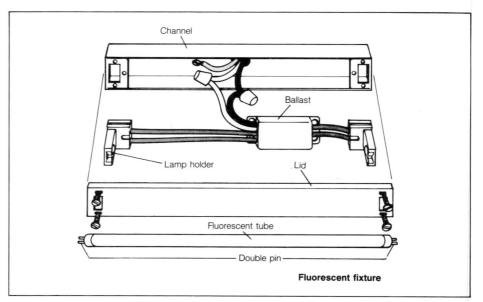

Fluorescent fixture

Shown is a fluorescent fixture with ballast and starter in one unit. This is a rapid-start fixture, because the tube ends have two pins. One pin on each end indicates an instant-start fixture.

The starter. The starter in a fluorescent fixture is a switch that closes when activated by electric current. After a momentary delay, the starter allows current to energize gasses in the tube. The electrodes need the delay to get hot enough to begin transmitting current.

There are two types of starters. Replaceable ones nestle in a contact seat in the fixture housing. The other type is called a rapid-start fixture. This starter is built into the ballast and cannot be replaced independently of the ballast.

Ballast. The ballast holds electric current to the level required to provide proper fluorescent light operation. Without the ballast, the amount of electric current flowing through the tube would exceed the capability of the tube, and the tube would quickly burn out.

There are two types of ballasts. Fluorescent fixtures that use small fluorescent tubes incorporate choke ballasts that have one purpose: to limit the amount of electric current flowing through the fluorescent tube. Fixtures holding large fluorescent tubes have ballasts that incorporate transformers and choke coils. When the fixture is turned on, the transformer steps up voltage to deliver a momentarily high surge of electricity. The surge is required to get the large fluorescent tube to glow as quickly as possible. Once the tube lights, a continued high electric flow could cause tube damage. Therefore, the transformer shuts itself off and the choke coil takes over to limit current input into the tube.

Replacing a Tube

On the outside ends of a straight tube are sets of 2 pins each. To set the tube into the fixture, simply rotate the tube into the holders at each end of the fixture.

Replacing the Starter or Ballast

When replacing either a starter or ballast turn off power to the fixture by deactivating the circuit breaker switch or fuse.

Starter replacement. Some early fixture models have their starters mounted externally. Here is how to replace the starter for those fixtures in which it is outside the ballast.

1. Remove the tube, or tubes.
2. Take off the cover plate.
3. Turn the starter one-quarter turn to the left (counterclockwise).
4. Pull the starter out of its seat.
5. Push in the new starter, turning it one-quarter turn to the right (clockwise).

Ballast replacement. To replace a ballast, proceed as follows.

1. Turn off power to the fixture by deactivating the fuse or circuit breaker.
2. Remove the tube, or tubes, and take off the cover plate.

3. The wire connections of the ballast you are replacing are the same or similar to one of those seen in this chapter. Notice that ballast wires of a given color are connected to fixture wires of the same color. A new ballast must be connected in the same way.
4. Disconnect the ballast wires from the fixture wires by removing the wire nuts or loosening the terminal screws.
5. The ballast will be heavy. Hold it securely as you remove the fasteners that attach it to the fixture. Take the ballast down.
6. Line up the new ballast so that it aligns with the position of the old ballast. Screw the new ballast to the fixture.
7. Connect all wires. Make sure that similarly coded wires are attached to each other.

Troubleshooting Fluorescent Fixtures

Fluorescent fixtures are easy to repair. However, when the faulty component is not obvious, troubleshooting them can be a hit-or-miss proposition. If you are unsure of the problem, replace one component after another until you hit upon the troublemaker. Begin with the most-likely-to-fail component.

The following chart lists possible fluorescent fixture failures, and their causes and repairs. Causes and repairs are listed in the order in which they should be done, assuming there is no indication of which component is faulty.

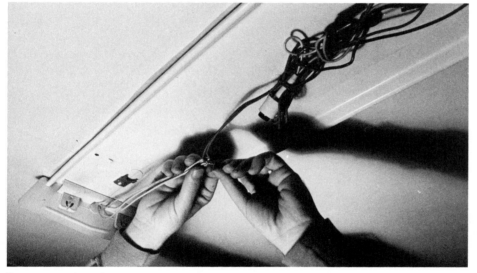

Do not worry about the maze of wires in an instant-start or a rapid-start fixture. It can be handled by matching and splicing wires according to their color.

Before attempting complicated repairs, check for signs of damage. Watch for signs of discoloration, wear or cracking. Be certain that contacts are clean and the holders lean inward.

If the tube flickers off and on, it may be because the pins are bent. Use a needle-nosed pliers to straighten them.

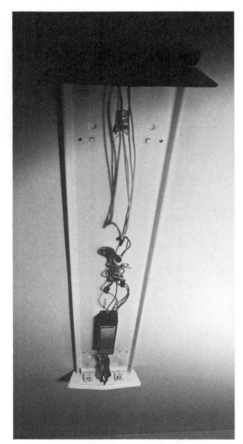

After the pins are straight, lightly rub them with a fine sandpaper to smooth the metal and to remove slivers left by the pliers.

A rapid-start or instant-start fixture has several wire splices. This ballast has wiring diagrams printed on it to aid installation.

FLUORESCENT FIXTURE TROUBLE SHOOTING*

Type of Failure	Causes	Repairs
Tube fails to light	1. Fuse has blown or circuit breaker has tripped	1. Replace fuse or reset circuit breaker. If problem recurs, check house wiring.
	2. Tube not seated correctly in sockets	2. If tube is straight, rotate off and reseat into sockets. If tube is circular, remove and reinstall; all pins should fully engage socket.
	3. Defective starter	3. If starter is independent of ballast, replace starter. If starter is part of ballast replace the tube before you replace the ballast.
	4. Defective tube	4. Replace tube with one of correct wattage, which is marked on old tube. If marking is unclear, check voltage marked on ballast.
	5. Defective ballast or starter in ballast	5. Replace the ballast. Check ballast connections.
Light flickers and swirls around in tube	1. New tube	1. Normal in new tubes; should clear up in a short time.
	2. Defective starter or ballast	2. Replace starter if it is independent of ballast; if problem remains, replace ballast.
Light blinks on and off	1. Low room temperature (below 50°F.)	1. To eliminate, install a low-temperature starter and ballast or replace entire unit with one designed for low temperature locations.
	2. Tube not seated properly	2. If tube is straight, reseat securely in sockets. If tube is circular, remove and reinstall. All pins must fully engage socket.
	3. Tube pins bent	3. Examine the tube pins. If bent, straighten with long-nosed pliers. Sand pins lightly; wipe away foreign matter. Insert pins securely into sockets.
	4. Sockets deformed or dirty	4. Turn off circuit (see Chapter 1). Socket contacts of a long fixture should lean inward. If deformed, try repairing them by bending with long-nosed pliers. Sand contacts lightly; blow foreign matter from sockets with an ear syringe.
	5. Loose connections	5. Turn off circuit; remove fixture cover. Remove wire nuts and check all wire splices. Reinstall wire nuts securely.
	6. Defective tube	6. Replace tube.
	7. Defective ballast	7. Replace ballast.

*Note: Directions given here are for fixtures with separate starter and ballast. If the two are combined, you will have to replace the entire ballast-starter unit in order to remedy a faulty starter.

FLUORESCENT FIXTURE TROUBLE SHOOTING*

Type of Failure	Causes	Repairs
Ends of tube light; center does not glow	1. Defective starter	1. Replace starter.
Tube seems to burn out rapidly.	1. Fixture is turned on and off at frequent intervals	1. Avoid turning fixture on and off so frequently.
	2. Incorrect ballast	2. If short tube life occurs after replacing ballast, ballast may be incorrect type for the fixture. Check ballast and fixture types. An electrical parts dealer can help you.
	3. Incorrect ballast wiring	3. Turn off circuit. Remove fixture cover and trace wire connections. Use earlier illustrations as guides.
	4. Mating tube failure	4. Replace a burned-out tube immediately, especially in some rapid-start fixtures holding two or more tubes. Otherwise, when one tube burns out, the other tube usually will fail prematurely.
	5. Defective starter or ballast	5. Replace starter; if condition continues, replace ballast.
Discoloration at tube ends	1. Normal condition	1. Brown or gray bands about two inches from tube ends are normal.
	2. Worn out tube	2. Gradually enlarging black bands at tube ends indicate tube is going bad. Replace tube.
	3. Defective starter or ballast	3. If black bands develop on new tube, replace starter; if condition continues, replace ballast.
Humming	1. Normal	1. Some humming is normal.
	2. Loose ballast wires	2. Loose wires can cause humming. Turn off circuit. Remove wire nuts and check connections. Secure wire nuts.
	3. Incorrect ballast	3. If humming started after installing ballast, it may not match the fixture type. Check ballast and fixture types.

To replace a toggle switch, release locknuts on the old switch. Then attach the wires to the terminal screws of the replacement switch.

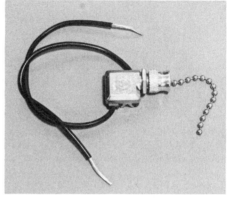

A pull-chain replacement involves internal wiring. Remove knurled nut and locknut; splice wires; replace the locknut and knurled nut.

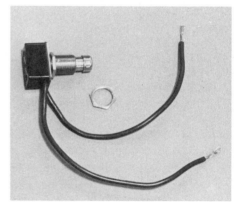

Perhaps you can replace a switch instead of an appliance. For safety, this push-button switch requires correctly made splices.

Outlets and switches, essentials in modern living, are not indestructible, though they sometimes seem that way. When you must replace one or the other, the task is fairly simple. Always follow established safety procedures: be sure the current in the circuit is shut off at the service panel, and doublecheck with a voltage tester, a device that is discussed in this chapter. Do not work in a wet or damp environment. Finally, always be sure the replacement parts bear the UL label and are rated for the amperage and voltage level of the circuit to which they are attached. Always practice safety as you work.

ANATOMY OF A SWITCH OR OUTLET
Junction Boxes

The finishing cover surrounding a switch or outlet is called a face plate. If you remove the face plate you will see the fixture itself. This is usually held to the wall by two screws in a metal mounting strap.

When the screws are removed, the fixture can be pulled (gently) from its housing. Every switch or outlet in your home is housed in a metal junction box. The box may be fastened to the wall with a special brace, but it is most likely that the box is fastened to a wall stud. One or more sets of wires feed into the junction box. To replace a switch or outlet, you don't have to do anything to the junction box or replace any wiring. Only the fixture itself is replaced.

The junction box may be tilted in the wall. Do not try to straighten it. A crooked box should not prevent you from aligning a receptacle or a switch. The wide mounting slots of the mounting strap allow you to shift the fixture to provide a straight installation. When the fixture is aligned, tighten the screws.

Wiring Layout

Although you don't have to replace any wires when you replace an outlet or switch, you do have to understand some facts about the position of the fixture on the circuit, because the position affects the way the fixture is wired up. A junction box will fall in one of two positions, either at the middle or the end of a circuit. Determine the position by the number of cables, or sets of wires, that enter the junction box through openings in the back and sides.

Neutral wires. Each set of wires will have two to four wires. One will be covered with white insulation. This is the neutral wire, which provides a normal path for return current. The neutral wire is designed to operate under normal conditions, not to handle a failure in the electrical system itself.

"Hot" wires. Also in the set will be one or two "hot" wires, which will be covered with black or red insulation.

Ground wires. Finally, there may or may not be a ground wire. This either will be enclosed in green insulation or will be a bare copper wire. Ground wires also provide a path to ground, but they do so when a failure occurs in the electrical system.

When the faceplate is removed, you can see the body of a switch or receptacle. A metal mounting strap holds the fixture in place.

A switch or receptacle sits inside a metal junction box in the wall. The box houses the wires and connections for the fixture.

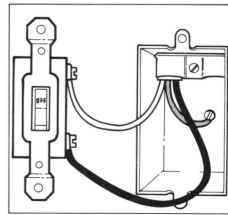

Inside the box are cable sets, which usually have two or three wires: a white neutral wire, a black hot wire and/or a green ground wire.

The path to ground minimizes the danger of shock.

End-of-the-run wiring. With this arrangement, only one set of two or three wires enters the junction box. The black and white wires attach to the terminal screws. The bare or green wire, the ground wire, loops around a screw attached to the metal box. If the box holds a switch, you have a "switch loop"; both wires are hot.

Middle-of-the-run wiring. With middle-of-the-run wiring, two sets of wires enter the junction box. The hookup itself will vary according to the type of switch or outlet and the type of ground system used. Wiring for each is covered separately, later in this chapter.

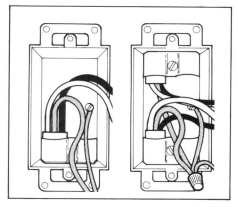

A junction box sits in two positions on a cable. At left is an end-of-the-run junction box. Only one set of wires comes into it. On the right is a middle-of-the-run junction box, which houses two sets of cables. The box's position affects the wiring methods inside it.

What looks like two separate outlets is actually two parts of a duplex receptacle. Both outlets are not necessarily on the same circuit.

REPLACING A RECEPTACLE

A receptacle is frequently called a wall outlet, or simply an outlet. It is the point of electrical service into which you insert the plug of a lamp, appliance, clock, or other electricity-using equipment. There are several varieties of receptacles. Some are designed exclusively for use out-of-doors, some are made to handle the heavy-duty requirements of major appliances, some are integrated into light fixtures, and some are combined with switches. But the most common home receptacle is the duplex receptacle that is rated at 15 amperes and 120 volts. A duplex receptacle has two outlets and accommodates two pieces of electrical equipment.

How to Test an Existing Receptacle

Because a receptacle has no moving parts, it rarely wears out. However, if you have trouble with a circuit, test it carefully to determine whether or not it is faulty. In time, plastic parts may become brittle and break off, or metal parts inside the receptacle can loosen and fail to make contact with plug prongs. If a receptacle shows physical damage, or if it seems to have an internal failure, it should be replaced. A bad receptacle cannot be repaired.

The lamp test. First, determine whether the problem lies with the outlet or the appliance plugged into it. The tester can be any lamp that you are sure is in good working condition. Turn off the circuit that governs the outlet. Plug in the lamp, reconnect the circuit, and turn on the lamp. If the bulb does not light, or if the circuit blows or breaks, you know that the problem is with the outlet, not with the appliance.

Replacement Parts Specifications

When you purchase a replacement receptacle, refer to the housing of the old one to be sure you get the one you need. The markings listed below are those found on both receptacles and switches. You should be familiar with all the abbreviations.

Underwriter's Laboratories (UL) and Canadian Standards Association (CSA) monograms. These indicate that the receptacle has been tested and listed by these organizations.

Amperage and voltage ratings. Such figures indicate the maximum amperage and voltage the receptacle is capable of handling. For instance, a rating of "15A-120V" means that the receptacle can con-trol a maximum of 15 amperes of current at no more than 120 volts.

Type of current. The current indicated on the receptacle is the only one that the receptacle can use. Receptacles that are used in houses and condominiums in the U.S. and Canada are marked "AC ONLY," which means they are designed for use with alternating current.

Type of wire. Check which wire the receptacle can handle, and determine what kind of wiring is used in your home (copper, copper-clad aluminum, or solid aluminum). Make sure the receptacle design accommodates that wiring.

Aluminum wiring. In selecting a receptacle to be used with aluminum wire (note: *not* copper-clad aluminum), follow the advice of Section 380-14 (c) of the 1981 National Electrical Code, which says use only receptacles marked "CO/ALR." This designation means the receptacle has been designed for use with aluminum wiring only, and that metal terminal screws are compatible with aluminum. Failure to select the correct receptacle may lead to overheating at terminal screw connections and, possibly, a fire. Conversely, receptacles marked "AL-CU" or with no type of wire designated should never be used with aluminum wiring. Use them only with copper and copper-clad aluminum wiring.

Types of Receptacles and How They Work

There are several styles of receptacles of which you should be aware.

Side-wired receptacles. The most com-

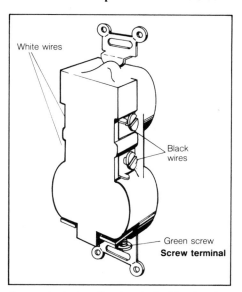

A receptacle has five terminals. The top two serve the top outlet; the bottom two serve the bottom outlet; the ground serves both.

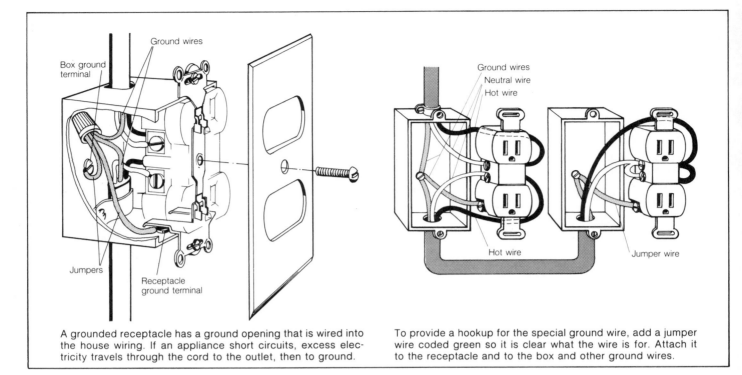

A grounded receptacle has a ground opening that is wired into the house wiring. If an appliance short circuits, excess electricity travels through the cord to the outlet, then to ground.

To provide a hookup for the special ground wire, add a jumper wire coded green so it is clear what the wire is for. Attach it to the receptacle and to the box and other ground wires.

mon style is the side-wired receptacle. It has four terminal screws, two on each side. Two of the four will be brass-or black-colored, and two will be silver-colored. The brass-colored terminals are hot terminals; the silver-colored terminals are neutral ones. The top pair of terminals serves the top outlet; the bottom pair serves the bottom outlet. In addition, there should be a fifth, green-colored screw on the bottom of the receptacle body. The green terminal is for a special ground wire. Receptacles having this fifth terminal have outlets with three openings. Receptacles without the ground terminal have only two openings.

Ground-wired receptacles. Receptacles that don't have the fifth screw for grounding purposes are obsolete. All receptacles included in new construction must have three openings to accommodate the ground prong built into most modern appliances. This provides protection from shock due to a short circuit in the appliance, by providing a continuous path from the appliance to the receptacle and then through the house wiring to ground. If your home has no grounded receptacles, you should replace them. Wiring details for replacement are given later in this chapter.

Back-wired receptacles. The wires to back-wired receptacles are inserted into holes in the rear of the receptacle housing. Spring clamps hold the wires in place. To attach or remove the wires, insert the blade of a knife or screwdriver into a re-

lease slot and press the spring clamp, thus releasing its grip. The wire is then either pushed into or pulled out of the housing.

Back-wired receptacles have a green terminal screw at the underside of the housing, to which a green ground jumper wire is attached. The wiring arrangement for hot and neutral wires is the same as with side-wired receptacles. Some back-wired receptacles also have terminal screws on the side of the housing, so you have a choice of how to make connections.

Polarized plugs and receptacles. A number of today's appliances, including radios, televisions, and portable lamps, have what is called a polarized plug. This safety feature enhances protection from electric shock. It is characterized by one prong that is wider than the other. This requires a special outlet whose openings match the plug. It is impossible to insert the plug the wrong way in such an outlet. Most homes built since the 1920s have receptacles with slots that accept polarized plugs. If a polarized plug does not fit an outlet, it is being inserted the wrong way. Reverse the position of the plug. Do not alter the configuration of a polarized plug by grinding metal from the wider prong; the safety feature then would be destroyed.

Preliminary Test for Safety

Using a voltage tester. Before you replace a receptacle, deactivate the fuse or circuit breaker that you think controls the

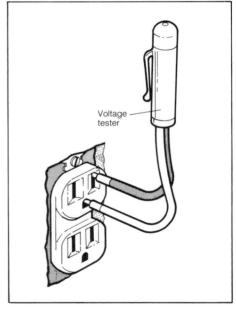

Insert one prong in the hot side of an outlet, the other in the ground or the neutral side. If the wiring is right, the bulb will light.

particular circuit (see Chapter 1). As an added precaution, use a voltage tester to see if electricity is present at the receptacle. The tester is a small bulb to which are connected two wires. Metal probes attach to each wire.

A voltage tester has no internal source of power. Thus, the light of the voltage tester will glow only if the probes connect points where voltage is present.

Caution: Handling. Be sure to hold voltage tester probes by insulation. Do not touch any metal part and do not touch the receptacle terminal screws. See that your hands are dry and that the spot on which you are standing is not wet.

How to test the circuit. To determine if the fuse or circuit breaker serving the circuit of a faulty duplex receptacle has, in fact, been deactivated, proceed as follows. (Do not touch the terminal screws or the circuit wires as you work through the steps.)

1. Remove the receptacle cover plate, loosen the screws that hold the receptacle in the junction box, and gently pull the receptacle out from the box until you can reach terminal screws. These will be silver-colored and black- or brass-colored. There also may be a green-colored screw.

2. Hold one probe of the voltage tester on the top black or brass terminal screw. Hold the other probe on the top silver terminal screw. The test light should *not* glow. If it does glow, the fuse or circuit breaker serving the circuit has not been deactivated. If you cannot determine which circuit controls the outlet, consult an electrician.

3. Now, hold the probes of the voltage tester on the bottom black or brass terminal screw and on the bottom silver terminal screw to see if voltage is present. To be safe, test for voltage at both the top and bottom outlets of a duplex receptacle. In rare cases, the individual outlets are controlled by different fuses or circuit breakers.

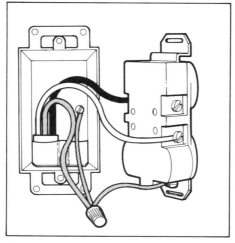

An end-of-the-run receptacle has only two main terminals occupied, one at the top and one at the bottom. Note the jumper wire.

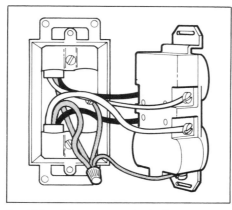

A middle-of-the-run receptacle has wires attached to all terminals. The ground is wired with jumpers. (If cable has two hot wires, join the silver screws with a jumper.)

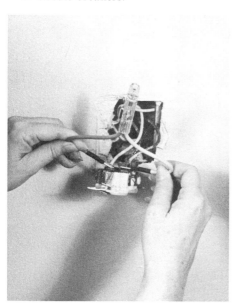

A second way to test an outlet is to touch the brass screw with one probe of the voltage tester and the silver screw with the other.

Attach wires to terminals in a clockwise direction. In that way, when the terminal screw is tightened, the wire will also tighten.

When you install a new receptacle attach black to brass and white to silver. The bottom screw shown here is for the ground wire.

How to Replace a Side-Wired Receptacle

Once you are sure the circuit is off, you can proceed. Replace a receptacle connected by side-terminal screws as follows.

1. Wrap a strip of masking tape around each of the wires connected to the receptacle. On the black (or red) wire connected to the top brass terminal screw, print the letter "T." On the white wire connected to the top silver terminal screw, also print the letter "T." On the black or red wire connected to the bottom brass terminal screw, print the letter "B." On the white wire connected to the bottom silver terminal screw, also print the letter "B." Wrap tape around the green wire and print the letter "G" on it for "Ground."

2. Loosen all terminal screws; remove and discard the faulty receptacle.

3. Hold the new receptacle in place. The ground openings in the outlets should be at the bottom. To make the hookup, connect the black and white "T" wires to the top terminal screws. Attach the black "T" wire to the brass screw and white to the silver screw. Then connect the black and white "B" wires to the bottom terminal screws. As before, attach these black wires to the brass screw and white to the silver screw. Finally, connect the green ground wire to the green (ground) terminal screw.

4. Set the receptacle in the junction box and secure it with the top and bottom

mounting screws. Before tightening the receptacle down, align it so it is straight. Then, tighten screws. You may not need the round "plaster ears" that are part of the receptacle mounting strap. There are four ears—one in each corner. Their purpose is to keep the receptacle flush with the wall if the box is recessed. However, if the box is flush with the wall, plaster ears may prevent securing the cover plate. If so, remove and discard the plaster ears by bending them back and forth with pliers until they snap off.

5. Mount the cover plate and reactivate the fuse or circuit breaker. Now, test to make sure that the installation is properly grounded.

Outlets with Openings for Grounded Appliances

Installing a grounded receptacle is a relatively simple task. You will need the new receptacles, a voltage tester, a needlenosed pliers, and a combination wire-cutter and wire-stripping tool. You also will need about six inches of wire for every receptacle you are installing. Ask for single conductor ground wire that is the same size as the circuit wiring. If you know the amperage level of the circuit, the dealer will know what size you require. Then, doublecheck the size with that printed on the wires attached to the existing receptacle.

In a typical grounded receptacle, the ground wire of the conductor that enters the receptacle box is spliced with two green jumper ground wires. The splice is covered by a wire nut. One of the jumper wires is attached to a ground terminal that screws into the metal junction box. The other jumper wire is attached to the ground terminal screw that is attached to the receptacle.

The first step of installing a grounded receptacle, as always, is to shut off the current to the circuit on which you will be working. Then, before you begin, doublecheck with the voltage tester to be certain that the current is off. If the tester light remains off, you may proceed with the following installation steps.

Removing an old outlet. First, take off the faceplate of the receptacle. Then remove the screws holding the receptacle in place, and pull the receptacle toward you. Tag the hot and neutral wires; loosen the screws on the receptacle and unhook the black and white wires. There may be a

ground wire attached to the back of the junction box. Leave this alone for the time being.

Jumper wires. In a wiring hookup, any piece of wire that is separate from circuit wires is called a jumper. You need one or two jumpers for this hookup. The number depends on whether the outlet is at the middle or the end of the circuit. There is also a separate process for grounding if the circuit wires have no ground wires of their own.

End-of-the-run junction. Using wire cutters, cut a six-inch piece of new wire. This is your jumper wire. Strip ½ inch of insulation from each end with the wire stripper. Do not do this with a knife. Using the needlenose pliers, make a loop in each end of the new wire. Attach one loop to the green screw of the new receptacle. As discussed earlier, the hook must run clockwise. As you tighten the screw, you will also tighten the wire around the terminal. Then connect the other end of the jumper under the screw at the back of the junction box in the same manner.

Middle-of-the-run junction. This hookup is more complicated than the first because here you must splice wires. In addition to the materials listed above, you will need electrician's tape and a wire nut for every receptacle.

Cut two 4-inch pieces of new wire. From one end of each, remove ½ inch of insulation. From the other end of each, strip 1 inch of insulation. Turn loops in the ½-inch ends. You now have Jumper #1 and Jumper #2.

Attach the looped end of Jumper #1 to the receptacle's green screw. Now loosen the screw at the back of the junction box and detach the two ground wires there. Fasten the looped end of Jumper #2 to this screw. Only Jumper #2 should be connected to the junction box itself. You now must splice together four ground wires— Jumper #1, Jumper #2 and the ground wires from the two cables that enter the junction box. Screw on the wire nut and cover the joint with electrician's tape. (Splicing is discussed in Chapter 3.)

Two-wire-cable junction. In a two-wire cable there is no independent ground wire. Instead, the metal casing that encloses the wires acts as a built-in ground. To ground the receptacle, cut a 6-inch piece of new wire and strip a half-inch of insulation from each end. Create a loop in one end and fasten it to the green screw on the

receptacle. Then, using a machine screw, fasten the other end to the back of the junction box.

Completing the installation. To complete the installation, attach the hot wires to the brass-colored screws and the neutral wires to the silver screws of the new receptacle. Fasten the receptacle to the junction box, reattach the face plate and test the ground system.

Checking for ground. After you have installed a grounded outlet, test it. Insert a probe of the voltage tester in the ground slot, which is the semicircular slot at the

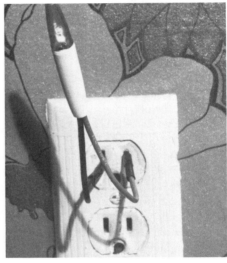

Use the voltage tester to test. Insert one probe in the right (hot) side and one in the left (neutral) side to light the light.

Then insert the probe in the outlet's left side (neutral) and the ground opening below it. The tester should not light up.

Finally, insert the probes in the right side and the ground opening. The light should light. If any tests fail, check wiring.

bottom of the outlet. Insert the other probe of the voltage tester in the slot to which the hot wire is connected. Normally, this is the slot on the right as you face the receptacle. In many cases, the hot slot is slightly shorter than the other (neutral) slot. The voltage tester lamp should glow.

Keeping the probe in the ground slot, insert the other probe in the neutral slot of the receptacle. The voltage tester lamp should *not* glow.

Check both outlets of a duplex receptacle. If you fail to get the results above, you have hooked up the new outlet incorrectly. Deactivate the fuse or circuit breaker and recheck your work.

Ground Fault Circuit Interrupter (GFI)

In most instances the normal grounding

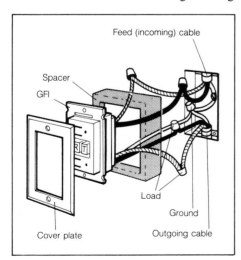

A Ground Fault Interrupter is required by code in all home locations subject to excessive dampness, such as a bathroom or patio.

system is a sufficient safeguard for all appliances. However, in certain circumstances, especially bathroom, basement and outdoor areas where the user can come in contact with water, the leakage in a circuit can be too small for a circuit breaker or fuse to respond, but large enough to kill the user. (Less than 1/10 of an ampere is required to light two Christmas tree bulbs; the same amount of current can kill a person after only two seconds of exposure.) Therefore, the National Electric Code now requires that in all new home construction there be special ground fault interrupters attached to all outlets in high risk locations, such as bathrooms, and to outdoor outlets.

How a GFI works. A ground fault circuit interrupter is a special device that is either built into an outlet or is added to an existing one. (It can even be built into your service box, although an electrician should do the job.) A GFI compares the amount of current entering a fixture on the black wire with the amount leaving on the neutral wire. Any discrepancy indicates leakage in the system. If the GFI detects as little as .005 amp difference between the currents, it breaks the current in 1/40 of a second, preventing serious shock. Although a GFI is not required equipment in a kitchen, you should seriously consider installing it, especially in receptacles near the sink area.

Procedure.
1. Turn off the power to the circuit; remove the old receptacle from the box. Label the wires, if necessary, before you detach the old receptacle from the wiring.
2. Measure the depth of the junction box. If it is not at least 2¾ inches deep, you will have to attach a special spacer plate provided with the GFI. The spacer plate creates the necessary space for the wiring.
3. To attach the outlet, you must determine which is the hot incoming (feed) wire and which is the hot outgoing wire. This is simple for an end-of-run receptacle. For a middle-of-the-run receptacle, follow this procedure. Use the voltage tester for this, and observe all the necessary safety precautions for this test. Do *not* hold the tester by the metal of the probes. Have a helper turn on the circuit at the service panel. Touch one of the wires with one of the probes. With the other, touch the junc-

tion box. If the tester lights up, the wire is a feed wire. If the tester does not light up, the wire is an outgoing wire. Turn off the circuit and label the wires accordingly.
4. The GFI has black and white wires marked LINE. Attach these to the corresponding black and white incoming house wires. Splice carefully; secure with wire nuts.
5. The GFI has black and white wires marked LOAD. Attach these to the corresponding outgoing black and white wires. If there are no outgoing wires, cover the end of each wire with a wire nut; secure with electrician's tape.
6. Cut a piece of ground wire that is 4 inches long, and strip 1 inch of insulation from one end, ½ inch from the other. Splice the 1-inch end with the ground wires in the housing wiring and with the ground wire in the GFI. Attach the ½-inch end to a screw in the junction box.
7. Fasten the GFI to the space. Finish off with a face plate.

REPLACING A SWITCH

A switch is a device that creates or interrupts a circuit to a lighting fixture, appliance or outlet. When the switch is in the ON position, the circuit is created; electricity flows from its source to an end point, where it is needed. This end point

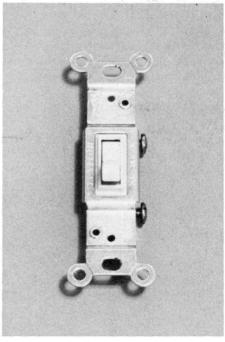

A switch that is the only control for an outlet or a light is called a single-pole switch. It will have only two terminals.

may be a wall outlet into which a lamp or appliance is plugged, or a lighting fixture mounted on the ceiling or wall.

How Switches Work

Switches in most homes are toggle types, or snap switches. Inside the switch are two contacts and an arrowhead-shaped metal device. One contact connects the switch to the service box by means of the circuit wiring. The other contact connects the switch to the end point. When the switch is in the ON position, the arrowhead-shaped metal touches both the incoming contact and the outgoing contact. Electrical current goes through the switch to the end point. When the switch is in the OFF position, the arrowhead touches neither contact; the electricity cannot reach its end point.

Types of Switches

The process for examining a switch is the same as for an outlet. Turn off the circuit to the switch before you begin. Then remove the faceplate and the mounting strap screws to release the switch. Pull it out toward you. The switch will be attached to the cable wires by either screw terminals or, less often, spring clamps like those in back-wired outlets. The number of connections tells you the kind of switch you have.

Single-pole switches. A switch with two terminals is called a single-pole switch. The incoming hot wire (remember: a wire and conductor refer to the same thing) is connected to one screw, and the outgoing hot conductor is connected to the other screw. The single-pole is the most commonly used household switch. It controls electricity to an outlet or light fixture from one location only.

Three-way switch. A switch having three terminal screws is called a three-way switch. One terminal is black- or copper-colored, while the other two are brass- or silver-colored. The black- or copper-colored terminal is labeled the common terminal. The hot conductor coming from the service box is attached to the common terminal.

Two three-way switches are used in combination to control electricity to an outlet or fixture from two locations. One of the brass- or silver-colored terminals of a three-way switch supports the hot wire that feeds an outlet or lighting fixture. The white wire here is recoded black because

it transfers electricity from the switch to an outlet or receptacle that is controlled by the switch. The other brass- or silver-colored terminal of a three-way switch holds the hot wire that goes to another three-way switch. Both switches control the same fixture. The third terminal screw is called a traveler terminal, because it transfers electricity from the switch to another switch. Notice also that the toggle on a three-way switch is not marked OFF and ON.

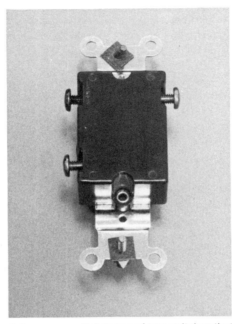

A three-way switch is one of two switches that control an outlet or light. There will be three terminals, one of which is marked COMMON.

Four-way switches. A four-way switch has four terminals. This switch works in combination with two three-way switches to control electricity to lights and outlets from three locations. All of the four terminals are brass-colored. They support hot conductors (traveler wires), which receive and transfer electricity from each of the three-way switches. The toggle on a 4-way switch also is not marked OFF and ON.

A double-pole switch. A double-pole switch also has four terminals and normally is used to control electricity to heavy-duty 240-volt appliances. Since most home appliances are not served by switches, the double-pole switch is rarely seen. It is mentioned here to warn you that if you are purchasing a four-way switch, do not buy a double-pole switch by mistake. The only clear indicator of a double-pole switch is the ON-OFF markings on the toggle. Otherwise, a four-way switch and a double-pole switch look alike.

Positions of Terminal Screws

The position of terminal screws varies to let you select a switch that permits the most convenient placement of wires in the switch box. No matter which switch you select, it will fit into a standard-size box.

Side-wired switch. One type of terminal arrangement has screws on one side of a single-pole switch or on both sides of three- and four-way switches.

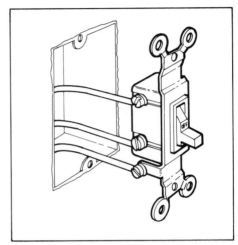

A side-wired switch has its terminals on the side as opposed to the top. Pull the switch out of the wall to see the terminals.

End-wired switch. Another type has screws on the top and bottom of the switch housing, with screw heads pointing up and down, respectively.

Front-wired switch. A third type of terminal arrangement has screws facing the front of the switch, with one screw at the top of the switch and the other at the bottom of the switch.

Back-wired switch. There is a fourth

A back-wired switch has openings in its back. The wires are inserted into the openings; a spring clamp holds them in place.

On the back of a back-wired switch you will find a line marked "STRIP GAGE ONLY." Strip only this amount of insulation from the wires.

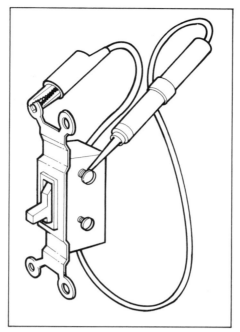

Use a continuity tester to see if the switch is working. With the toggle at ON, touch the two terminals. The light should light.

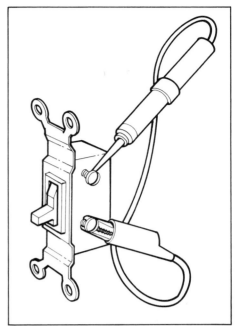

Flip the toggle to OFF. Again touch both of the terminals with the probes. If the wiring is right, the light should not light up.

setup, a back-wired switch. It doesn't have terminal screws. Instead, it has holes in the rear of the switch into which wires are pushed. Adjacent to each hole is a slot. To release a conductor, use the end of a paper clip, screwdriver, or similar tool to press the tang in the slot. To insert a conductor, press the tang in the slot, push the wire into the terminal hole, and release the tang.

Note: Switches other than back-wired switches often have both terminal screws and the back-wired feature to give you a choice.

Caution, aluminum conductors. If your house or condominium is equipped with aluminum conductors, don't use back-wired switches or the back-wired switch feature of a switch that has both terminal screws and terminal slots. Use back-wired switches only with solid copper or copper-clad conductors (see the earlier discussion of aluminum wire). Check with the contractor who built your home or with the municipal building inspector to determine the kind of wires that you have.

How to Test a Single-Pole Switch
A switch may be faulty when electricity fails to reach an outlet or fixture, or the defect may lie with an outlet, fixture, appliance or lamp. To determine if the switch is causing a circuit to fail, use the continuity tester to test the switch. If the switch proves faulty, replace it. Do not try to repair a faulty switch.

1. Turn off the power to the switch by deactivating the appropriate fuse or circuit breaker (see Chapter 1). If there is any doubt as to which fuse or circuit breaker controls electricity to the switch, disconnect the main fuse or deactivate the main circuit breaker, shutting off all power.

2. Remove the faceplate. Two screws, one at the top and one at the bottom, hold the switch in the box. Loosen the screws until you are able to pull the switch out of the box far enough to extend the wires.

3. Loosen both terminal screws and (if present) the ground terminal screw at the base of the switch. Open the loops of the hot wires with a pair of needle-nosed pliers. Detach the wires from the screws and remove the switch. Do *not* do anything to any other wires present in the box.

4. When the switch has been removed from the box, use a continuity tester to determine if the switch is faulty. First, attach the tester alligator clip to one of the terminal screws. Hold the tester probe to the other screw. Flick the toggle between OFF and ON. If the switch is in good condition, the tester light will glow when the toggle is in the ON position, but will not glow when the toggle is in the OFF position.

5. If the switch passes this test, attach the alligator clip to the metal mounting strap. Touch the probe to one of the switch terminals and move the toggle between OFF and ON positions. If the switch is in good condition, the tester light will *not* glow with the toggle in either position. Now, touch the probe to the other switch terminal and move the toggle between OFF and ON. Again, if the tester light does not glow, the switch works. Replace the switch if it fails to pass any of these tests.

How to Buy a Replacement Switch
Purchasing a replacement switch is simple. With the circuit off, remove the old switch from the junction box and take the switch to a hardware or electrical supply store. Match the data stamped on the new switch to the data stamped on the old switch. This follows the data included on replacement receptacles. Be sure that the new switch bears the UL (or CSA) emblem. Match amperage, volt and wire types, for a compatible hookup. Be sure the switch is for AC current. (Also available are several specialized switches. Their installation is discussed in Chapter 7.)

Replacing a Single-Pole Switch
It is not difficult to replace a single pole switch. The process will vary somewhat, depending upon your house wiring system. The requirement also will be different for a grounded switch as opposed to an ungrounded one. A grounded switch looks just like an ungrounded one, except that

a grounded switch has an extra terminal screw at the switch's base. This terminal screw is colored green or identified by the letters GR. (Some brands possess both means of identification.) This type of grounding system offers redundancy and is, therefore, more reliable than other ground systems that do not connect up with the switch.

When replacing a switch, it is wise to purchase one having a ground terminal screw, even though it may be necessary to modify the wiring arrangement, as explained below. Whether the old switch is grounded or not, remember that you detach only those wires that are connected to the switch itself. Do not disturb any others, such as joined white neutral wires or green ground wires, unless you are specifically instructed to do so.

Installing an ungrounded switch. It is not uncommon to find an ungrounded switch when the house wiring is enclosed in metal sheathing. In this case, only two wires complete a set, and the sheathing acts as a ground system. Even so, a grounded switch is recommended here since the sheathing doesn't reach all the way to the switch. However, if you choose to stay with an ungrounded switch, here are the steps to follow to install it.

Set the switch at the OFF position. The toggle will be aimed downward. Connect

the hot wires to the switch terminal screws. It doesn't matter which wire is connected to which terminal. However, be sure that wire ends are connected properly to the terminal screws, that is, with looped wire ends facing clockwise, the same direction that the screws turn. Mount the switch in the junction box, and align the switch so it is straight. Then attach the face plate and reactivate the fuse or circuit breaker.

Installing a grounded end-of-run switch. When installing a new switch that possesses a ground terminal screw, in a box that did not previously have this type of switch, you will need to buy single conductor ground wire that has the same amperage as the house wiring. Buy about 4 inches to make a jumper wire for each switch you are installing.

Hook up the hot wires to the switch. Using the combination tool, cut the ground wire to length. Strip ½ inch of insulation from both ends of the jumper. Then simply run a length of ground wire from the switch ground terminal to a screw in the junction box. Normally there is more than one screw holding the box; you can attach the jumper to any one of them.

Installing a grounded middle-of-the-run switch. The existing ground system in a middle-of-the-run junction box will consist of the two ground wires emanating from each cable and a jumper that is attached by a screw to the metal box. The three wires will already be joined together.

To attach a ground wire to a middle-of-the-run switch, you again need to purchase extra ground wire. Using the combination tool, cut a 4-inch jumper. Strip ½ inch of

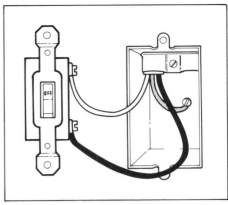

An end-of-the-run switch has wiring that looks like this. Do not touch the wires unless you are certain that the current is off.

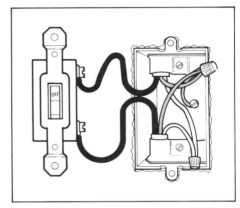

A middle-of-the-run switch will have two hot wires attached to it. You do not need to bother with any wires but those two.

insulation from one end of the wire and 1 inch from the other. Then unscrew the wire nut holding the ground wires in the box and, using pliers, twist the end of the new wire firmly around the original splice. Attach the wire nut. (If the old nut can't be tightened, you may have to buy a larger

Be certain that the power to the circuit is off. Label the wires HOT and NEUTRAL; then back out the terminal screws to release the wires.

Hook up the new switch. Be certain that the toggle is set so that it is down when the switch is at OFF and up when the switch is at ON. Attach wires in a clockwise direction.

wire nut.) Now, attach the ½-inch end of the new ground wire to the switch ground terminal. Finish up the installation as described above.

Replacing a grounded switch. There is very little difference between this installation and the other two. When you remove the old switch you must also detach the ground wire on the old switch. Then re-attach the hot wires and the ground wire to the new switch. You do not need to disturb the rest of the wiring setup.

Replacing Three- and Four-Way Switches

When a three-way switch may be causing a problem, you must ask yourself this question: Which of the two three-way switches is at fault? Use a continuity tester to test both switches, as described below.

When a four-way switch is involved, before you begin working, you must identify the four-way switch and the three-way switches. Turn off the electricity and remove the cover plates from all switches. A four-way switch possesses four terminal screws; the three-way switches have three. Test the two three-way switches first. If both pass the test, assume that the four-way switch is causing the trouble and replace it.

Removing a three-way switch. The procedure involved in replacing a three-way switch doesn't differ significantly from replacing a single-pole switch. Follow the procedure outlined above, but observe a few additional steps. Remember that there are two types of terminals in a three-way switch: one common terminal and two traveler terminals.

1. Shut off the power, remove the cover plate, release the switch, and pull it from the box.
2. Identify the common (hot) terminal screw. It is usually black or copper in color, but in any case, it is always darker in color than the other terminals. The other terminals, which are the traveler terminals, are usually silver- or brass-colored.
3. After identifying the common (hot) terminal, wrap a piece of masking tape around the wire attached to the terminal, and as a precaution, write the word "HOT" on the tape. You will now be certain to re-attach this wire to the common terminal. The traveler wires can be crossed, so that each is connected to a different traveler terminal

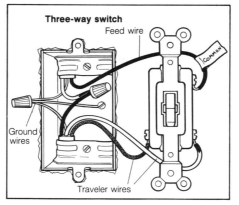

Three-way switch
Feed wire
COMMON
Ground wires
Traveler wires

Before you back out the terminals and release the wires to a three-way switch, identify the black wire that is called COMMON.

than on the old switch, and you will have no problem—the switch will still work. However, if the hot wire is inadvertently connected to a traveler terminal and a traveler wire is connected to the common terminal, the switch won't work.

4. Disconnect wires from terminals and remove the switch. Do not disturb any other wires in the box.

Testing a three-way switch. To test this switch, you will need a vise and a continuity tester.

1. Place the switch in the vise, but do not overtighten the vise or you may crack the housing. Attach the alligator clip of the continuity tester to the common terminal.
2. Set the toggle in one of its positions; touch the probe of the continuity tester to one of the traveler terminals. Note whether the light in the tester lights up. Flip the switch and repeat the test. If the switch is in good condition, the continuity tester will glow when the toggle is in one position or the other. If the tester does not glow, the switch is faulty and should be replaced.
3. Leave the toggle in the position that makes the continuity tester glow. Now, hold the tester probe to the other traveler terminal. The tester should not glow. Flick the toggle to the opposite position. The tester should glow. If this does not happen, replace the switch.

Installing a three-way switch. To install a three-way switch, connect the hot wire to the common terminal and traveler wires to traveler terminals. Check that the wire ends are looped around the terminal screws in the same direction that the screws turn.

Replacing a four-way switch. If you test the two three-way switches and neither is

defective, replace the four-way switch as follows.

1. With a new four-way switch in hand, disconnect the wires attached to the top terminal screws of the old four-way switch. Immediately attach and tighten wires to the top terminal screws of the new four-way switch. Be sure wire loop ends face clockwise, so that they tighten when the screws turn.
2. Disconnect wires attached to the bottom terminal screws of the old four-way switch. Attach these to the bottom terminal screws of the new four-way switch. Again, see that the wire loop ends face the direction in which the screws turn.
3. Place the switch in the box, and install the cover plate. Turn on the circuit and try the switch. If it fails to perform properly, the new switch may require a different wiring arrangement. Turn off power and pull the switch from the box, again. Disconnect two of the wires on *one* side of the switch and reverse their positions. Replace the switch and turn on power. Now the switch should function.

A Word About Testing Back-Wired Switches

Back-wired switches are tested in the same way as switches with terminal screws; however, the continuity tester must have two probes that can be inserted into the terminal holes. Keep in mind that with a back-wired three-way switch, the common (hot) terminal is marked COMMON or COM.

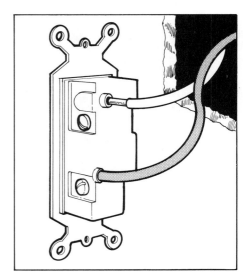

When you install a back-wired switch, be certain that no exposed wire extends beyond the outside edges of the terminal openings.

This chapter deals with replacing a home's existing switches with special switches that provide extra convenience. Unless otherwise stated, the wiring connections required for installing specialized switches are the same as those for installing wiring connections of a replacement switch (see Chapter 4). The main purpose of this chapter is to acquaint you with the variety of special switches that are available, so you can select and install the one that most nearly meets your needs.

For the sake of clarity, switches described in this chapter will be referred to either as conventional or special switches. A conventional switch is the ordinary clicking switch installed by builders in houses and condominiums. A special switch provides a feature not included in a conventional switch.

SPECIAL SWITCHES THAT USE REGULAR WIRING

When purchasing a special switch, always choose a single-pole switch to replace a single-pole switch, or a three-way switch to replace a three-way switch. The wiring arrangements are not interchangeable (see Chapter 4).

Purposes of Specialized Switches

There are two reasons for replacing conventional switches with specialized switches. You can acquire a convenience or advantage a conventional switch is not giving. If you install decorative switches, you can give walls a more attractive appearance. Of course, you often can achieve the same effect by replacing only the faceplates with more decorative covers.

Switches and "quiet switches." Most conventional switches being installed in new homes and sold in hardware stores are called "quiet switches". This is a misnomer, since quiet switches make noise. At one time, a quiet switch was considered a special switch. Many older houses that possess original switches do not have quiet

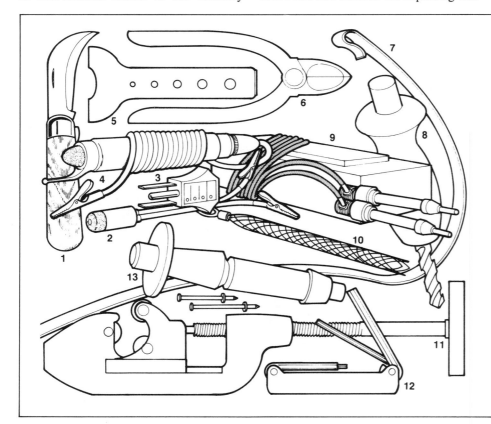

1. **Electrician's knife:** curved blade locks into position; simplifies stripping insulation from cable and wires
2. **Low voltage tester:** checks circuits such as in stereo switching systems
3. **Receptacle analyzer:** shows if wiring is correct; notes five possible problems
4. **Continuity tester:** sends battery signal through circuit before hookup
5. **Cable ripper/wire gauge:** clip shaped; fits over cable to cut away insulation
6. **Diagonal cutting pliers:** designed with long handles and short jaws to increase leverage when cutting wires
7. **Fishtape:** draws cable and wires through and between walls
8. **Hammer drill:** drives holes in masonry walls; needs no electricity
9. **Bar meter voltage tester:** measures voltage between 120 and 600 volts
10. **Wire basket:** method of attaching cable or wires to fishtape
11. **Pipe cutter:** designed specifically to cut through metal conduit
12. **Hex wrench:** used to tighten terminals for heavy cable
13. **Drive pin set:** small version of a hammer drill; drives holes for light items such as anchor cables

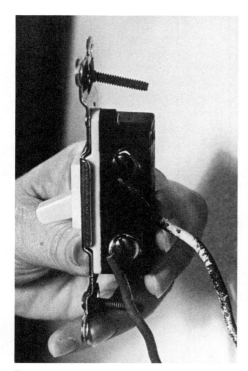

The common toggle switch can be replaced with one of a number of specialty switches that add convenience. The wiring is often the same.

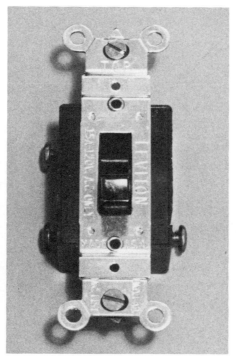

A "silent switch" replaces the armature of a toggle switch with a mercury bulb. The mercury creates the circuit operating the switch.

A rocker arm switch such as this is especially convenient in areas where one often has full hands, such as a laundry or nursery.

switches. Instead, they have snap switches.

A snap switch has a strong spring and knife-blade contacts that make loud clicking noises when the switch is engaged and disengaged. Quiet switches produce less noise than snap switches. This is due to less forceful springs and silver-alloy contacts, which do not make as much noise when they are engaged.

A quiet switch and a snap switch have one other main difference. The snap switch can serve with either alternating current or direct current. Each one is marked "AC-DC" to indicate that it can be used where either type of electrical service prevails. A quiet switch is marked "AC ONLY." If the noise created by a snap switch is annoying, and you wish a quieter switch for minimum cost, replace snap switches with quiet switches. The wiring connections are the same.

Silent switch. A silent switch, or mercury switch, is a toggle switch that looks like a snap or quiet switch. However, it makes no noise. The switching mechanism relies upon a sealed container of mercury, which flows from one end of the container to the other as the toggle is flipped ON and OFF. The flow of mercury completes or breaks the circuit between the switch contacts. There is no spring. Some designs have toggles that glow in the dark to pinpoint switch location.

A silent switch costs more than a quiet switch. On the other hand, it will seldom, if ever, fail. Because of its structure, practically no wear is placed on its parts. Some manufacturers of silent switches guarantee them for as long as 50 years.

Silent switches are available in single-pole and three-way models. Each is installed in the same way as a conventional single-pole or three-way switch. However, a silent switch must be put into place right

Wire an illuminated switch exactly as you do a regular switch. The illuminated switch is handy in a bathroom or garage.

side up. To ensure that you install the switch right side up, the word TOP is on the upper switch mounting strap. Keep the switch vertical. If it is installed at an angle, it may not work.

Locking switch. A locking switch is a tamper-proof switch that you must unlock with a key before the power can be turned on. Those wishing to prevent someone from using a device, such as a stationary power tool like a lathe or a drill press, can replace a conventional switch with a locking switch. Both are wired in the same way.

Rocker-arm switch. A rocker-arm switch combines decoration and convenience. It has a flat push-button ON-OFF panel rather than a toggle. The switch is activated by pushing lightly on a section of the panel. This can be done with a finger or, if your arms are full, with your elbow. Rocker-arm switches are silent. They come in a variety of colors, and on some the panels glow in the dark. These switches are installed the same way as conventional switches.

Time-delay switches. A time-delay switch contains a timer that keeps a light on for a period of time after you switch it off. Do not confuse time-delay switches with time-clock switches. Time-clock switches can be set to turn light or appliances ON and OFF. Time-delay switches turn lights or appliances OFF only. They are installed the same way as conventional switches and come in two styles, automatic and manual.

Automatic delay. The automatic time-delay switch possesses a time control of about 45 seconds. When the switch is flipped to either OFF or DELAY, depending on design, the timer starts running and keeps lights on for about 45 seconds. The automatic time-delay switch is useful in basements, garages, in outdoor areas, such as patios and decks, or in any location in which you desire a light that remains on for a brief period while you get to another lighted area.

Manual delay. You can set a manual time-delay switch for a period of time ranging from minutes to as long as 12 hours. The switch can be wired to control receptacles into which appliances are plugged or into circuits that control lights. If you have occupied a motel or hotel room having overhead infrared "sun" lamps in the bathroom, you are familiar with manual time-delay switches. They are specialty items usually sold only at electrical supply stores.

SPECIAL SWITCHES REQUIRING SPECIAL WIRING
Advantages of Time-clock (Timer) Switches

A time-clock switch combines a wall switch and timer in one unit. It is expensive and relatively difficult to find, so you may have to visit an electrical supply store rather than a hardware store to purchase one. However, no other switch provides the

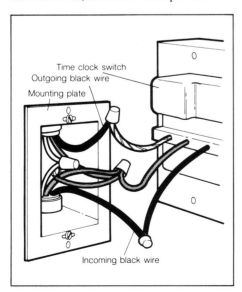

The wiring for a time-clock switch is complex. Be sure to attach the black wire of the switch to the feed wire in the box.

service of a time-clock switch. It has an automatic "ON-OFF" control that can be set to turn lights or appliances off and on by themselves at prescribed times. As a result, the switch can turn on a room air conditioner, attic fan, or other appliance before you return home from work or turn lights on and off when you are not home to make burglars think someone is there.

Safety procedures. Time-clock switches fit standard junction boxes. However, because of the clock's motor, a deviation in switch wiring is required. Before you make this hookup, use a voltage tester. When you use the tester, remember these safety rules:

(1) Do *not* touch any wires;
(2) do *not* touch the junction box;
(3) do *not* push the two black wires together, so that they touch;
(4) be sure your hands are dry and that you aren't standing on a wet surface.

Installing a Time-clock Switch

As always, the first step is to turn off power to the switch by deactivating the fuse or circuit breaker (see Chapter 1). Then proceed as follows:

1. Take off the switch cover and pull out the old switch so you can examine the wiring arrangement in the junction box. You can install a time-clock switch only if the wiring is middle-of-the-run. (For a description of middle-of-the-run wiring, see Chapter 3.) If wiring is middle-of-the-run, disconnect and remove the switch.

2. Determine which of the two black wires in the junction box is the hot feed (incoming) wire, that is, the one entering the box from the fuse or circuit breaker panel. The other black wire is the hot outgoing wire, which leads to other fixtures. Be sure the two black wires do not touch. Then, reactivate the fuse or circuit breaker.

3. To avoid receiving a serious shock, hold the two probes of the voltage tester by their insulation. Do not touch any metal, either in the junction box or on the wall. Touch one probe to the end of one of the black wires, and the other probe to the metal switch box. If the junction box is plastic, touch this probe to the ground wire instead.
   If the voltage tester light glows, you are touching the hot feed wire. Make a mental note of which wire it is, and

turn off the circuit. Then, so you will not confuse this wire with another, wrap a piece of masking tape around the hot feed wire.

If the voltage tester light does not glow, the other black wire is the hot feed wire.

4. Remove the wire nut from the two neutral (white) wires in the box and separate the two.

5. Time-clock switches come with a special mounting plate. The slots at the top and bottom of this plate line up with the screw holes of the junction box. Match these slots to the screw holes in the junction box and attach the mounting plate.

6. Straighten the wires in the box. Now connect the wires of the time-clock switch to the wires in the box. Splice the black wire of the switch to the circuit feed wire; then, connect the red wire of the switch to the circuit outgoing wire. Finally, connect the white neutral wire of the switch to the two white neutral wires in the junction box. Splice the ends of all the connections securely together.

7. Cover the wire ends with wire nuts; cover the nuts with electrical tape.

8. Attach the switch to the mounting plate and turn the electricity back on.

Adding a Pilot-light Switch

Pilot-light switches, available in single-pole and three-way models, have small bulbs that shine to tell you when the switch is ON. The light is separate or is built into

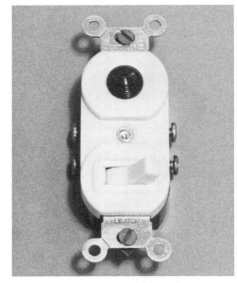

A pilot light switch can help you remember if you turned out the garage light on your way into the kitchen. The switch is simple to add.

the toggle. A pilot-light switch reveals that a light is on when the light cannot be seen. It is used primarily to turn basement, attic, garage, or outdoor lights on and off from a location that is remote from the lights. A pilot-light switch can only be installed in a junction box served by middle-of-the-run wiring. To complete the installation, you will need the replacement switch, a voltage tester, a wire nut, electrician's tape, and about 6 inches of wire covered with white insulation. Purchase No. 14 AWG for a 15-amp circuit, No. 12 AWG for a 20-amp circuit. AWG means American Wire Gauge and is a standard for wire thickness (see Chapter 9 for a longer discussion of wire gauge).

Installing a pilot-light switch with a separate light. As always, turn off the circuit controlling the switch box. Find the incoming feed wire and label it, as discussed above.

1. Be sure the electricity to the switch box still is turned off.
2. On one side of the switch is a brass terminal and a silver terminal. Connect the black hot feed (incoming) wire to the brass terminal screw.
3. On the other side of the switch are two brass terminal screws. Connect the black outgoing hot wire to one of the two brass terminals. Since these two terminal screws are connected together by a brass strip, it does not matter to which screw the wire is joined.
4. Strip ½ inch of insulation from one end of the white jumper wire and 1 inch from the other end. Connect the ½-inch end of this wire to the silver terminal screw on the switch. Splice the 1-inch end with the white neutral wire in the switch box.

Installing a pilot-light switch with a bulb in the handle. This switch only has two terminal screws. Both are brass. Connect each black house wire to one of the screws. Turn on the power and try the switch. If the pilot light in the handle stays on when the switch is in the OFF position, turn off the power and switch the hookup of the black wires.

Types of Dimmer Switches

A dimmer switch allows you to select various intensities of light to create a mood and conserve electricity. The switches reduce the number of watts that fixtures consume when maximum light intensity is not needed. The switches are used pri-

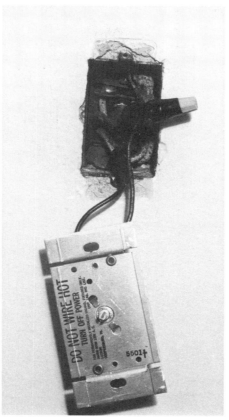

To add a dimmer switch, the power to the circuit must be off. Remove the old switch from the box, and splice in the new.

When you splice wires together, screw on the wire nut securely. The splice is then finished off with electrician's tape, as at left.

If the junction box cannot hold the dimmer housing and the wire nuts, do not use splices without nuts. Instead, enlarge the box.

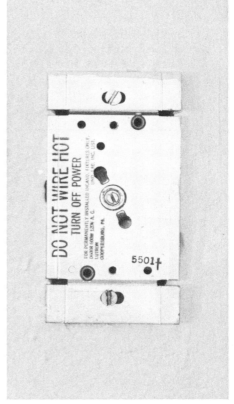

Push the wires carefully into the back of the box. Then fasten the dimmer housing to the openings provided for a mounting strap.

marily to control incandescent or fluorescent overhead and wall fixtures. Do not use them to control receptacles into which you may plug appliances or power tools. Using a dimmer switch for this purpose will damage the dimmer.

Hi-Lo switches. One type of dimmer

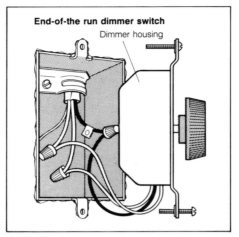

End-of-the-run dimmer switch
Dimmer housing

An end-of-the-run installation looks like this. If the dimmer has no built-in ground, attach the cable ground wire to the junction box.

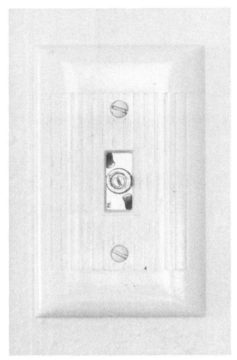

Install the cover plate over the control knob of the dimmer. The cover plate may also be replaced with a more decorative one.

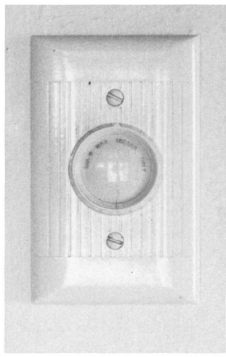

Finish with the control dial. Push the dial in to activate the circuit. Turn the dial to the right to brighten, to the left to lower.

switch has a toggle that lets you select one of three positions: OFF, LOW, and HIGH. This is referred to as a "Hi-Lo" switch. Although readily available, this type of dimmer is not the most popular.

Rotary switches. The most popular dimmer switch provides a rotary, rather than a toggle, control. You can set the control to provide a light output that is fully on, fully off or at any intensity in between. The light on some rotary control dimmers is turned off by turning the rotary fully to one side. With others, the rotary has to be pushed to turn the light off and on. You can, therefore, dial a desired light level, push the control to turn the light off, and push it again to turn on the light at the same intensity as before.

Size. A dimmer switch is somewhat larger than most other conventional or special switches. In most cases it will fit into a standard junction box; however, an older box can present a problem because old boxes are smaller than new ones. You will be able to get the switch into the box, but you may have no room left to hold the wire nuts over the wiring splices. It is, therefore, a good idea to measure the inside dimensions of the box, including its depth, and take the measurements with you when buying a dimmer switch. You may have to replace the box or do without the dimmer. (See Chapter 9 for a discussion of new junction boxes.)

Information markings. A dimmer switch has markings that are similar to those of conventional switches, with one notable exception. A dimmer switch has data relating to the switch's maximum-control wattage. This tells you the maximum wattage of bulbs that may be used with the

switch. For example, a hanging lamp is controlled by a dimmer switch with a maximum-control wattage of 600 watts. That means that the maximum wattage of the bulbs in the lamp cannot exceed 600 watts.

Cost. Dimmer switches cost more than conventional switches. They are available in single-pole and three-way models. As was pointed out before, never install a three-way dimmer switch in a box that originally possessed a conventional single-pole switch. Nor should you install a single-pole dimmer switch in a box that originally possessed a conventional three-way switch. The switch will not work.

Interference problems. Before deciding to install a dimmer switch, you should know that the addition of a dimmer may result in interference with television, radio and stereo systems. To dim or brighten a light, the switch possesses an electronic device similar to a rheostat. This regulates the strength of the current entering a light by varying the resistance in the switch. Although dimmer switches usually possess a filter to ferret out signals created by the rheostat, these signals may penetrate the filter, enter house wiring, and create interference with radio, TV and stereo systems.

One way to lessen interference is to plug television, radio and stereo equipment into a circuit other than the one serving the dimmer switch. If this does not work, purchase a power-line filter from a TV supply store and attach it, as directed, between the equipment and the receptacle into which you plug the equipment. A power-line filter traps interfering signals created by dimmer switches before they reach the radio, TV or stereo.

Installation for fluorescents or incandescents. The procedure involved in installing a dimmer switch to control incandescent lights may differ somewhat from installing a conventional switch for incandescent lighting. The procedure involved in installing a dimmer switch to control fluorescent lights differs significantly. Instructions for installing incandescent and fluorescent dimmer switches are given separately.

How to Install Incandescent Dimmer Switches

Always deactivate the fuse or circuit breaker serving the switch before you do any work on the switch.

Installing a single-pole dimmer. If the

dimmer switch is a single-pole device, install it the same way as you would a conventional single-pole switch. However, the dimmer switch may not have terminal screws. It may, instead, be equipped with wire leads that are to be spliced with the hot wires in the switch box. Then, join them with the proper-sized wire nut.

Installing a dimmer in a three-way system. If you are installing a three-way incandescent-light dimmer switch, determine which one of the three-way conventional toggle switches you wish to replace. Replace only one of the two conventional switches. To function correctly, a three-way dimmer switch must be paired with a conventional three-way toggle switch.

Turn off the power. Tag the black wire attached to the common terminal. Then disconnect the switch. Connect the hot wire of the dimmer switch to the tagged hot (common) wire in the junction box, and connect the two traveler wires of the dimmer switch to the two traveler wires in the switch box, as shown in Chapter 4.

How to Install Fluorescent Dimmer Switches

Fluorescent dimmer switches control the light output of fluorescent fixtures in areas where the intensity of the light is uncomfortably bright. A fluorescent dimmer switch can control as many as eight fluorescent bulbs simultaneously. However, the ballast of every fluorescent fixture you want to control must be replaced with a special ballast having dimmer capability. Special dimmer ballasts are available for 48-inch, 40-watt fluorescent fixtures. This size is the most common of fluorescent fixtures.

The fixture (or fixtures) you wish to control also must be of the rapid-start fluorescents. Fluorescents with external starters or instant-start require extensive work to be adapted for a dimmer. This involves replacement of the fixture terminals that hold the fluorescent lamp, grounding of the fixture (if it isn't already grounded), and installation of a different lamp. In other words, you must make a 40-watt rapid-start fixture out of the external starter-type or instant-start fluorescent fixture. Considering the time and expense involved, it seems more practical just to replace the fixture.

Types of fluorescents. The types of fluorescents are discussed in Chapter 3. To review them briefly, a fixture possessing

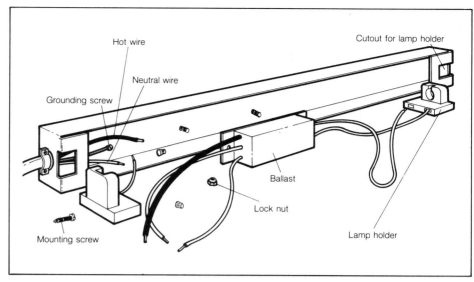

A dimmer switch to a fluorescent will not work unless the ballast in the fluorescent is changed. To remove the old ballast, unscrew its locknuts and slip the lamp holders out of position.

a small removable canister near one of the lamp terminals is an external starter-type fluorescent fixture; a fluorescent lamp having a single pin on each end and terminals for a single pin is an instant-start fluorescent fixture. If the fixture possesses neither of the characteristics just described, it is a rapid-start fluorescent.

Another way to identify a rapid-start fixture is to remove the cover. If the fixture is rapid-start, two wires will run from both sides of the ballast to the lamp terminal at each end of the fixture.

Installing the dimmer ballast. The following instructions describe how to provide a single 48-inch, 40-watt rapid-start fluorescent fixture with dimmer switch capability.

1. Cut power to the fixture by deactivating the fuse or circuit (see Chapter 1). To doublecheck, turn on the switch to make sure no electricity is present at the fixture.
2. Remove the fluorescent lamp and the metal lid to uncover the ballast and wiring.
3. Screws hold the lamp terminals in place. Remove these to free the terminals from the fixture.
4. Wire nuts cover the splices connecting the neutral and the hot wires of the ballast and the house wiring. Unscrew the wire nuts and untwist the wires so you can remove the ballast and lamp terminals from the fixture as an assembly. You don't have to disconnect the ground wire.
5. Locking nuts hold the ballast in the fixture. Remove these with pliers. (Be

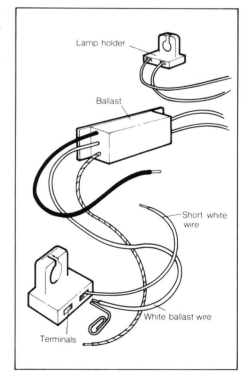

Then detach the lamp holders. This is done by inserting a wire such as the end of a paperclip into the opening beside the ballast wire.

careful, since the ballast is heavy.) Then, lift out the ballast and the lamp terminals.

6. You now have to disconnect the lamp terminals from the ballast. First, however, note the wiring setup: four sets of wires extend from the ballast, two on each end. The two wires at one end have identically colored insulation. The two at the other end will be color-coded white or one will be white and the other will be color-coded with dif-

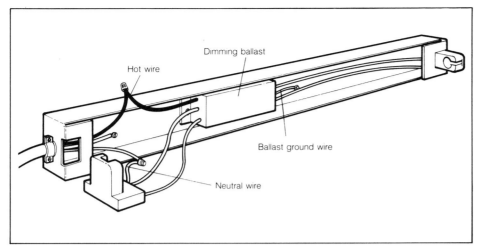

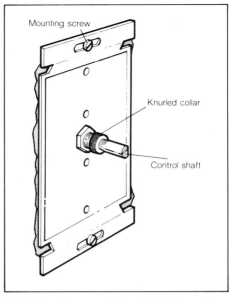

Reverse the process to install the dimmer ballast. Attach ballast wires to the lamp holders; slip holders into position; fasten down ballast. Then splice house wires and ballast wires.

Adjust the dimmer switch so the lights work as you want. Do this by manipulating the knurled nut on the control shaft of the switch.

ferent color. The colors (except for the white) will vary by manufacturer.

7. Disconnect all these wires from the lamp terminals. Align the dimmer ballast wires with those in the old ballast, so the new hookup will be identical with the old. If there is a short white wire protruding from one of the lamp terminals, leave it alone. Don't detach it.

8. In some fixtures, wires are held to lamp terminals by screws. However, in most fixtures, wires are held to terminals by small spring clamps. To release the wires, insert the end of a paper clip into the terminal slots located alongside the wires and press the clamp to release the tension. Pull the wires free.

9. Wire the new dimmer switch ballast to the lamp terminals by pressing the clamps, pushing the wires into their respective slots, and releasing pressure from the clamps.

10. Attach the dimmer switch ballast to the fixture with the locking nuts. Notice if a short piece of bare-metal wire is attached to the ballast. This is a ground wire. Wrap it around one of the ballast locking nuts before the nut is secured.

11. Reinsert the two lamp terminals in their housings and secure them with screws. Now, connect ballast wiring to house wiring by wrapping the hot wire around the house hot wire, and wrapping the ballast neutral wire around the house neutral wire. Secure the wire ends with wire nuts; cover them with electrician's tape. Re-install the fixture cover and the fluorescent lamp.

Installing the dimmer. Install the dimmer switch as described earlier. Then, adjust the switch for its minimum illumination level to make sure the fluorescent lamp won't turn off until the dimmer control is turned to OFF. To make this ad-

justment, activate the fuse or circuit breaker and turn the dimmer switch control shaft all the way clockwise so the lamp is at its brightest. Using long-nosed pliers, turn the knurled adjustment nut of the control shaft fully clockwise.

Now, turn the dimmer control to the lowest possible setting without having the lamp go out. Using long-nosed pliers, turn the knurled adjustment nut slowly counterclockwise until the lamp just begins flickering. Then, turn the adjustment screw clockwise until the lamp stops flickering. The adjustment is made.

More than one fluorescent. If there are several rapid-start fluorescent fixtures connected together and controlled by the same switch, replace the ballasts of all of them with special dimmer ballasts if you want to install a dimmer switch.

INCANDESCENT FIXTURES

You should have few problems, if any, when you want to take down an outmoded or damaged overhead or wall incandescent fixture in order to replace it with a modern unit. The task generally is easier than replacing a switch. The physical circumstances may be more difficult, however, because you may be working on a ladder. The fixture also may be too unwieldy to hold by hand. Furthermore, if the new fixture is a different shape, size, or weight from the old fixture, the new fixture will require different mounting hardware. These annoyances, and others, can be overcome by following the recommendations in this chapter.

Before turning attention to the job, let's say a word about problems that may afflict an incandescent fixture. Although fixtures are durable, suffering no greater problem for years than burned-out light bulbs, they may sustain physical damage that would necessitate their repair or replacement. You may also wish to replace a simple fixture with one that is more complex, such as a chandelier or a wall fixture that incorporates an outlet. Both these installations are fairly complicated; they are discussed separately.

Caution: Safety Procedures

Before you attempt any repairs to a lighting fixture, be sure power to the fixture is turned off by deactivating the fuse or circuit breaker serving the fixture circuit (see Chapter 1). Merely turning off the wall switch or pull chain that turns the fixture on and off is not good enough. In some installations, this will not turn off power to all wires of a fixture. Flip all switches to the fixture to doublecheck that the power is off.

During restoration this gaslight chandelier was converted to electricity. A dimmer switch varies light from very bright to the level of a soft glow.

TROUBLESHOOTING INCANDESCENT FIXTURES

Problem	Causes	Remedies
Light bulb does not go on.	1. Burned out.	1. Replace.
	2. Bad wall switch.	2. Test. If faulty, replace (see Chapters 4 and 5).
	3. Loose or broken wire.	3. Remove fixture (see below); tighten or repair affected wire.
Light bulb flickers.	1. Loose bulb.	1. Tighten.
	2. Loose fixture wire.	2. Remove the fixture (see accompanying text below); tighten the affected wire.
	3. Bad fixture socket.	3. Test (see text). Sockets of some fixtures can be replaced; sockets of others cannot—replace the fixture.
Fuse blows or breaker trips when fixture is turned on.	1. Bad fixture	1. Test (see text). If the socket is defective, replace it, if possible, or replace the fixture.
	2. Wire insulation has melted, creating a short circuit.*	2. Remove the fixture (see accompanying text) and inspect the wires. Use electrician's tape to cover the bad wire.

*Bulbs that exceed wattage specifications are the primary cause of damaged fixture wires. This specification is usually imprinted on the fixture housing. If bulbs more powerful than those specified are used, the fixture cannot withstand the heat created by the lights. In some instances, the heat can melt the wire insulation and cause a short circuit and, possibly, a fire.

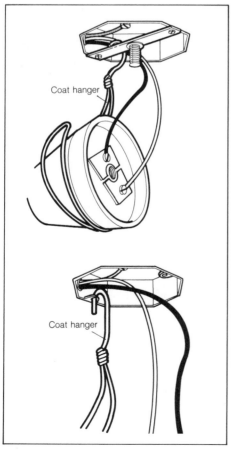

While you work on a ceiling fixture, hold it up with a bent coat hanger to support the fixture's weight and to protect the wiring.

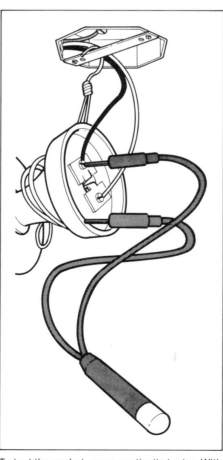

To test the socket, use a continuity tester. With the circuit power off, touch the black wire and the fixture housing.

How to Test Fixture Sockets

Test the sockets of incandescent fixtures in the following way.

1. Deactivate the power to the fixture by turning off circuit (see Chapter 1).
2. If possible, remove the socket without taking the fixture down from the ceiling or wall. If this is not possible, remove the fixture (see below).
3. Remove the bulb and connect the alligator clip of a continuity tester to the metal socket housing. Touch the probe of the continuity tester to the silver-colored terminal screw, if it is accessible. If it is not, touch the metal probe to the base end of the white wire.
4. The continuity tester bulb should glow. If it does not, an open circuit in the socket needs to be replaced. If the structure of the fixture is such that it is not possible to replace the socket, you will have to replace the fixture.

How to Remove an Incandescent Fixture

The following description applies to fixtures other than chandeliers. Installing a chandelier is somewhat more involved than installing an ordinary ceiling or wall fixture and is explained later in this chapter.

1. Turn off all power to the fixture (see Chapter 1). In the case of a broken fixture, test it with a voltage tester to be sure the fuse or circuit breaker has been deactivated (see step 4, below).
2. Loosen the mounting screws or nuts holding the fixture housing to the ceiling, but do not remove the fasteners just yet. First, fashion a double hook using a metal coat hanger. Straighten out the coat hanger and bend each end into a hook shape.
3. Remove the fixture mounting screws or nuts. Hook one end of the wire hanger to the fixture and the other end to a mounting strap of the fixture's junction box. In this way the fixture does not have to hang by its wires. Excessive stress will damage the wires; in addition the wires can pull loose from terminals and the fixture might fall.
4. If the fixture is not working, use the voltage tester to see if any power is present before you handle bare wires. With the fixture hanging by its coat hanger hook, hold one probe of the tester against a metal part of the fixture. Touch the other probe to the bare

end of the black wire where it attaches to the fixture terminal screw.

If the terminal screw is not visible, carefully unscrew the wire nut from the house black (hot) feed wire and the black fixture wire. DO NOT TOUCH THE BARE ENDS OF THE WIRES. Touch one probe of the voltage tester to the bare ends of the black wires and to a metal part of the fixture.

5. If the voltage tester bulb glows, power is present at the fixture. You have failed to deactivate the right fuse or circuit breaker. Work through the circuits until the fixture's power is off.

6. Disconnect the house wires from the fixture. There are two ways that the wires are connected: (1) by terminal screws, which are part of the fixture; (2) by house wires attached to fixture wires, with wire nuts covering connections. *Important:* Disconnect only those wires attached to the fixture. Do not disconnect any other wire in the fixture box.

Replacing a Single Porcelain Fixture

In a single porcelain fixture generally used in basements and garages, house wires are connected to fixture terminal screws. The hot wire is attached to the brass-colored terminal screw. The neutral wire is attached to the silver-colored terminal screw. Two mounting screws attach the fixture to the fixture junction box. To take down the fixture, remove the screws.

To install a fixture of this type, attach house wires to the proper terminal screws and line up mounting holes in the fixture with mounting tabs in the fixture box. Then, insert and tighten the mounting screws.

Installing Fixtures Requiring Mounting Hardware

If a new fixture does not line up with existing hardware and is a different size, shape or weight from the one which has been removed, you must judge how best to mount the fixture. There are two ways, both of which require additional hardware that is available from the electrical section of a hardware store. These methods are: (1) using screws that pass through the fixture housing and attach to an added metal mounting strap; (2) adding a threaded nipple to the junction box; a cap nut is screwed to the threaded nipple to secure the fixture.

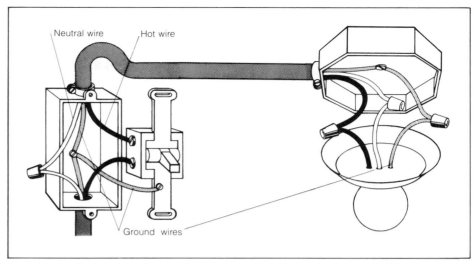

To replace a single center fixture, simply remove the old fixture. Then wire like-colored wires together. If the fixture has no built-in ground wire, attach the house ground to the junction box.

Steps for adding a mounting strap. A fixture that is held in place along its sides must have a mounting strap.

1. Measure the opening of the ceiling junction box and bring this dimension with you to the electrical parts store to assure that you get a mounting strap of the correct size. You will also need wire nuts and electrical tape.

2. Examine the fixture wires. If the wire ends are covered with insulation, strip off about ¾ inch. Twist together the fixture wire ends with house wire ends—black-wire-to-black-wire, white-wire-to-white-wire. Cover the splices with wire nuts.

3. If a threaded stud is protruding from the junction box, attach the mounting strap to the stud with a locknut. Threads are standard, so you do not have to worry that the locknut won't fit the stud. Notice that there are threaded holes on each end of the mounting strap. These will mate with holes in the new fixture. Tuck the house wires carefully inside the junction box. Position the fixture so its mounting holes align with the threaded holes of the mounting strap. Insert the mounting screws and tighten them securely.

4. If no threaded stud is protruding from the fixture box, you still can use a mounting strap. Notice that the strap is provided with elongated slots. Also notice that the fixture box has threaded ears. Just align the slots with the ears and attach the mounting strap with screws. Then, install the fixture with screws which are long enough to assure a secure hold.

Measure the diameter of a side-anchored fixture in order to be certain that the mounting strap you purchase is the right size.

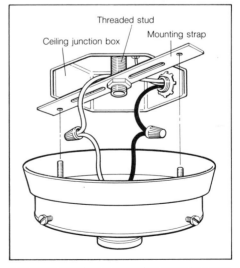

A locknut attaches a mounting strap to a center stud. Or, fasten the mounting strap to small "ears" on the edge of the junction box.

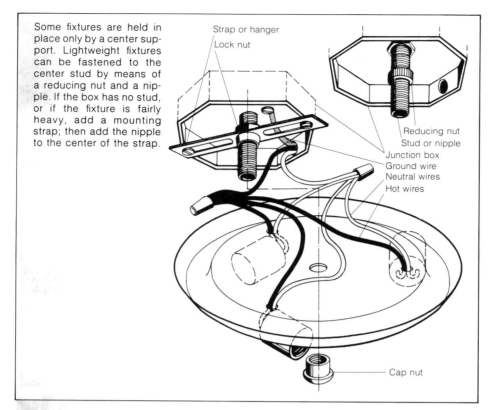

Some fixtures are held in place only by a center support. Lightweight fixtures can be fastened to the center stud by means of a reducing nut and a nipple. If the box has no stud, or if the fixture is fairly heavy, add a mounting strap; then add the nipple to the center of the strap.

Strap or hanger
Lock nut
Reducing nut
Stud or nipple
Junction box
Ground wire
Neutral wires
Hot wires
Cap nut

A hickey is necessary if you plan to install a chandelier that weighs more than ten pounds. It must be fastened to a center stud.

Installing fixtures that attach to a threaded nipple. A fixture that is held in place by a center support requires a threaded nipple.

1. Look for a stud in the center of the junction box. If one is present, buy a reducing nut and nipple. The reducing nut is threaded on both ends. One end is designed to fit the stud. The other end matches the threads of the nipple. Screw the reducing nut to the stud and screw the nipple to the reducing nut.

2. If the fixture has two or more sockets, it also has two or more black wires and two or more white wires. Strip off insulation, if it has not already been done, and splice together like-colored wires from the fixture with the corresponding house wires. Secure wire ends with a wire nut. Lift the fixture into place, so the nipple passes through the hole in the center of the fixture. Tuck all wires neatly into the fixture box and secure the fixture to the box with a cap nut. The cap nut is threaded to mate with the threads of the nipple.

3. If there isn't any stud in the ceiling junction box, buy a nipple and a mounting strap, that is large enough to fit the box. Be sure the nipple is long enough so that it can be tightened securely to the strap and still have ample length to provide a mounting for the cap nut.

Screw the nipple into the center hole of the mounting strap. Use screws to attach the mounting strap to the ears of the junction box.

4. Connect wires and mount the fixture by passing the nipple through the center hole of the fixture. Secure the fixture to the box with a cap nut.

Attaching a Chandelier

There are several things to consider before replacing one chandelier with another. If you are replacing chandeliers that weigh approximately the same, there is no problem. The mounting hardware is already in place and will provide adequate support. You need only substitute one chandelier for the other. Replacing a fixture with a chandelier that weighs less than ten pounds also presents no problem. Use the threaded nipple and mounting strap method described earlier.

However, if you are replacing a fixture or lightweight chandelier with a chandelier that weighs ten pounds or more, you must use a different mounting procedure. Hopefully, the junction box will have a threaded stud to which you can attach a nipple. If there is no threaded stud, remove the old box and install a new box that possesses a stud. This installation is discussed in Chapter 9.

If the junction box has a stud, prepare it to accommodate the heavier chandelier as follows.

1. Take down the old chandelier or fixture as described earlier in this chapter. Examine the chandelier. The line cord, which will fasten to the house wiring, comes up the chain from the lights. It passes through a collar, which is a finished lock-nut piece. Directly above this is the canopy, a dish-like shape designed to cover the ceiling junction box and the wiring. These parts are important components.

2. Buy a hickey, which is a bracket-shaped adapter that screws to the stud in the junction box. Screw a nipple onto the other end of the hickey. You may have to experiment until you have the proper spacing. The nipple must be screwed into the hickey far enough so the chandelier canopy, when in place, will be held securely against the ceiling. At the same time, the end of the nipple protruding from the box must have sufficient thread to secure itself firmly to the collar of the chandelier. The nipple and collar are the only two parts that hold the chandelier to the ceiling. After screwing the nipple to the hickey, secure the nipple to the hickey with a locknut.

3. Strip about ¾ inch insulation from the fixture wires. Insert the chandelier

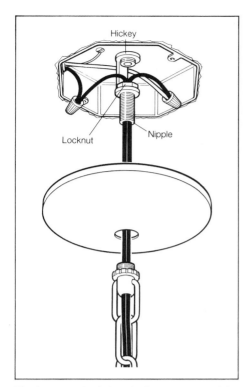

The lower end of the nipple must extend far enough to reach through the collar and to accommodate the finishing cap nut.

wires through the chandelier collar and through the nipple and lower part of the hickey into the junction box.

4. Secure the chandelier wires to house wires. If the chandelier wires are color-coded black or white, see that they match the color-coded house wires; that is, black-to-black and white-to-white. (If the chandelier wires are the same color, the neutral wire will be indicated by a filament called a tracer.) Secure the wire ends with wire nuts.

5. Hold the chandelier canopy in place and screw the chandelier collar to the nipple. Make sure fasteners are tight.

Replacing Wall-Mounted Fixture-and-Receptacle Combination Units

Note: When used in the following discussion, the term "fixture" refers to an incandescent light fixture.

Wall fixtures that incorporate a receptacle are a bit more cumbersome to handle than fixtures by themselves, but only because of the extra wiring needed to serve the receptacle. There are two ways in which combination units are wired: (1) end-of-the-run; (2) middle-of-the-run.

End-of-the-run installation. The term "end-of-the-run" refers to wiring that enters the combination fixture and receptacle box and terminates at this point. The

A chandelier or hanging lamp is an excellent way to illuminate a dining area. The hardware needed depends upon weight of the fixture. The installation itself is not difficult.

wiring serves only the fixture and receptacle; just one cable enters the box.

The fixture and receptacle are served by a wall switch. Unlike a receptacle in a middle-of-the-run installation, a receptacle in an end-of-the-run installation is not hot at all times. Instead, power to the outlet is controlled by the switch that controls the light. If the light is on or off, so is the outlet.

Replacing a combination fixture and receptacle wall unit having end-of-the-run wiring is less complicated than replacing a unit having middle-of-the-run wiring.

1. Shut off all power to the circuit by removing the fuse or tripping the circuit breaker (see Chapter 1). To make sure the power is off, turn on the wall switch

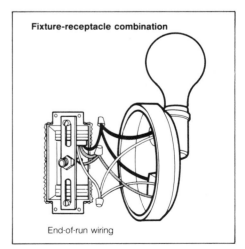

Fixture-receptacle combination

End-of-run wiring

If a receptacle combination has end-of-the-run wiring, the switch controls the light and the outlet.

controlling the fixture and also plug a lamp or electric shaver into the receptacle. Nothing should work.

2. Unscrew the cap nut holding the unit to the wall and draw the unit away from the wall. Identify the unit as end-of-the-run.

3. Undo each wire nut. There are three. Free the wires from one another and remove the unit.

4. Join the black wire attached to the fixture and the black wire attached to the receptacle to the incoming cable black wire. These are all hot.

5. Join the white wire attached to the fixture and the white wire attached to the receptacle to the incoming cable white wire. These are all neutral.

6. Join the single green wire from the combination fixture-receptacle unit to the green jumper wire attached to the screw in the junction box and to the bare wire from the incoming cable. These are ground wires.

7. Be sure all splices are tight. Cover them with wire nuts; secure the nuts with electrical tape.

8. Tuck the wires carefully into the junction box, position the combination unit, and secure the unit with the cap nut.

Middle-of-the-run installation. In a middle-of-the-run combination fixture and receptacle installation, two cables are contained in the fixture-receptacle box. One cable is the incoming cable, bringing electricity to the box. The other cable is the outgoing cable, taking electricity away from the box to other electrical components.

With a middle-of-the-run installation, only the light fixture is controlled by the wall switch. The receptacle is hot at all times. You can plug in and use a lighted make-up mirror, for instance, without having to turn on the wall switch and, hence, the fixture. This characteristic affects the roles of various wires in the house cable hookup.

House cables. In a typical installation, the incoming cable has 3 wires: (1) a black hot wire that brings electricity to the unit, (2) a white neutral wire, (3) a ground wire. The outgoing cable also has three wires: (1) a black hot wire that carries electricity out of the box to other receptacles; (2) a white hot wire that connects to the wall switch which in turn controls the light; (3) a ground wire.

Note: If it has not already been done,

wrap black electrician's tape around a portion of the outgoing cable white wire to identify it as hot. This process is called recoding, and it is a necessary safety precaution required by code.

Unit wiring. The combination fixture and receptacle unit possesses five wires: two white neutral wires, one of which attaches to the fixture and one that attaches to the receptacle; two black hot wires, one that attaches to the fixture and one that attaches to the receptacle; and one green ground wire.

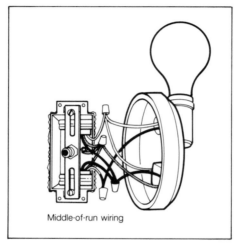

Middle-of-run wiring

To wire a combination fixture to middle-of-run wiring, identify the incoming hot wire. Remember to recode the outgoing neutral wire.

Inside the fixture-receptacle box is also a green jumper-ground wire. It is attached under the head of a screw that is screwed into the back of the box.

Procedures. If you want to replace a wall-mounted fixture and receptacle combination unit which has middle-of-the-run wiring, proceed as follows:

1. Turn off power to the old unit by deactivating the fuse or circuit breaker (see Chapter 1). To make sure power is off, turn on the wall switch controlling the fixture and also plug a lamp or electric shaver into the receptacle. Nothing should work.

2. Unscrew the cap nut holding the unit to the wall and draw the unit away from the wall. Identify the unit as middle-of-the-run.

3. Undo each wire nut. There are four. Free wires from one another and remove the unit.

4. Be sure all wires are separated. Then with the assistance of a helper, determine which cable is the incoming (feed) cable, as discussed in Chapter 5. Tag the cable if necessary.

5. Join the white wires from the fixture and receptacle to the single white wire from the incoming cable.

6. Join the black wire from the light fixture part of the unit to the white hot switch wire of the outgoing cable. As noted above, this is the white wire around which you should have wrapped black electrician's tape in order to identify it as hot.

7. Join the black wire from the receptacle part of the unit to the black wires from both the incoming and outgoing cables.

8. Join the green wire from the unit to the green wire attached to the screw in the box and to the bare wires from both the incoming and outgoing cables.

9. Make sure wires are securely twisted to each other. Cover wire ends with wire nuts.

10. Complete the installation by setting the combination unit in place and securing with a cap screw.

REPLACING AN INCANDESCENT FIXTURE WITH A FLUORESCENT FIXTURE

Sometimes it is desirable to remove an incandescent ceiling fixture in a kitchen, utility room or workshop and replace it with a fluorescent fixture. This is as easy to do as replacing an outmoded incandescent ceiling fixture with a modern incandescent ceiling fixture.

Installing a Circline Fluorescent Fixture

Follow these instructions to install a circline (circular) fluorescent fixture:

1. Turn off power to the incandescent fixture by removing the fuse or tripping the circuit breaker serving the fixture (see Chapter 1).

2. Remove the incandescent fixture as discussed earlier. Then determine which cable is the incoming cable.

3. Examine the fixture box. Is there a threaded stud? If there is, screw a reducing nut onto the stud. Then, screw a nipple into the reducing nut. When in place, the nipple will pass through the center hole of the circline fixture. Thread a cap nut onto the nipple to hold the circline fixture in place.

4. If the fixture box does not possess a stud, purchase a mounting strap long enough to fit across the box. Using screws, attach the strap to the two ears of the box. Now, screw a nipple far

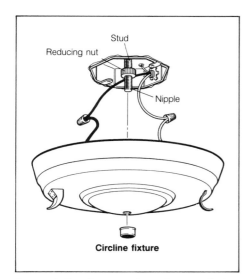

A new circline fluorescent requires a reducing nut and a nipple. Splice like-colored wires together. Attach the ground to the box.

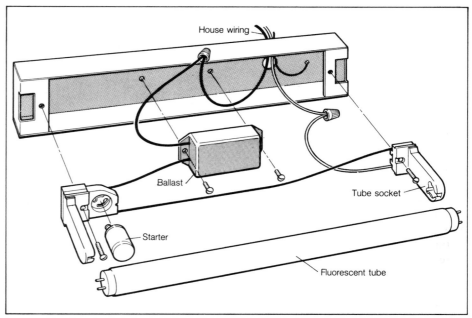

enough into the center hole of the mounting strap to be sure the nipple is secure. Extend the nipple a sufficient length to accept the cap nut that holds the circline fixture.

5. To connect the circline fixture to house wiring, splice the incoming black (hot) wire to the black wire of the fixture and connect the incoming white (neutral) wire to the white wire of the fixture. The ground wire arrangement varies from installation to installation (as follows).

6. If the circline fixture is equipped with a green ground wire, splice the wire together with the incoming ground wire and a short jumper wire. Attach the other end of the jumper wire to the screw in the junction box.

7. If the circline fixture is not equipped with a ground wire, disconnect the incoming cable ground wire from the screw. Cut *two* jumpers of green wire. Attach one jumper with a screw to the fluorescent fixture housing. Attach the other jumper to the ground screw in the junction box. Now, using a proper-sized wire nut, connect the two jumpers with the incoming ground wire.

Installing Straight-Tube Fluorescent Fixtures

The same general procedure used to install circline fluorescent fixtures applies if you want to install a straight-tube fluorescent fixture. However, there are some differences worth noting. These tips will help you avoid potential problems. Because of the fixture's size, work with a helper.

Installing a single-tube fixture. Consider, first, the installation of a fluorescent fixture that has just one tube.

1. Turn off power and remove the old incandescent fixture (see Chapter 1).

2. If the junction box is equipped with a stud, screw a hickey onto the stud. Then screw a nipple into the hickey, securing the nipple to the hickey with a lock nut. The nipple will serve as the securing medium for the nut that holds the fixture to the ceiling.

3. If the fixture box does not have a stud, buy a mounting strap and attach it to the ears of the box. Screw a nipple into the center hole of the strap, as explained above.

4. Now, remove the cover from the new fluorescent fixture and punch out one of the tabs in the fixture mounting plate. Remove the center tab, unless you are dealing with an off-center installation. In that case, remove whichever tab is applicable. Use a screwdriver or punch to knock out the tab.

5. If you use a channel other than the center channel to mount the fixture to the ceiling, use screws on each end to hold the fixture in place. These must be fastened to ceiling joists. Locate the joists and insert screws into the wood so that the fixture is held firmly to the ceiling. (See Chapter 9 for locating joists.)

6. Notice the black, white and green wires in the fluorescent fixture. Insert their ends through the channel in the fixture mounting plate and up through the cen-ter of the nipple, into the junction box.

7. The wiring connections are no different from those explained earlier. Black and black wires go together; white and white wires go together; green and green (or bare) wires go together.

8. Raise the fixture to the ceiling so the nipple passes through the channel in the fixture mounting plate. Place a washer around the nipple and over the channel. Secure the fixture to the ceiling with a nut.

Installing a multi-tube fixture. Replacing an incandescent fixture with a straight fluorescent fixture having two or more tubes is done in much the same way as above. However, if the fixture has a large cutout in the center of the mounting plate, attach it only to a fixture box that has an octagonal shape and is equipped with a screw stud. If the junction box is not the correct shape, install a new one. (See Chapter 9 for instructions.) Then mount the fixture as follows:

1. Screw a reducing nut onto the stud in the fixture box and screw a nipple into the reducing nut.

2. Wire the fixture to house wiring, as explained above.

3. Hold the fixture against the ceiling and screw a mounting strap onto the nipple. The mounting strap has to be long enough to stretch across the large channel. Its purpose is to provide a firm hold for a fixture.

4. Screw a locknut on the nipple until it is secure against the mounting strap.

SURFACE WIRING

In every home, there are some locations that need switches or outlets. The usual way to solve the problem is to extend an existing circuit. Circuit cables are run through the walls to the place where you want the new receptacle, switch or fixture to be. One end of the cable is attached to an existing receptacle or other power source. Then the new item is wired in. Such a project can be fairly complex, for it involves opening up walls or ceilings, or both. Procedures that permit you to do this in the most efficient manner are outlined in Chapters 9 and 10.

There is, however, an alternative method of adding circuits, and it requires no carpentry work. The method is called surface wiring, and it is done by means of a type of hardware called raceway. According to the National Electrical Code, a raceway is "any channel that holds wires, cables, or bus bars. Raceway may be of metal or insulating material and the term includes rigid metal conduit, rigid nonmetallic conduit, flexible metal conduit, electrical metallic tubing, underfloor raceways, cellular concrete floor raceways, cellular metal floor raceways, surface metal raceways, structural raceways, wireways, and busways." (In electricity, the term "bus" refers to a conductor or group of conductors serving as a common connection for three or more circuits. A bus comes in the form of a metal bar, thus, the term "bus bar.")

A Raceway vs. an Extension Cord

As complicated as the National Electrical Code definition may appear, do not let it discourage you. In actuality, a raceway is like a protected extension cord, but the differences between the two are significant. Instead of cord, the raceway usually

relies on wires. These wires are enclosed in a protective casing of plastic or metal. The casing is attached to walls, baseboards, ceilings or even floors, to create a permanent installation. A raceway can include outlets, switches or ceiling fixtures. Special connectors turn corners or provide intersections for extending branches from the basic pathway. Another major distinction between a raceway and an extension cord is that a raceway is grounded, either with a ground wire, metal casing, or both. Only heavy-duty extension cords offer such protection.

There is one way in which an extension cord and a raceway are the same. A raceway is not a new circuit. It is an extension of an existing circuit. You do not have more electricity at your disposal; you only have more access points.

Uses of Raceways

Raceways were developed primarily for use in nonresidential buildings where cables are normally embedded in concrete. Concealing new cables requires breaking up the concrete—a horrendous task. Metal or plastic raceways allow offices, stores and factories to place cables in relatively unobtrusive channels that are mounted on walls, along floors and on ceilings.

Most municipalities have no regulations

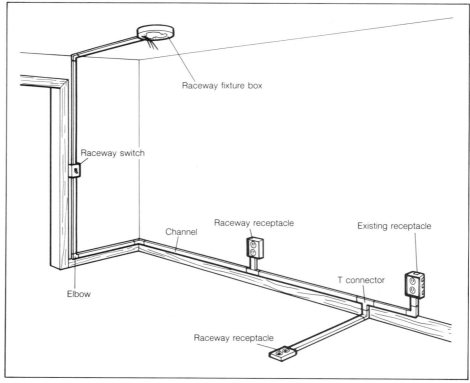

Raceway provides an efficient method to add receptacles, switches and fixtures. The metal or plastic track contains single conductor wires; special housings hold the equipment desired.

that prohibit homeowners from using metal or plastic raceways if they want to avoid the job of concealing cables. Homeowners themselves, however, sometimes are reluctant to add a raceway on the grounds that they find the channels unattractive and distracting. Before ruling out its use, see if you can conceal raceway channels behind your furniture at the baseboard level. You also may be able to run wiring vertically up a wall behind draperies.

Even if you still find raceways unappealing for use in the main rooms of your home, consider using them in areas where the appearance may not be objectionable. For example, many homeowners do not mind surface wiring in home workshops, garages, utility rooms or basements.

Regulations Governing Raceways

NEC regulations. If you decide to install a raceway, be aware that there are limitations to its use. The National Electrical Code specifies that metal raceway be installed in dry locations and then only so long as it will not be subject to physical damage. The metal sections must be installed in such a way that they form a secure mechanical and electrical coupling in order to protect the wires inside the raceway from abrasion. The holes for the screws that hold raceway against walls or ceilings have to be flush with the metal channel surface to provide added protection against cable abrasion.

The National Electrical Code also spells out limitations for plastic raceway. It must be flame retardant, and resist moisture, impact and crushing. As with a metal raceway, a plastic raceway should be installed in a dry location.

Both metal and plastic raceways are designed in sizes to contain wires or cable of a specific size. You must adhere to these specifications. Furthermore, the number of wires installed in a raceway should not be more than the number for which the raceway is designed. If you are guided by these limitations, you should have no problem installing or using a raceway.

Local codes. Although most local electrical codes allow homeowners to use surface wiring, some do not. Still others establish limitations over and above those set down by the National Electrical Code. You must determine what, if anything, the electrical code of your municipality says about raceways and/or surface wiring before you begin to install it in your home.

Which Raceway to Buy

Size. There are several different raceway sizes and connector sizes designated by numbers from 200 to 3000. The numbers are based on the size and number of wires a given raceway can handle. Usually size 200 raceway will serve if you are using No. 14 or No. 12, Type TW wire. Type TW wires is the one used in most home circuits. No. 14 and No. 12 wires are standard sizes for 120-volt circuits that are used to provide electricity for lighting and for receptacles for small appliances. (A more detailed discussion of wire and cables is presented in Chapter 9.)

Types. One type of raceway consists of tubular channel clips that have been fastened to walls or ceilings. Wires or cable are threaded through the channels and connected to a source of electricity. Another type of raceway consists of two major components: (1) a backing that is attached to the wall, and (2) a front cover plate that is snapped onto the backing after wires or cables are laid.

Meeting your needs. A talk with the dealer of your local electrical supply store can help you select the type of raceway that is best for the task at hand. Before you go, draw a sketch of what arrangement you want. Locate the position of receptacles and/or switches you want to install, and measure between the spots where you want them. Since the raceway will get its power from an existing circuit, decide upon the existing receptacle that you are going to tap for power. The dealer should be able to advise you concerning what type of raceway is best for your use, how much of it you will need, and what accompanying hardware (connectors) will be required.

INSTALLING A PLASTIC RACEWAY

Generally, the procedure for installing a raceway involves several steps: (1) determine if the circuit you wish to tap has sufficient electrical capacity to permit hooking up to the circuit; (2) prepare an existing hot receptacle to accept new wiring; (3) install new receptacles; (4) measure, cut and attach the raceway; (5) connect the wires; and (6) finish off the junctions with cover pieces.

Step One: Purchasing Materials

If your plan is fairly thorough, you will be able to determine the amounts of materials needed in order to complete the in-

stallation. Measure the total distance that the channel will travel, and purchase channel lengths to equal that plus an extra 5 to 10 feet to allow for possible breakage.

You also must purchase the housings for the receptacles, switches, or fixtures you plan to include in the raceway. Ask for pieces compatible with raceways.

Connectors. There are two types of special hardware that you may need, a raceway elbow connector and a raceway T-connector junction box. The elbow connector is used to connect two pieces of raceway that join at right angles. The T-connector junction box is used to connect a new middle-of-the-run receptacle. You will need a number of reducing connections to connect the larger junction and fixture boxes to the smaller raceway openings. The number depends upon the complexity of the installation.

Wire. Finally, you will need to purchase single conductor black wire, white wire and green wire. Request Type TW. If the circuit that you are tapping is a 15-amp circuit, ask for No. 14 wire; if it is 20-amp, ask for No. 12 wire. To the total of the channel lengths, add at least one-third more for hookups and general wastage. You will also need wire nuts and electrician's tape.

Selecting the tools. You will also need basic tools for installing the raceway, such as a screwdriver and masonry or wallboard anchors. To cut the raceway to size, use a hacksaw with a fine-toothed blade that has 40 teeth per inch. You will be using a wire cutter and stripper to finish the wire connections. To pull the wires through the raceway, you need what is called a fish-tape, which is a long, thin metal wire that ends in a fishhook shape.

Step Two: Selecting the Circuit

The power source for a raceway installation must be carefully planned before you begin work. To select an appropriate circuit, consult your circuit map and the Wattage Table in Chapter 1 to find out which circuit can provide enough wattage to supply the outlets, light fixtures or appliances the raceway will serve. If you do not take this step, you can overload the circuit and it will break constantly. If you are drawing power for surface wiring from an existing switch, use the same kind of adapter. The procedure is the same. A ceiling box requires a specially shaped adapter; the process, again, is the same.

Step Three: Preparing the Receptacle

The raceway connects to an existing junction box. Usually this holds a receptacle or, less often, a ceiling fixture or switch. To make room for the connections and the raceway housing, you will be provided with a backing plate and an adapter extension. The backing replaces the receptacle's faceplate. The raceway will fit into a shaped opening between the backing plate and the extension plate.

Backing plate. First turn off the circuit controlling the existing receptacle. To install the adapter, remove the receptacle cover plate and unscrew the receptacle from its mounting strap. Without disconnecting the wires, pull the receptacle from the junction box. Slip the receptacle and wires through the raceway backing plate so the backing plate mounts against the wall.

Extension piece. There are a number of knockout sections cut into the extension to allow the raceway to enter from the bottom, sides or top of the adapter. Use a pliers to remove the section through which the raceway will pass. Then slip the receptacle and wires through the hole in the extension plate. Clip the extension to the backing plate.

Step Four: Installing New Receptacles

You now have to install the new receptacle, or receptacles. This is done before installing the raceway channels. Each section requires a receptacle mounting plate and a receptacle cover.

Positions of receptacles. As with receptacles of any normal circuit, receptacles on a raceway fall into one of two positions—middle-of-the-run or end-of-the-run. A middle-of-the-run receptacle is one that receives power from a source through an incoming cable. But power does not "terminate" at the receptacle. Rather, it is transmitted to another receptacle, switch, or fixture through an outgoing cable. Conversely, an end-of-the-run receptacle receives power from a source through an incoming cable, but there is no cable going to another receptacle, switch or fixture.

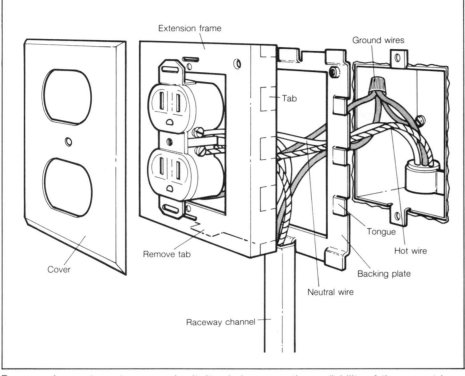

Raceway does not create a new circuit; it only increases the availability of the current in an existing circuit. The raceway wiring attaches to an existing receptacle.

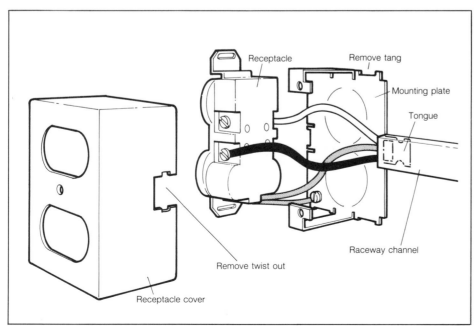

Receptacle covers house a receptacle. Remove all tangs on the backing plate except the one that fits into the channel; in the cover, remove only the tang that fits over the channel.

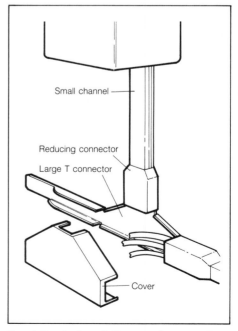

Specially designed T-connectors create a junction between the main channel of the raceway and the channel feeding a receptacle.

To install a middle-of-the-run receptacle, you will need a T-connector piece and two reducing pieces on either side of the T-shaped base. An end-of-the-run receptacle will require only an elbow connector.

Mounting plate. The receptacle mounting plate is outfitted with a series of tangs. Twist off all of these, except the one to which the raceway will connect. Then, attach the mounting plate to the wall at the spot your plan indicates. The mounting plate must be fastened securely to the wall. Use molly bolts to install the plate in gypsum wallboard. These bolts fasten into an expandable shank that spreads out as the

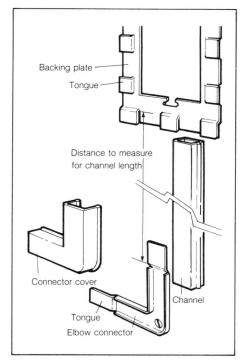

When you purchase raceway materials, be sure that you have all the pieces you need. Install cover pieces before stringing wires.

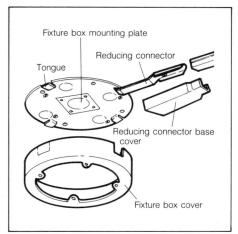

A ceiling fixture requires a mounting plate and a cover. A reducing connector joins the mounting plate and the channel itself.

screw is tightened. To install the plate in plaster or other masonry walls, use masonry anchors. These are expandable shafts that are sunk into a drilled hole. As the screw is tightened in the anchor, it spreads and tightens against the surrounding surface.

Switches and fixtures. These two items also come with backing plates and covers. Install them exactly as you would the receptacle mounting base. Use a reducing connector to connect the wider tongue of the mounting plate to the smaller opening of the channel base.

Step Five: Installing the Channels

Marking the channel lines. The channels must be laid in straight lines from one location to the next. To do this, measure up from the floor to the position of the proposed location of the top of the horizontal channel. Use a spirit level and a long metal straightedge to draw in a level line as long as the channel's path. You will also need vertical lines in those locations that require a vertical channel, such as the junction between a channel and a receptacle or a switch.

Snapping chalkline. The easiest way to assure a straight line is to use a plumb-and-chalkline. This is an inexpensive tool that holds a line of string in a spring-controlled container. As the string is pulled out, the container automatically covers the string with chalk. At the end of the string is a weight, so it will hang straight. Pull a length of string from the container so the string measures slightly past the horizontal channel's position. Let it hang on either side of the tang to which the channel will connect. Tack down the weighted end; snap the string to create a straight chalkline.

Placing the channels. Using proper fasteners, as you did for the mounting plates for receptacles, install all corners and elbows. Align the edges carefully. Then measure to determine the length of channel that is required to go from one connector to another, as shown. Cut pieces to size with the hacksaw. If some lengths are longer than the pieces that you have, join two with special channel joiners.

Once the pieces are cut, install the backings. In locations where there are tongued couplings, you will have to remove the screw holding down one of the tongues to complete the connection.

Once all the backing pieces are in place,

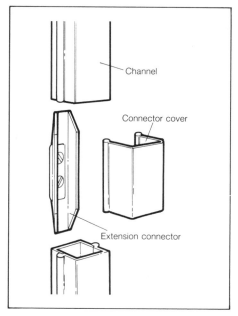

If you require a run of channel that exceeds the 10-foot lengths, purchase special channel extensions. All screws must be flush.

snap on the channel covers. Do not install the covers for any of the junctions, however. These will be placed after the wiring connections are made.

Step Six: Fishing the Wires through the Channels

Running wires is fairly simple if you use a fishtape, as described here. You will run the vertical lines first and then the horizontal lines. Once the lines are in place, the connections will be made and the final finishing completed.

Using the fishtape. A fishtape can greatly simplify the task of running wires through a raceway channel. To pull the wires through, push the tape from one channel opening to the next. Remove 3 inches of insulation from one end of each of the three wires. Pass the stripped ends through the tape's hook, fold the wires over and secure them with electrician's tape. You can then draw the wires through with no trouble. If you want to, coat the wires with lubricant that has a wax base before you draw them through long stretches of channels, such as from a switch to a ceiling fixture. This will make them easier to pull through. Do not use a lubricant with a petroleum base; the chemical structure will damage the insulation.

Wiring the new receptacles, switches and ceiling fixtures. Cut a wire of each color so that it is 16 inches longer than the channel. This will give 8 inches of leeway at each end to make the wiring hookups. Use the fishtape to pull the wires up from the horizontal junction to the new receptacle. Fasten the receptacle to the mounting plate. Then hook up the wires as you would for an end-of-run receptacle—hook the black wire to the brass screw beside the top outlet and the white wire to a silver screw beside the bottom outlet. Finish by hooking up the green ground wire. (For illustrations of these hookups, see Chapters 3 and 4.) If there is no green ground screw (which is sometimes true of a ceiling fixture), fasten the ground wire to the back of the mounting plate. Once the connections are complete, position the cover plate over the installation.

Wiring the T-connectors. You now must fish the horizontal wires. Measure from the center of a T-connector to the center of the next T-connector; add 8 inches to the total to allow 4 inches at each end for the wiring connections. Run wires through all the channels before you begin to make any wire connections.

At each T-connector there will be three wires of each color—two from the horizontal channels and one from the vertical channel. Splice like-colored wires together, cap with a wire nut and secure the nut with electrician's tape.

Step Seven: Connecting to the Existing Power Source

An end-of-the-run outlet. As stated earlier, this hookup is simple. It requires 2 green jumper wires that are 4 inches long and one wire nut. Strip 1 inch of insulation

from one end of each jumper wire, and ½ inch from the other.

First, attach the house wires to the top receptacle (as always, connect black to brass and white to silver). Next, connect the black and white raceway wires to the bottom receptacle. Then connect the black and white raceway wires to the correct screws at the bottom outlet.

Now connect the ½-inch end of a jumper to the back of the junction box. Connect the ½-inch end of the other jumper to the green ground screw on the receptacle base. Splice the two jumpers together with the ground wires from the house circuit and the raceway. Cap with a wire nut; secure the nut with electrician's tape.

Middle-of-the-run receptacle. This hookup is more difficult because it requires one splice for connection of each of the three colors of wiring. Cut 4-inch jumpers of black, white and green. Strip 1 inch of insulation from one end of each wire and ½ inch of insulation from the other. Detach the black and white wires from the bottom receptacle. Splice all the like-colored wires together with the 1-inch ends of the jumpers. Then hook the ½-inch ends of the jumpers to the proper terminals.

Step Eight: Finishing Off
Once the wiring hookups are finished, install the faceplate over the receptacle and the raceway is done.

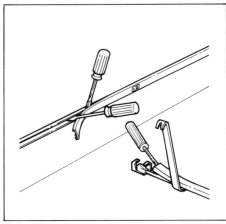

To add to a prewired raceway after it is installed, turn off the circuit. Pry away the cover with one screwdriver; hold the loosened cover with another. To lift the cover off a floor channel, use a prybar.

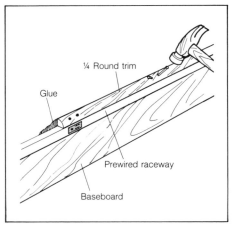

One way to hide a raceway is to fasten it to the top of the baseboard. Then install quarter round above the raceway. The trim conceals and protects the installation. Be sure to nail at an angle to protect the raceway.

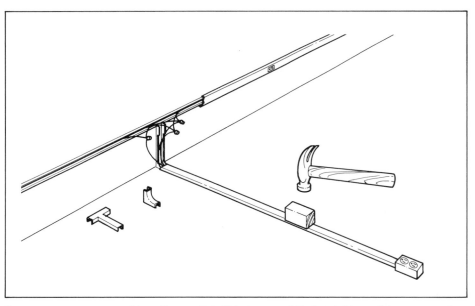

In a prewired raceway, the wires are installed before the cover channel is installed. Receptacles and switches are built into the channel, rather than added onto it. This characteristic increases the raceway's usefulness.

Some raceways can provide a floor outlet. This is especially helpful in a dining area or in a playroom where an outlet is needed to operate a small appliance, such as a coffeemaker, or an electric motor. Use a wood block and hammer to snap the cover in place.

FUNCTIONS OF A PROGRAMMABLE THERMOSTAT

Most homeowners today are concerned with rising heating and cooling costs. One helpful and money-saving project, which is easy to add to your home, is a programmable thermostat. This can be set to adjust the temperatures in your home automatically for waking and sleeping hours. The thermostat also can include indicators that set temperatures for those hours when the house is usually occupied and for those hours when it is not. Since your heating-cooling system will not use as much energy when the house is empty, you will reduce fuel usage and cut costs.

Types of Thermostat Units

The units come in a variety of styles and are produced by several manufacturers. There are some units that replace heat-only thermostats, which have two or three wires. Other units will replace thermostats

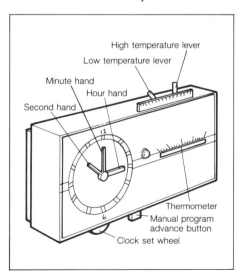

A programmed thermostat is designed to regulate the temperature of your home according to your schedule and living patterns.

that are combination controllers for heating and air conditioning. The latter may have four or five wires. Since energy-saving, programmable thermostats vary considerably from one brand to another, be sure to get full instructions with the unit when you buy it.

Components. All the models come with a wall plate that is fastened in place over an opening through which the existing thermostat wires run. On top of the wallplate, you attach a subbase that is wired to be compatible with your thermostat. The actual programmable thermostat then fits over the subbase. Contacts on the back side of the new thermostat touch contacts on the front of the subbase to complete the necessary circuits.

Installation Guidelines

The unit described here is made by Honeywell. One major requirement for the thermostat is that it be exactly level, because the mercury switches used as controls must be level to operate properly. A mercury switch is a glass bulb inside which there is a small pool of mercury and two wire conductors. When the bulb is tipped, the mercury runs down to immerse the conductors. Electric current then passes through the mercury from one conductor to another. When the bulb (switch) tips back, the mercury moves away so the conductors are separated and the electric current stops. ("Silent" light switches work on the same principle. The switch toggle shifts a small container of mercury up and down to control the light.) To insure a level thermostat, use a small spirit level.

Information You Must Know

Before you buy the new thermostat, you need certain information about the exist-

ing one in order to purchase a programmable thermostat that will properly replace your existing one. Note the brand name and model number of the existing thermostat. Then remove the cover so you can determine how many wires are in the thermostat connection. If the thermostat controls heat only, there will be two or three wires; if it controls both heating and air conditioning, there may be four or five.

Check also to see if you have the instructions that came with the existing thermostat. They will help when you wire the new programmable unit. If you do not (and most of us will not, since the previous owner or builder will have discarded them), installation instructions for the new unit usually include "typical" wiring diagrams.

INSTALLATION PROCEDURES
Removing the Old Thermostat

We will repeat: programmable thermostats vary from one brand to another, so be sure to get complete instructions with your unit. However, the following is a general breakdown of the steps involved.

When you install the new thermostat, be sure that the electric power is off. To accomplish this, remove the fuse or pull the circuit breaker that runs your furnace fan. Lift off the cover plate from the old thermostat. Carefully note which wires go to which connection in the existing thermostat. The connections will be numbered or lettered, and comparable identification marks will be on the connections of the new programmable thermostat. The easiest way to keep track is to tag each of the lines.

Inspect the condition of the wires carefully. If they are discolored, or if the insulation is cracked or broken, you must either cut back the wires to solid material, or you must replace the wiring leading from the furnace fan to the thermostat.

Now remove the old thermostat base from the wall. Plug the wall opening through which the wires come. This is important. Otherwise, a warm or cold draft through the opening could affect the operation of the thermostat.

Installing the New Unit

The Honeywell thermostat pictured here has a built-in clock. This, coupled with the

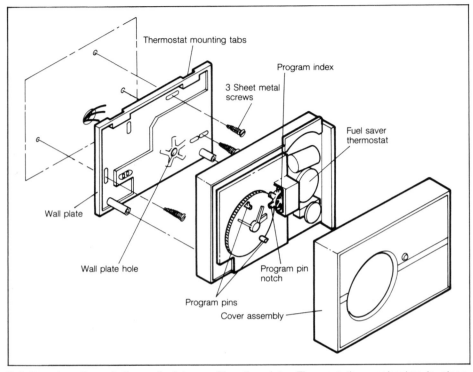

Pull the wires through the wall plate; position the plate. Then set the mechanism in place. Program pins set into the clock wheel turn the system on and off at predetermined times.

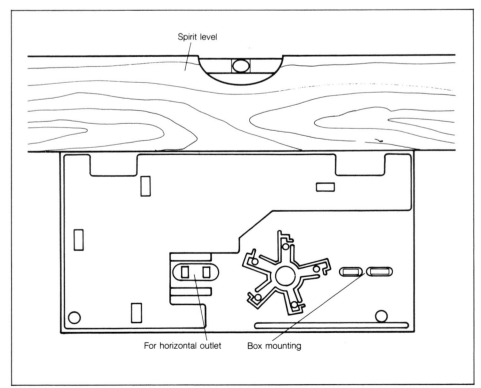

A programmable thermostat is controlled by a mercury switch. Therefore, the wall plate must be perfectly level for the thermostat to function correctly. Check with a small level.

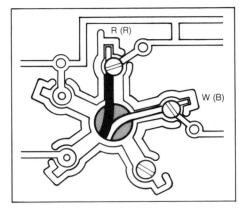

The wires must lie within the design ridges. This arrangement will prevent interference with the thermostat mechanisms.

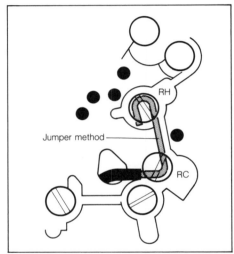

If your system has a single transformer for heating and cooling, strip enough insulation from the wire to connect terminal RC and RH.

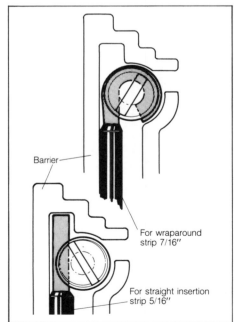

Wires can be fastened to the terminal screws in two ways. Either curl them around the terminal post or insert them beside the post.

programming, governs the heating and cooling cycle. The clock is run by a small battery, which must be charged before the thermostat can function. From then on the battery recharges while the thermostat is working. Methods for acquiring the initial charge will vary according to manufacturer; see the instruction sheet for your model.

Connecting the Wires

Draw the wires through the opening in the wallplate and fasten the wall plate loosely in place with the screws provided. Level the plate and secure it firmly, but do not overtighten the screws or the wall plate threads will be stripped. Fasten the wires as shown.

Then tuck the wires back into the hole—without dislodging the patching material there. Protruding wires can catch on the mechanisms in the thermostat and cause it to malfunction.

Attaching the Base

At the back of the thermostat base are small spring fingers. These match up with terminals on the wallplate you just positioned. Install the base carefully so you do not damage the springs.

Setting the Heat Anticipator

Check the primary control or gas valve of your heating system to find out how much current it draws when it is operating. This is your heat-anticipator rate. On the lower right side of the base is a dial. Set this to match the rating you found.

If you cannot find a rating, check with the instruction sheet of your unit to find how you can set this dial.

PROGRAMMING THE THERMOSTAT

The programming for the Honeywell unit is handled by three interrelated functional components. The first is the built-in clock. This is set up in two 12-hour sections, one light-colored for daylight hours, the other dark-colored for nighttime hours. The second component consists of two temperature levers, one of which is blue for the lowest temperature level, and one of which is red for the highest temperature level. The third component is a set of pins that fits into cogs built into the clock wheel. These send a signal to the control mechanism, indicating that either the red or blue temperature level should govern the system. The pins are color-coded red or

blue to indicate which level is being signalled.

Keep in mind that it will take approximately one-half hour for the temperature to change from one level to another. (For this reason, two pins cannot be closer to each other than one hour.) Therefore, if you set the night temperature for your furnace at 60° and you want that to switch to 68° F. by 7 o'clock in the morning, the red pin would be set at 6:30.

Multiple settings. The thermostat can handle more than two pins. If the house is empty from 8:30 to 4:30 every day, set a blue pin at 8:30 and a red one at 4:00. In that way you can have a warm house in the morning and in the evening, while you are there, and a cool one while everyone is either gone or asleep.

Recalibrating the Thermometer

If you suspect that the thermometer on the thermostat is inaccurate, it can be recalibrated. To do so, remove the thermostat cover and open the lens protector. Set the thermometer next to another thermometer that you know is functioning properly. Since the thermometer will have absorbed heat from your hand, let the two sit for 5 to 10 minutes before you compare the readings. Then insert a small screwdriver into the slot in the back of the thermostat thermometer and adjust the indicator until it matches that of the test thermometer.

Again let the two thermometers rest for 5 to 10 minutes. Recalibrate if necessary. Reinstall the thermometer and replace the thermostat cover.

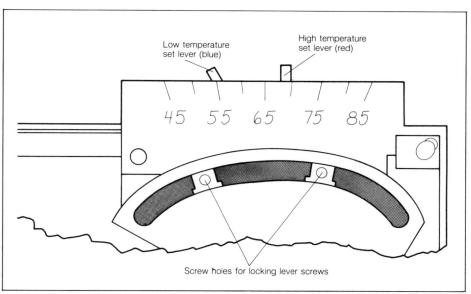

Built into the temperature control are two color-coded levers. The blue lever sets the cool temperature; the red lever sets the warm temperature. If desired, lock the levers in place.

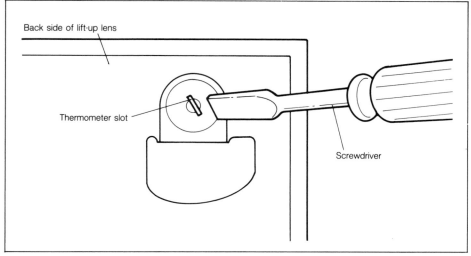

If the thermometer is not accurate, adjust it with a small screwdriver. The special slot built into the thermometer realigns the temperature indicator.

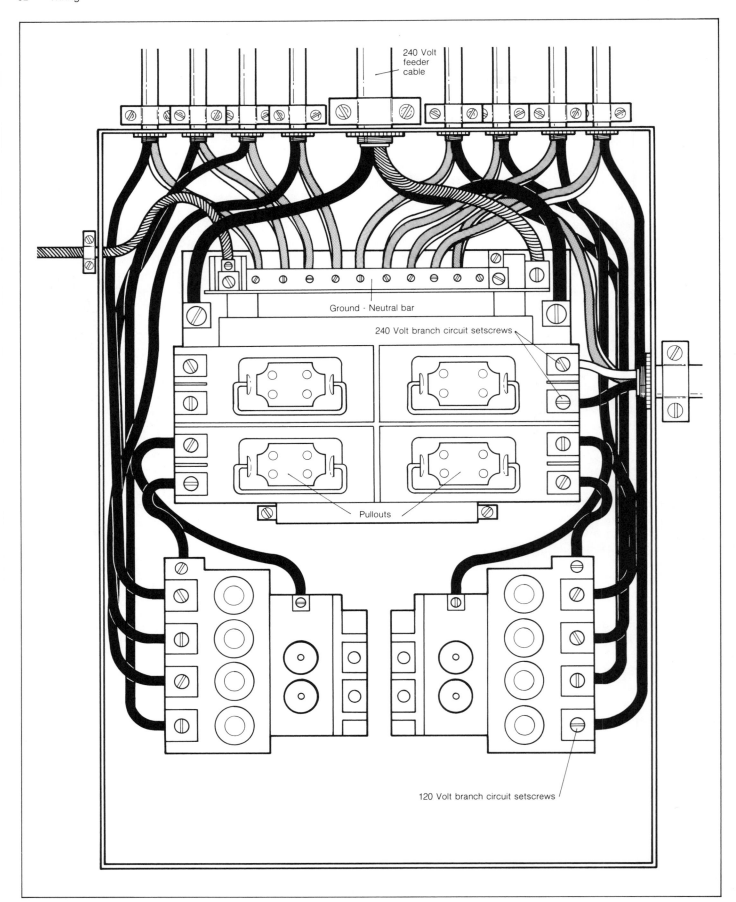

240 Volt feeder cable

Ground · Neutral bar

240 Volt branch circuit setscrews

Pullouts

120 Volt branch circuit setscrews

If your service panel looks like this one, take care when you work on your wiring. The only way to turn off all power entering the house is to remove all four pull-out boxes in the top section. These hold cartridge fuses. Standard plug fuses control the circuits themselves.

Adding Receptacles

If there are not enough outlets in a room, but you do not want to install a raceway, you can acquire the extra receptacles by extending an existing circuit. This means that you will run wires through the walls of your home, install a new junction box and hook the new wires to both a new and an old junction box. The existing circuit will then feed the receptacle in the new junction box. In order to carry out a project like this, however, you must first know about cables and wires, junction box installation and fishing cable through walls.

WIRES AND CABLE
Definitions: Avoiding Confusion

Wires conduct electric power from the point where it is generated to the point where it is used. The National Electrical Code makes little mention of the term "wire" as such, but speaks in terms of "conductors," which the NEC defines as "wire or cable or other forms of metal suitable for carrying current." Therefore, all wires are conductors, but not all conductors are wires. For instance, the copper bus bar in your service panel is a conductor, but it is not a wire.

To confuse matters, the terms wire and cable, in particular (and sometimes conduit), are often used interchangeably. For our purposes, a *wire* is a single strand or several strands of conductive material enclosed in protective insulation. A *cable* consists of two or more wires grouped together within a protective sheathing of plastic or metal (usually galvanized steel). Conduit is a galvanized steel or polyvinylchloride pipe through which wires are threaded. Some local electrical codes require the use of conduit in homes; others do not. Check code requirements for your locality.

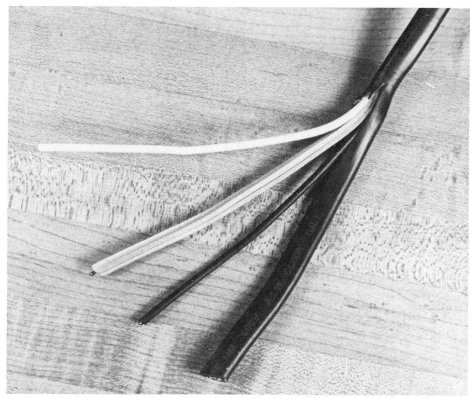

Before you can add to the wiring in your home, you must distinguish between the terms *wire* and *cable*. A cable contains several wires that are color-coded according to function.

Types of Wires

There are three different types of house wires—copper, copper-coated aluminum and aluminum. For any project, you should always use the same type of wires as already exists in your system.

About aluminum wire. Use special care with aluminum wire—it has very special properties. If your home uses copper-clad aluminum wire, do not add aluminum wire. Use only copper or copper-clad aluminum wire.

If your home does already have aluminum wire, check to see that switches and receptacles are designated CO/ALR or CU/AL. The CO/ALR marking is used on switches and receptacles rated up to 20 amperes; the CU/AL marking is used on switches and receptacles rated at more than 20 amperes. If the switches and receptacles do not bear these markings, replace them with those that do.

Never use aluminum wire with any back-wired switch or receptacle that requires pushing the wire into the device. Aluminum wire must connect to terminal screws.

When using aluminum wire, be awar that recommendations regarding wire sizes are generally for copper and copper-clad

WIRE SIZE GUIDE

Copper Wire AWG Number	Copper Wire Ampacity	Comparable Aluminum Wire AWG Number	Common Uses
6	55 amps	4	Electric ranges, central air conditioning systems, heat pumps, water heaters
8	40 amps	6	Same as No. 6 copper and No. 4 aluminum when ampacity permits
10	30 amps	8	Dishwashers, clothes dryers, washing machines, 240-volt window air conditioners
12	20 amps	10	Receptacles, lighting circuits, refrigerators
14	15 amps	12	Lighting circuits; heavier-duty extension cords
16	10 amps	—	In stranded form, for lamp cords and lighter-duty extension cords
18	7 amps	—	Door signaling devices, intercoms

wire. Readjust the designation to the next larger size according to the recommendations in the accompanying chart. For example, if AWG No. 14 (copper) wire usually is recommended and you are using aluminum wire, you must use AWG No. 12 wire instead.

Wire size numbers. The wires with which you will be most concerned carry even numbers and range in size from No. 18 to No. 6. *Remember:* the term *wire* refers to a single conductor. In a cable containing two wires, both wires will be of the same size.

Wire numbers are based on the American Wire Gauge (AWG) system. When comparing AWG numbers, keep in mind that the larger the number, the smaller the wire; conversely, the smaller the number, the larger the wire. For example, No. 14 wire is 0.064 inch in diameter, while No. 4/0 wire is about 0.5 inch in diameter. Wire sizes proceed from the larger numbers (smaller wires) through No. 0. Sizes after No. 0 are No. 00, No. 000, and No. 0000. These are commonly referred to as No. 1/0 (one-aught), No. 2/0 (two-aught), No. 3/0 (three-aught), and No. 4/0 (four-aught).

Ampacity. In determining the size wire you need for a job, consider the wire's ampacity, or the maximum current in amperes that a particular wire size can safely handle. If a wire is too small for the job, it will present a greater-than-normal resistance to current. This causes friction, which generates heat and destroys insulation. As a result, undersize wire could lead to a fire.

Ampacities for copper and aluminum wire sizes used most often in the home are summarized in the accompanying table, along with wire sizes and common uses. Notice that an aluminum wire with the same AWG number as a copper wire has less ampacity.

All About Cable

Local codes. There are three basic types of cable for circuits. As discussed in an earlier chapter, inside the cable are two or three wires that are color-coded. Black (or sometimes red) stands for the hot wire, white for neutral, and green for ground. In a two-wire cable, there will be no ground wire. The kind of cable in your home most likely is determined by local code. For any of the projects included in this chapter, find out the code requirements for your particular area.

Note: matching cable. If cable in your home is plastic-sheathed, use plastic-sheathed for any job you do. If cable in

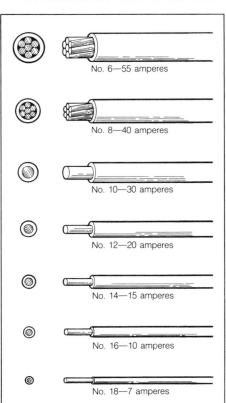

No. 6—55 amperes

No. 8—40 amperes

No. 10—30 amperes

No. 12—20 amperes

No. 14—15 amperes

No. 16—10 amperes

No. 18—7 amperes

The size and makeup of a wire determines the number of amps it can safely carry without overheating and causing a fire hazard.

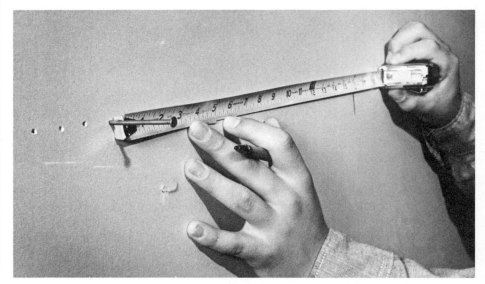

Studs (and most framing members) are evenly spaced 16 inches apart from center to center. (This is called "on center.") Find one stud and you can easily find the others.

your home is armor-wrapped, use armor-wrapped for all electrical work.

Location restrictions. Once you know code requirements, you also need to determine under what circumstances the cable will be used. According to the National Electrical Code, "circumstance" is defined as either a dry, damp, or wet location. A *dry* location is one that is indoors and is not normally subjected to dampness or wetness. Usually the environment is above ground level, in the living quarters of a home.

A *damp* location is an indoor location that is subjected to a moderate degree of moisture. The environment usually is below ground level, such as in a basement.

A *wet* location is an area where cable is liable to be saturated by water. Falling into this category are outdoor areas, areas beneath the ground, and concrete slabs or masonry that are in direct contact with the earth.

Types of Cable

BX cable. Armor-wrapped cable, which is commonly called BX (a trade name), consists of an outer wrapper of flexible galvanized steel that contains two or three wires. Each wire will be individually wrapped in insulation and then with paper. When a ground wire is present, it is sometimes bare. If the cable does not have a ground wire, the metal sheathing serves as a ground wire whenever it comes into contact with metal junction boxes.

BX flexes to turn easily around corners. It is good for use in dry indoor locations, especially in areas where wires need protection from nails due to later carpentry or decorating projects. In some localities, it cannot be strung more than three feet in any exposed area. Despite its appearance, armor-wrapped cable is not indestructible. When it is used in wet locations, the dampness may cause the steel jacket to corrode. Wire sizes in armor-wrapped cable are AWG No. 12 and AWG No. 14.

Plastic-coated cable. Plastic cable is often called Romex, which is a trade name. This cable is enclosed in a plastic sheath. All three wires inside are paper-wrapped or embedded in plastic. Romex is very flexible. The size of the wire is stamped along the outside of the cable, as are designations for use areas. There are three plastic-cable categories.

Type NM. This cable is for use only in dry locations. It is used most often in house circuits. Each wire (with the possible exception of the ground wire) is wrapped in its own plastic sheath. The three wires are then wrapped in a paper insulator, and the paper wrapping is covered over with plastic. The wire in Type NM cable is either AWG No. 12 or AWG No. 14 for normal house circuits; larger sizes, such as No. 10 or more, are used for heavy appliances. In either size, NM cable is available with two or three conductors plus a ground wire. A ground-wired system is highly recommended. Use three-conductor NM cable for heavy-duty circuits, especially where two hot wires are needed.

Type NMC. This cable is for use in damp locations, but it may also be used in dry areas. The distinguishing characteristic of this cable is that the individually insulated wires are embedded in solid plastic to provide protection against moisture. As a result, it is appropriate for basement installations, where codes permit. As with Type NM cable, Type NMC is also available with two or three conductors plus a ground wire, and in AWG No. 12 and AWG No. 14.

Type UF. For use in wet locations, including burial under ground, UF cable is the alternative to conduit. The distinguishing characteristic of this cable is that the individually insulated wires are embedded in water-resistant solid plastic that is heavier than that used in Type NMC cable. Type UF cable is also available in AWG No. 12 and AWG No. 14 as well as others. It contains two or three conductors plus a ground wire.

Abbreviations. Markings on the outside of the plastic sheathing or nonmetallic cable explain what is inside. Consider the following designation: "14/2 WITH GROUND TYPE NMC 600V (UL)." The first number tells the size of the wires in the cable, in this case No. 14. The second number tells you there are two conductors in the cable. There also is a ground wire, as indicated. The type of cable is listed; the number following indicates the maximum voltage allowed through the cable. Finally, the UL notation assures you the cable has been rated as safe for the uses for which it was designed.

Conduit. In place of BX or Romex cable, in homes with very thin walls, single conductor wires are usually enclosed in galvanized steel pipe called thin-walled conduit. In some areas, conduit is required

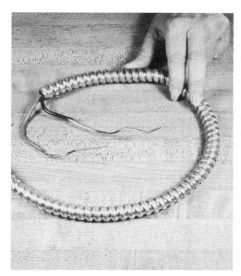

Some BX cable comes with only hot and neutral conductors, or wires. The metal sheathing itself becomes the ground for the cable.

Stamped along the outside of Romex cable are abbreviations indicating size and number of wires inside, the appropriate location, and the maximum voltage load the cable can handle.

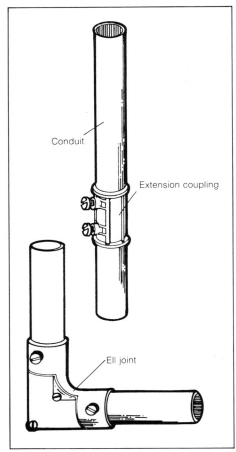

Conduit

Extension coupling

Ell joint

Conduit is joined with a variety of connectors, depending upon whether the end is threaded or not. Also available are elbow pieces.

when more than three feet of BX cable will be exposed in a basement. When using conduit, run insulated conductor wires of black, white and green through the conduit pipe. Do not try to run BX or Romex cable through a conduit.

Since conduit comes in a variety of sizes, it can hold a number of sets of wires. The straight pieces come in 10-foot lengths. Couplings and joint pieces make it adaptable to most settings. It also can be bent to shape with a special tool called a hickey. This is a difficult tool to learn to use, so, unless the local electrical code requires EMT (electrical metal tubing), stay away from it—unless you have had prior experience working with it.

How Much to Purchase

In estimating the amount of cable you will need for doing this or any job, measure the distance between the new outlet and the power source. Add an extra foot for every connection you will make. Then, to provide a margin for error, add 20 percent. For example, if you measure for 12 feet of cable between a new and existing re-

ceptacle, add another two feet for the two connections, making the total 14 feet. Then, add 20 percent (roughly 3 feet) to the total. To do the job, therefore, you should start with 17 feet of cable.

Working With Cable

Romex. To prepare plastic-sheathed (nonmetallic) cable for installation, you need a sharp utility knife and a wire stripper.

1. Set the cable on a flat hard surface.
2. Measure about eight inches from the end of the cable.
3. Press the utility knife into the middle of the plastic sheathing, just enough to penetrate. Slowly draw the knife down to make a shallow cut in the plastic.
4. Go over the cut in the sheathing, pressing a bit deeper each time, until you are able to peel back the plastic and reveal the insulated wires beneath. *Caution:* Use care as you cut through the plastic sheathing. If you penetrate too deeply and nick one of the conductors, cut away the section with the nick and start over from the beginning.
5. Grasp the loose plastic and paper jacket. Bend it back and cut it off. You can now work on the two or three individual conductors and the ground wire.
6. Tear off the paper insulation from around the ground wire, and use a wire stripping tool to strip the plastic insulation from the hot and neutral conductors. Do *not* use a knife to strip insulation. You can easily nick the conductors, thus creating an electrical hazard.

BX cable. To prepare armor-wrapped cable for installation, you need a fine-toothed hacksaw blade and a wire stripper.

1. About eight inches from the end, cut through the armor with the fine-toothed hacksaw blade. Make the cut diagonally across one of the metal ribs, and stop sawing as soon as the blade cuts through the metal. Avoid cutting any of the wires inside the cable.
2. Place a thumb on each side of the cut and bend the cable back and forth until the metal armor snaps. Then, slide the armor off the cable and remove the insulation from the conductors.
3. The amount of insulation you strip off the conductors, once the plastic or armored covering is removed, depends on what you plan to do with the ends of the wires. If you are going to attach

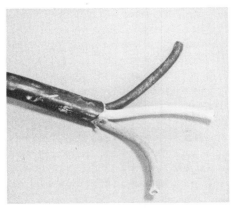

Cable covered with plastic sheathing will contain three or more wires. Each wire is encased in color-coded insulation.

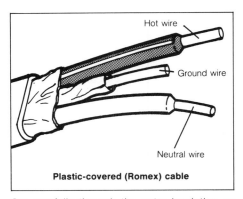

Hot wire

Ground wire

Neutral wire

Plastic-covered (Romex) cable

Cut carefully through the outer insulation so that you do not knick the wires inside. Then remove the insulation with a wire stripper.

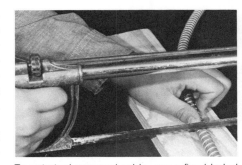

To cut steel-wrapped cable, use a fine-bladed hacksaw. Cut diagonally across one of the rings. Bend the cable to snap the cover.

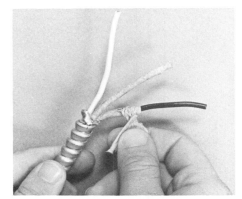

Armored cable, often called BX, contains two or three wires. Each will be encased in paper and insulation.

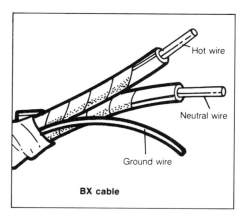

BX cable

BX cable sometimes has a bare ground wire. The spiral casing is designed to flex around curves and corners for easy installation.

them to screw terminals, strip off only about ½ inch, enough so you can wrap the bare ends three-quarters of the way around the terminals. If you are going to insert bare ends into push-in terminals, lay the wires across the strip gauge found on this type of receptacle in order to measure the amount of insulation to be stripped.

4. If you are going to splice the wires to the house cables, strip off about ¾ inch of insulation. Then splice the wires together as discussed in Chapter 3.

Anchoring and Supporting BX or Romex

Parallel to studs or joists. When the cable is to run parallel with studs or joists, support it with metal clamps (available at electrical supply houses) or electrician's staples, which are flattened to protect the cable. Cables are most often secured with staples because this is the fastest way; however, the best way is to use clamps. Tap the staples around the cable lightly; do not puncture the cable or press into it.

When you secure cable parallel to a joist or stud, space the cable supports four feet apart, or less. There also should be a support not more than one foot away from any junction box.

Perpendicular to studs or joists. When the cable must go in a direction perpendicular to wall studs or ceiling or floor joists, drill ¾-inch holes through these members. Use a power drill or a hand drill (brace and bit). Cables strung through joists or studs are supported by the members themselves.

Precautions when drilling through 2x4s. When you cut through studs or joists, you must observe a code regulation set by the National Electrical Code. This regulation states that when you drill through small members, such as 2x4s, you must cover the front edge (the edge that faces the finish material) with a 1/16-inch thick metal plate. This is necessary so that you do not hit the cable with a nail when you (or others) nail finish materials over the members. The metal plates, available at electrical supply houses, come with built-in spikes so the plates can be hammered to the studs or other small members. The rule is that the plates should be used wherever the drilled holes for cable are less than 2 inches from the finished surface. This would apply if you string cable through the center of the 4-inch face of a stud. Obviously, you do not need to use the metal plates on joists, since—when the holes are drilled in the center—there will be more than 2 inches between the cable and any finished surface in which nailing might occur.

Using furring strips for perpendicular alignment. If you are unable to drill through framing members when you are stringing cable perpendicular to the members (such as in the attic, where insulation may get in the way), you can first nail a furring strip (typically a 1x3) perpendicular to the members and then attach the cable to the strip with clamps or staples. However, these furring strips will interfere with surfacing materials. As a result, if you plan to finish over the joists or studs with flooring, panelling or other materials, your only alternative is to route the cable

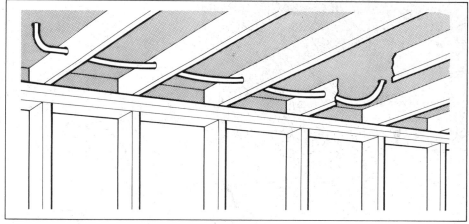

If the cable runs perpendicular to the joists, you must cut openings through the joists to support and protect the cable. Then fish the cable through over to the new outlet.

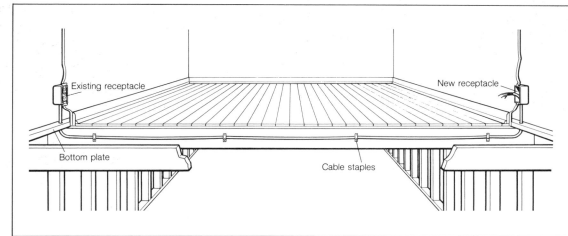

Existing receptacle   New receptacle   Bottom plate   Cable staples

If your installation requires that you run cable parallel to the floor joists in order to connect the old and the new receptacle, you cannot allow the cable to hang loose. Instead, hold the cable in position with cable staples. Be careful as you install the staples so that you do not pierce the insulation. If you do, you must replace the cable.

in locations that are out of the way and are protected.

How to Use Conduit

As mentioned earlier, you may be required by code to use conduit. The code will also specify which kind of conduit you can use, typically electrometallic tubing (EMT) or Type AC armored cable.

Conduit is easiest to use if you remove the wall surface and expose the studs. The conduit is then fitted into notches in the studs. Because the notches weaken the studs, a better method is to run the conduit above the ceiling and down between the studs to the location of the switch, receptacle or light fixture. If you are working on the first floor of a two-story house, conduit can be run up through the wall from the basement.

Both plastic and metallic conduit are strung in about the same manner as BX or Romex. If the conduit is parallel with the studs or joists, hang it with clamps or staples. These should be no less than 4½ feet apart. In addition, place a support no more than one foot from all boxes.

Run conduit through the framing members if the direction of the wiring is perpendicular to the framing.

An alternative method is to run conduit perpendicular to framing and to notch the framing enough so that the conduit running perpendicular to studs or joists will be flush with the face of the framing. Then cover the conduit and the notch with a metal protective plate, as described for BX and Romex.

To run conduit perpendicular to the framing, use a spade bit to drill holes through the members. The members then support the weight of the conduit. An alternative method is to notch the edge of the stud or joist; then seat the conduit into the notch so that the conduit is flush with the edge of the member. This installation requires that the conduit and the notch be covered with a metal protective plate, as described for BX and Romex.

Bending conduit. Bending conduit requires the use of a hickey conduit bender. This is a simple tool shaped roughly like a "T," except the top of the T is curved and has a clamp attachment. The handle of the hickey, which creates the leg of the T is about 30 inches long. The procedure is a fairly simple one, but it requires patience and muscle. Attach the conduit through the clamp attachment; put the conduit on the ground or floor; with your foot on the conduit, push the handle down, bending the conduit.

Conduit connections. Connections between lengths of conduit are made with

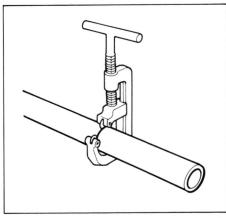

A special pipe cutter has a cutting blade built into its jaws. Circle the cutter, tightening the pressure until the cut is complete.

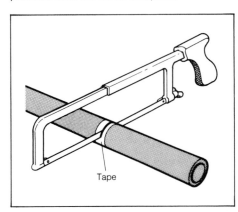

Tape

If you use a hacksaw to cut through conduit, first lay a piece of masking tape over the cut mark. This keeps the saw from slipping.

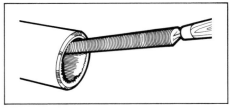

In order to protect the wires inside from rough edges, use a half-round file to finish the end of a cut piece of conduit.

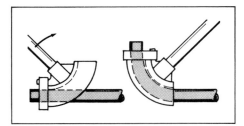

A hickey is a tool used to bend metal conduit. Slide the conduit into the holder and pull the handle toward you to create the curve.

compression fittings. Each fitting has a nut that clamps down on a metal ring which in turn clamps onto the conduit. Metallic conduit does make a safe and neat job. When all connections are made tightly, the conduit itself becomes a "third wire" that creates a ground.

SELECTING A POWER SOURCE

Your primary consideration here is to tap an existing box that is closest to your new receptacle. The second consideration is ease of installation—some junction boxes will be easier to work with than others. Your third consideration will be finding the route that involves the least amount of damage to the ceilings and walls. The best routes are those that run parallel to the joists of an unfinished basement or attic. However, one cannot always take advantage of such paths.

Switches and Outlets

End-of-the-run receptacle. The easiest place to attach your new cable is to an end-of-line receptacle, as long as it is not controlled by a switch. (If it is, once the switch controlling the old outlet is off, no power will go to your new outlet either.) As explained earlier, an end-of-line receptacle will have only one cable entering the box. Two terminals on the receptacle will be vacant.

Middle-of-the-run outlet. If the receptacle is at the middle of the line, two cables will enter the junction box and all terminals will be occupied. Since you will be adding to the number of wires and splices in the box, you may have to add another box onto the existing box. This is called ganging the box.

Middle-of-the-run switches. You can extend the circuit from a middle-of-a-run switch. This switch will have a cable both at the bottom and the top of its junction box. If the box is small, it may have to be ganged just like an outlet.

Ceiling fixtures. You can attach the cable to a ceiling fixture, although this is the least desirable choice because it is so inaccessible. The ceiling fixture must have middle-of-the-run wiring. Otherwise, your new receptacle will receive power only when the particular switch to that fixture is on.

It is not as easy to determine a ceiling fixture's position in the run of cable as it is a switch or receptacle, for the number of cables is not an indicator. Several cables

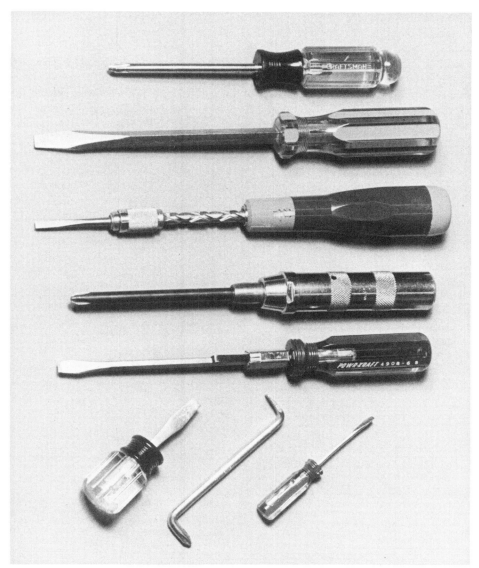

An ideal screwdriver selection includes (from top): Phillips head, standard blade, spiral ratchet, changeable blade, screw holding, stubby standard, offset and small standard blade. Offset screwdrivers are handy for working inside a junction box. Do not use any screwdriver for anything other than driving screws—no screwdriver can protect you from shock.

A standard junction box has ears at the top and the bottom. These are adjustable so the box can be installed flush with the wall.

A junction box for wood paneling has clamps along the sides. When the screws are tightened, the clamps expand to secure the box.

may simply indicate that the ceiling fixture is controlled by more than one switch rather than its being in the middle of the run. Examine the cable connections very carefully to determine the fixture's position. Coming from the fixture itself will be a black and a white wire. If these both attach to the same cable, the fixture is at the end of the run. If the black wire attaches to one cable into the fixture's junction box, and the white wire attaches to another cable, the fixture is at the middle of the run. Note: some ceiling boxes will have recoded wires. A wire will be white, but near its terminal or splice there will be black paint or electrician's tape. This wire is now a hot wire, having been recoded black. Do not misinterpret the wiring or the outlet will not work.

Main Junction Boxes

Below the floor of your home (probably in more than one location) are what are called main junction boxes. Cable from one or more circuits will route through this box. You can attach new cable into this box, but be sure it connects to the correct circuit.

HOW TO ADD JUNCTION BOXES

The new receptacle must be housed in a junction box. These come in three basic designs, each of which is best suited for a particular type of wall construction.

Box Styles

Standard box with adjustable ears. The junction box used most often is a simple rectangular structure with screw openings at the top and bottom front edges. The sides are straight up and down; there are no brackets or clamps. This box is appropriate for plastered walls, since the walls are sturdy enough to hold the box in place. This box also is used for drywall, along with two side brackets, which are purchased separately. The brackets give the box the support that drywall alone cannot.

Box with side clamps. This box resembles the first except that it has screw-activated clamps on the front side edges. When the screws are tightened, the clamps come forward and spread out to hold the box in place. This box is used in paneling or hardboard that is attached to studs. Both wall coverings are sturdy enough to hold the box securely.

Box with side flange. A junction box with an external flange running along one side is used in locations in which one has easy access to a wall stud, such as an unfinished basement or attic. The box is simply nailed to the side of the stud. A second style of this box is held in place by metal teeth, which are pounded into the stud. If you intend to add wall covering after you have installed the wiring in an area, recess the box so there is ample space for the finishing work.

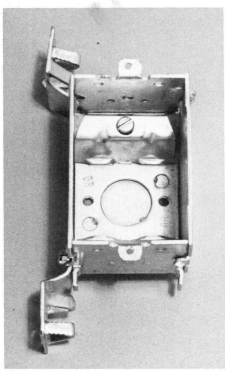

In new construction, use a junction box with a side flange. This is nailed to the side of the exposed stud; brackets fasten to the stud.

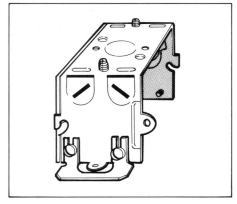

Use the U-shaped opening in a junction box for a saddle clamp; the round-shaped knockouts require two-part connectors.

Cable Knockouts

Built into the walls of a junction box are several knockouts. They will be either round or U-shaped. Round knockouts accommodate BX cable and conduit; U-shaped knockouts accommodate BX and plastic-coated cable. Before you install the box, remove the knockout appropriate to your installation.

Judging Box Capacity

There is another aspect of this job to consider before starting to work. You have to determine if the existing junction box can accommodate additional wiring. Any box can hold only a certain number of connections. These are limited by physical space and by regulations set down by the National Electrical Code. The charts below outline the maximum number of connections that junction boxes can accommodate when you are using AWG No. 14 or AWG No. 12 cable. If you are going to use a larger size cable, discuss the project with your electrical parts dealer. He can tell you the maximum number of connections that are safe to use in an existing box. Overcrowding can cause damaged insulation, which is a real fire hazard.

Definition: connections. In judging what is and what is not a connection, use the following guidelines:

    (1) count each conductor in the box as one connection;

    (2) do not count a ground wire that enters the box and is connected directly to the receptacle, switch, or fixture;

    (3) do not count a jumper wire as a connection;

    (4) count a ground wire that is connected to the box as one connection;

    (5) count cable clamps or lighting fixture mounting devices that are inside the box, such as a nipple or hickey, as one connection;

    (6) count a receptacle or switch as one connection.

Add the total number of connections and check the accompanying chart to determine if you can add connections to a box. For example, suppose you are dealing with a 4x1½-inch junction box in which there are two AWG No. 14 conductors, one ground wire connected to the box, and a hickey. There is a total of four connections. The maximum the box can accommodate is six. You can, therefore, make up to two additional connections.

Enlarging ("ganging") a junction box. If the junction box you wish to tap is too small to hold extra connections, it is possible to enlarge the box. This is called "ganging." Enlarging the box means you will have to open up the wall around the existing box and repair the wall later. For this reason, some people simply select another location, rather than go to the trouble required. Ganging involves attaching one or more boxes to an existing box of the same size. It is done as follows:

1. Turn off the power to the circuit feeding into the box (see Chapter 1).

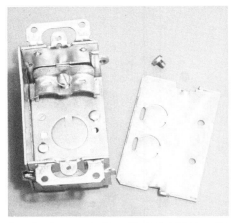

Junction boxes can be enlarged. Unscrew the side screw to release a side panel; lift the panel free. Discard the panel, but save the screw.

Place the open side of the two boxes next to each other. The notch on one will fit into the flange on the other, hooking them together.

MATCHING CONNECTIONS TO JUNCTION BOXES

Box Size (inches)	Maximum Number of Connections: AWG No. 14 Wire	Maximum Number of Connections: AWG No. 12 Wire
WALL BOXES		
3 x 2 x 2½	6	5
3 x 2 x 2¾	7	6
3 x 2 x 3½	9	8
CEILING BOXES		
4 x 1¼	6	5
4 x 1½	7	6
MAJOR BOXES		
4 x 1¼	9	8
4 x 1½	10	9
4 x 2⅛	10	9

2. Make space for the new box alongside the old box by removing enough of the wall to accommodate the new box.

3. Disconnect all wires, and remove the receptacle. Withdraw the box from the wall. This often requires that you remove even more of the wall surface in order to uncover the stud to which the box is attached.

4. Remove the corresponding sides of the old and new boxes. The sides of the box are held by screw and notch combination.

5. Holding the boxes together, place the notch of each box under the corresponding screws of the other box. Tighten the screws to fasten the two boxes together, making them one.

6. Install the enlarged box in the wall.

Attaching Cable to a Junction Box

Using an internal clamp. Attach Romex or BX cable to the receptacle box with an

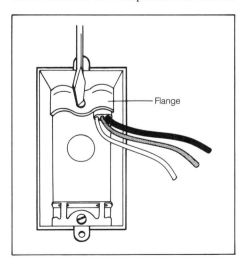

A convenient cable clamp is an interior saddle clamp. To use with plastic cable, remove the loops on the clamp with wire cutters.

internal clamp called an internal saddle clamp. For plastic-sheathed cable you will have to use metal cutters to remove the metal strip containing the two loops that extend down from the solid section of the clamp. To use the clamp, screw it loosely to the inside of the box. Then, pull the cable into the box through a U-shaped knockout. The cable should fit between the clamp and rear wall of the box and extend far enough above the clamp for you to see the plastic sheathing. Tighten the screw to secure the cable to the box.

To use a saddle clamp with BX cable, use the entire metal clamp. The cable slides up against the round openings; the clamp is then tightened up against the cable to hold it securely in position.

Using a two-part clamp. Two-part clamps attach the cable to the box through one of the round knockout holes. The larger section of the clamp is applied to the cable. The cable then passes into the box, where the second section of clamp, a nutlike fastener, tightens and holds the cable in place. Strip off about 6 inches of the outer sheathing from the cable. Slip the larger piece of the connector over the wires and the sheath. The threaded end of the connector faces the same direction as the stripped wires. The sheathing should not extend beyond the threading. Firmly tighten the screws on each side of the round knockout opening, along with the threading. Slip the nut over the wires and tighten it over the threading, using a screwdriver.

The cut metal edge of BX cable can cut or chafe through the insulation on the wires that extend from it. Therefore, if you are using BX cable you must install a standard plastic insulator that slips over

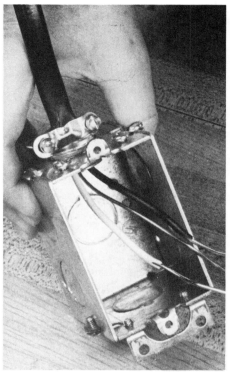

Slip the larger part of a two-part clamp over the sheath of the cable. The sheath should extend out about ½ in. Tighten the connector.

Be sure that the cable cover extends through the sides of the opening. Then, install the locknut on the inside of the box.

the wires and sits between them and the sharp end of the metal sheathing. Do this *before* clamping the BX or installing a BX connector over the sheathing.

Attaching conduit. Conduit also is attached to a junction box with a connector. A steel nipple connector screws into the box. It is held in place with a locknut on the inside of the box. Over this, protecting the wires from abrasion, is a plastic protector. A set screw secures the locknut.

OPENING UP THE WALLS

The next step is to open up the wall at the location of the new junction box. The procedures will vary according to the materials of which the wall is constructed.

Anatomy of a Wall

No matter what materials create a wall or floor, the interior framework remains constant.

Studs. Studs are the vertical wood beams, generally 2x4s, mounted 16 inches apart, center to center. All wall materials are secured to studs. In some localities, where high humidity has an adverse effect on wood, metal studs instead of wood studs are used to support walls. In most cases, the best electrical installations are those in which junction boxes are mounted on the side of a stud, although this is not required—and is oftentimes not possible in a finished room.

Joists. Joists are the horizontal wood beams mounted 16 inches apart, center to center, in attics and basements. Ceiling material and flooring are nailed to joists. Cable often runs either parallel or perpendicular to floor or ceiling joists.

Types of Wall Materials

Before 1950, walls and ceilings of houses were generally constructed of plaster over wood or metal lath. In this type of construction, lath, which is the base material to which several layers of plaster are applied, is nailed to the studs.

Homes built since 1950 generally have walls and ceilings of gypsum wallboard, which is also called drywall or plasterboard. The panels come in 4x8-foot, 4x10-foot or 4x12-foot sizes, and are made of compressed gypsum sandwiched between layers of heavy composition-type paper. The panels are nailed directly to wood studs and ceiling joists. From an electrician's standpoint, wood paneling and hardboard fall into the same category as dry wall. They, too, are fastened to wood studs and joist.

Working with Drywall

Plan the location of the junction box for the new receptacle, so it will fall between the wall studs. If the receptacle is to be placed near the bottom of a wall, position the box 12 to 18 inches off the floor. If you want the receptacle at a midbody height—for example, in a kitchen, dining or dressing area—position the box 10 to 12 inches above the surface of a nearby table or counter.

Locating studs. In order to position the opening correctly, you first must locate the studs. You will then position the box between the studs. Side brackets hold the standard box with adjustable ears in place in the wall.

You can buy a magnetic stud locator for not much money, and sometimes one works. You move the device along a wall and when the magnetic finder goes over a metal nail a small needle in the finder wiggles. The wiggle can indicate the stud location; however, it could be indicating some other metal object, such as a pipe.

Another way to locate a stud is to pound on the wall with your fist. The thump will sound hollow until you hit a stud, then the thump will sound solid.

Still another way is to measure from a corner out across the wall. The corner is framed with double studs and the next stud out will be 16 inches—or at least it ought to be.

One other quick method is to pry off the baseboard along the wall in which you want to locate the studs. The baseboard covers the vertical untaped joints of the gypsumboard. These joints are supposed to be spaced 48 inches apart. Then measure from the seam. There should be a stud 16 inches either way from the seam.

The best way. Measure out from a corner 16 inches. Drive a nail, such as a 10d finishing nail, into the wall at this point. If you hit something solid, it probably is the stud. If you do not hit something solid, keep trying until you do. Then mark this location on the wall. You can always patch the nail holes with a daub of spackling compound, and you will be sure of the stud location.

All other stud locations can be measured from the first stud you found with the nail. The studs will be spaced every 16 inches on center across the wall.

Creating a template. Place the junction box, open face down, on a piece of lightweight cardboard, and trace an outline of the box onto the cardboard. Do not trace the outlines of the ears on the top and bottom of the box. The outline transferred to the cardboard should be rectangular. Set the box aside and fill in any blank areas. Cut around the outline to make a template. Place the template on the wall so the hole you drilled in the wall for probing falls at the center of the template. The template should be as straight and level as possible. Now, trace the outline of the template onto the wall.

Cutting the wall opening. You are now ready to cut out the section of wall into which the receptacle box will go. To do this, drill ½-inch holes in each corner of the outline and use a utility knife to cut along the outline from one hole to another. If the piece of wallboard does not fall free after the cut is made, hold a block of wood against the cutout and tap the block with a hammer. The piece of drywall will fall behind the wall, where it will not cause any problems. Use the utility knife to cut away any protruding fragments and trim the edges of the hole so that they are straight and clean.

Once the opening has been created, you are ready to fish the electrical cable from one location to the other (this procedure is discussed later in this chapter). Then you can install the new junction box in the wall.

Inserting the junction box. Insert the box into the opening, and bring the front of the box flush with the edges of the wall. The ears on the top and bottom of the box will keep it from falling inside the wall. In fact, you may have to adjust the mounting brackets around the ears to position the box so it is flush with the wall.

Hold the box in position with one hand. Slide one of the two metal side brackets, which you purchased when you bought the new receptacle, into the wall opening along one side of the box. The bracket is longer than the opening in the wall; you will tilt it to get it into position. Do not let the bracket fall. To assure that the

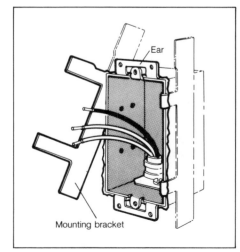

To hold a junction box in drywall, you will need side brackets. Slide one in on each side. Do not drop them in the wall space.

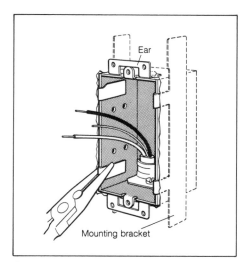

Once the bracket is in position between the wall and the box, bend the side extensions tight and flush against the side of the box.

bracket tabs hold the box securely, pull the bracket toward you until it is pressed firmly against the back of the wallboard. To secure the bracket and the box, use a needlenose pliers to bend the tabs as tightly as possible around and against the inside wall of the box. Insert another bracket on the other side of the box in the same way. Be sure the bracket arms are tight and flush; otherwise, they could interfere with the cable wires.

Working with Plaster and Wood Lath

To install the box, follow these steps.

1. Check the location for the new receptacle to make sure there are no obstructions behind the wall that will interfere with the receptacle box. Follow the stud location probing procedure outlined above for drywall.

2. If there are no obstructions, use a chisel and hammer to remove the layer of plaster from above and below the drilled hole. (A concrete chisel, commonly referred to as a cold chisel, is best.) The purpose of doing this is to expose an entire width of a single wood lath strip and portions of lath above and below it. You will probably have to chip away 1½ to 2 inches of plaster above and below the drilled hole. Extend the opening ¾ to 1 inch out from the sides of the drilled hole.

3. Pencil in a mark at the center of the exposed width of wood lath. Then, make a template of the junction box, as described under the procedure for drywall. Include the outlines of the top and bottom ears.

4. Cut a small hole in the center of the template. Position the template against the wall, so the hole in the center is over the mark you made in the wood lath. Trace the outline of the template onto the wall.

5. Place strips of masking tape so that the tape is outside the box and the inner edges fall next to the outline. Tape helps prevent plaster from crumbling as you make the opening for the box.

6. Drill ½-inch holes through the wall at each corner of the outline and in the areas designated for the top and bottom ears.

7. Use a utility knife to score the plaster along the outline. Repeat the scoring process several times. This step minimizes the pressure needed for cutting out the opening and, thus, reduces the chance of damaging the plaster.

8. With a hacksaw or keyhole saw, saw through the plaster and wood lath from drilled hole to drilled hole. Use even, firm strokes; otherwise the movement of the saw may splinter or crack the lath and chip the plaster adjoining the work area.

9. When the area for the box has been cleared, remove the masking tape and insert the box as far as it will go into the opening. The mounting brackets above and below the ears of the box will prevent the box from slipping through the opening.

10. Remove the masking tape. Trace onto the wall the outline of the mounting brackets at the top and bottom of the box.

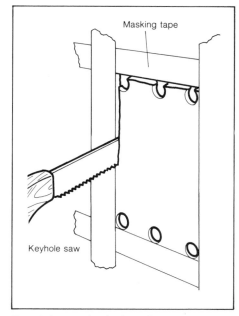

To cut the opening in drywall, outline the template. Bore starter holes around the edges of the outline. Cut the hole with a keyhole saw.

11. Remove the box. Working inward from the outline, chip away the plaster within the outline; do not chip away the wood lath underneath the plaster. The purpose of doing this is to set the box far enough into the wall so that the front of the box is flush with the wall. The cutout also allows the mounting brackets to be screwed to the lath.

12. Insert the box into the wall, and see that it fits properly. Make marks for the mounting screws through the holes provided in the mounting brackets.

13. Remove the box, and drill ⅛-inch pilot holes for screws.

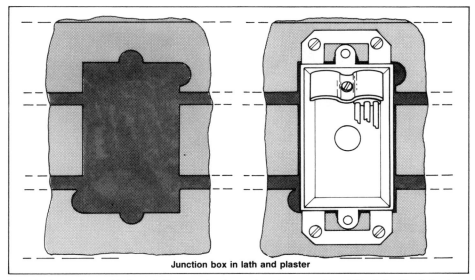

Junction box in lath and plaster

In a plaster and wood lath wall, the opening is centered over a strip of the lath. The lath above and below are only notched. Adjust the top and bottom ears of the box so it is flush.

14. Fish cable through the wall and secure it to the box with clamps (see below).

15. Insert the box in the wall. Use No. 5 wood screws through holes in the mounting brackets in order to secure the box in the wall to the wood lath.

Working with a Plaster/Metal Lath Wall

The procedures for installing a junction box in a plaster wall laid on metal lath are virtually the same as for a plaster wall over wood lath, discussed above.

1. Locate an unobstructed position for the junction box as described earlier. Create the template, and trace its outline

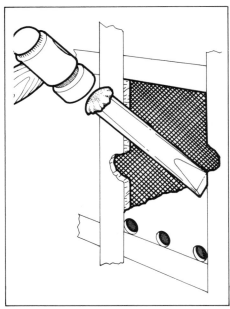

Edge the outline of the template with masking tape. Then carefully chisel the plaster away to expose the metal lath underneath.

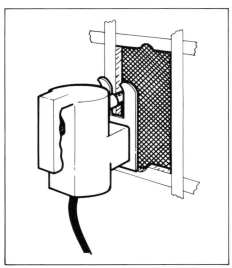

Once the plaster is chipped away, cut through metal lath with a sabre saw. Work carefully; otherwise you will crack the existing wall.

on the wall. Outline the outline with masking tape.

2. Drill holes in the four corners and the ear openings; use a ⅜-inch metal bit. Chisel out the area with a cold chisel. Clear the area completely in order to expose the metal lath.

3. You must exercise care when you cut through the metal lath. The job requires a metal blade in a sabre saw, or a reciprocating saw. Insert the saw blade through one of the corner holes, and cut away the lath. Work very slowly; otherwise the plaster along the edges will break and chip away.

4. Insert and fasten the same type of junction box and side brackets as you would for a drywall installation.

Working with Wood Paneling and Hardboard

To install a side-clamped receptacle box in wood paneling or hardboard walls, proceed as follows:

1. Make sure there are no obstructions behind the wall where you plan to locate the junction box. Follow the probing procedure described under drywall.

2. Make a template of the box as explained under drywall. Include the outlines of the side flanges, but do not include outlines of the ears on the top and bottom of the box.

3. Place the template on the wall, so the center of the template is aligned with the hole you drilled for probing. Trace the outline on the wall.

4. Drill holes through the wall at each corner of the outline and at the locations of the side clamps. Use a ⅜- or ½-inch bit.

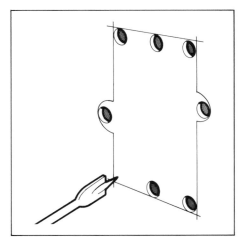

Bore starter holes around the outline on a wood panel wall. Also bore openings to allow room for the side clamps to pass through.

5. Using a keyhole saw, cut along the outline.

6. Fish the cable through the wall and secure it to the box (see below).

7. Insert the box into the wall, bringing it flush with the surface of the wall.

8. Turn the screws of the side clamps. As you do, the clamps will expand and secure the box to the wall. You do not have to screw the box to the wall with screws inserted through the ears.

FISHING THE CABLE

After the opening for the new wall receptacle box is made, you have to decide which of the two cable running options to use. To review, they are:

(1) running cable from an existing duplex receptacle that is in the same room as the new receptacle;

(2) running cable from an existing duplex receptacle that is in an adjacent room.

Safety. No matter which location you utilize, before working at an existing receptacle, be sure to deactivate the circuit breaker or fuse that serves the receptacle (see Chapter 1).

Tapping Off an Existing Duplex Receptacle in the Same Room

Select an existing receptacle that is as close as possible to the new receptacle. Check to determine the type of wiring, and gang the box if necessary. You generally have a choice of three ways to run cable from the power source to the new receptacle. (See Chapter 10 for instructions for tapping a ceiling fixture.)

Up through the basement. Bring the cable from the power source down through the wall into the basement, run the cable along joists to an area below the new receptacle, and bring the cable up through the wall to the new receptacle. This method may be used if the existing receptacle and the new receptacle are on walls that face each other or are on walls that butt each other. It is applicable both for drywall and for plaster and lath construction.

Along the base of the wall. Bring the cable along the base of the wall from the power source to the new receptacle. This method may be used if the existing receptacle and the new receptacle are on the same wall, for either plaster and lath or drywall construction.

Through the wall studs. Bring the cable

through the wall studs from the power source to the new receptacle. This method may be used in drywall construction if the existing receptacle and the new receptacle are on the same wall, whether they are positioned at table/counter height or near the floor.

Receptacle to Receptacle Through the Basement

This first of the three alternatives described above can be used only when the room in which the receptacle is being installed is above a basement or crawl space with exposed joists. It may be used whether the receptacle is to be mounted near the floor or at table or counter height.

Do the following after you have made the opening for the new receptacle. However, before installing the box, turn off power to the existing receptacle (see Chapter 1).

1. Remove the baseboard below the existing receptacle.
2. In line with the receptacle, drill a 1/16-inch hole through the floor at the base of the wall. Insert a thin piece of wire through the hole.
3. In the basement, find the wire.
4. Aligning with the wire, locate the bottom plate, which is the support for the wall studs. The plate will be approximately ½ inch from the protruding wire.

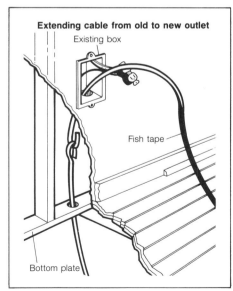

Extending cable from old to new outlet

Push one tape through the knockout and into the wall; push the other up through the plate hole. Hook the two; pull into the basement.

5. In line with the wire, use a spade bit to drill a ¾-inch hole up through the bottom plate. When the bit breaks

through the bottom plate, the drill bit will be in the empty wall space between the wall studs. Withdraw the drill bit.
6. Repeat this locating and drilling procedure below the opening for the new junction box.
7. At the existing receptacle, loosen the receptacle and withdraw it from the box. Do not disconnect the wires.
8. Using a hammer and punch, knock out the appropriately shaped tab in the base of the box. You will bring a cable through this opening into the box.
9. Thread an electric fishtape, which is hooked on the end, through the knockout opening and into the wall space. Have a helper in the basement push another fishtape up into the wall space through the hole that was drilled in the bottom plate. Maneuver the tapes until they hook together. Then, draw the end of the upstairs tape down through the hole in the bottom plate and into the basement. Unhook the two fishtapes.
10. At this point, prepare the cable you will use for connecting existing and new receptacles. Strip off three inches of plastic sheathing and remove the insulation from the wires. Take the cable into the basement.

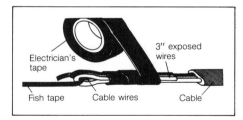

To fasten cable to a fishtape, remove 3 in. of sheathing and insulation from the cable end. Loop wires through the hook, and tape.

11. If you are using BX cable, remove 11 or 12 inches of the armored sheathing. Install the plastic protector between the wires and the sheathing. If you are using a two-part clamp, install the larger of the two pieces that clamp the cable to the junction box. Then strip away 3 inches of insulation from the wires and proceed.
12. In the basement, thread the bare wires through the fishtape hook. Bend back the ends of the bare wires over the hook and wrap masking or electrician's tape around the cable wires and the fishtape to join them securely.

13. Draw the fishtape and cable up through the wall space and out into the room. Have your helper in the basement guide the cable through the hole in the bottom plate. Draw the cable through the knockout hole in the receptacle box. Then, separate the fishtape and the cable.

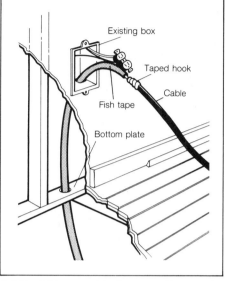

Pull the fishtape up into the room. Remove the fishtape; strip 8 in. more of cable from the wires; hook them to the receptacle.

14. Strip another eight inches of sheathing from plastic cable, but do not remove the insulation from the wires. (BX cable needs no further work.)
15. If you are using plastic cable, pull the cable into the box, so that it fits between the internal saddle clamp and rear wall of the box. The cable should extend far enough above the clamp for you to see the plastic sheathing. Tighten the screw to secure the cable to the box. Do not tighten the clamp to the wires themselves. If you are using BX cable, pull the cable into the box until the large clamp connection is seated firmly in the knockout opening. Slip the locknut of the cable connector over the ends of the wires; screw it tightly in place.
16. In the basement, run the cable along the joists to the area below the opening for the new receptacle. Repeat the procedure given above to bring the cable up the wall to the opening.
17. If you have to run cable at right angles to the joists, drill a ¾-inch hole into each joist and thread the cable through the holes. If you have to run cable parallel to a joist, attach the cable to

the joist with electrical staples or clamps placed 48 inches apart. In either case, see that the cable is taut.

18. With the cable in place at the opening for the new receptacle, attach the cable to the new box and insert the box in the wall in the manner best suited for the wall materials. Install the new receptacle just as you would any standard receptacle. Instructions for hooking up the cable to the existing cable and for repairing any damage to the wall are given below.

Receptacle to Receptacle Through the Wall

If the room in which you are working is on the upper floors of a home or is over a finished basement, you will not have access to the studs or to the joist area. Therefore, you will have to cut access openings in through the wall. Since these openings cause extensive damage, this process requires extensive repairs. However, in some cases you have no choice.

Working on drywall. Prepare the location for the new receptacle as described above.

1. Locate each stud lying between the existing receptacle box and the opening for the new box. Once you have located the first one, the process should be fairly simple. In standard construction, studs are installed 16 inches apart, although in some homes they may be spaced either 12 or 18 inches.

2. At each stud, mark off a rectangle that is centered on the stud and is 2 inches high and 4 inches wide. The width is critical. Once the rectangle has been cut out, both sides of the stud should be exposed.

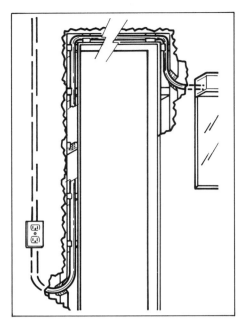

For a path around a door frame, remove the trim. Notch out channels for the cable into the framing spacers, headers and uprights.

3. Use a utility knife to cut out rectangular access holes.

4. With the studs exposed, use a spade bit to drill a ¾-inch hole from side to side in each stud.

5. Fish the cable from the existing box to the access hole in the wall. Then, thread the cable through the holes in each stud until you reach the opening for the new box.

6. Make the electrical connections to both of the receptacles.

7. Now, make patches to cover access holes in the wall. This involves cutting out appropriately sized rectangles from a panel of drywall. Nail the patches to the studs. Fill the cracks around the patches and over nailheads with spackle. Finally, sand and paint.

Working behind the baseboard. If you are working on a plaster and lath wall, extend the cable behind the baseboard. This keeps all the repair work hidden from view.

1. Remove the baseboard from under the existing receptacle box and from under the opening for the new receptacle. Slide a wide, thin-bladed chisel behind the wood strip and tap gently with a hammer as you pull the baseboard free.

2. Prepare the existing box to receive the new cable, as explained above.

3. Just above the floor and aligned with the existing outlet, chip out a hole that is 1 inch high and deep enough to break through behind the plaster and lath.

4. Continue chipping out until you form a channel that extends from the existing outlet to the position of the new one. This channel should be 1 inch high and ½ to ¾ inch deep.

5. Drop one fishtape into the wall through the appropriate knockout hole in the receptacle box and push one fishtape up into the wall through the channel opening just below it. Hook the two together.

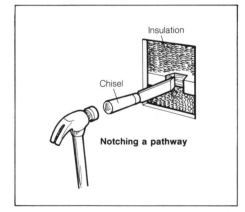

To route cable along a stairway or past an obstruction, put notches into the framing members; then fit the cable into the notch.

6. Fish the cable down through the knockout hole to the channel. Run the cable along the channel to the area of the new box, pushing the cable into the wall. At the opening for the new box, use the fishtape method to pull the cable up the wall to the opening.

7. When the new box has been installed and electrical connections have been made, cover the opening with a 1/16-inch thick metal plate fastened in place with small finishing screws. Instead of nails, use a contact adhesive to attach the baseboard to the wall. Nails may

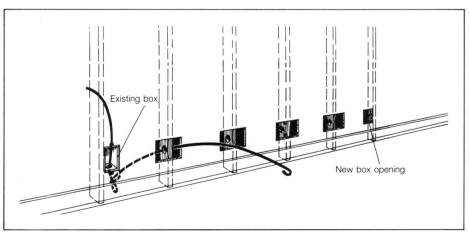

To route through a wall, cut rectangles to expose both sides of each stud. Then drill holes through each stud. Remove a knockout in the existing box; fish the cable through.

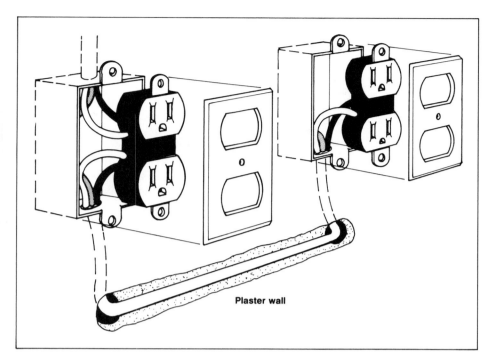

In a plaster wall, to extend cable from an old outlet to a new one, cut a channel to hold the cable. Punch holes for box connections. Hook up the wires; repair the plaster.

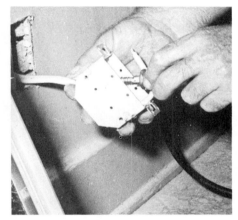

When fishing the cable to the new junction box, allow yourself at least 6 in. of extra length. This will give you ample working room.

accidentally puncture the cable and create a fire hazard.

Use a similar procedure to extend cable from an existing receptacle to a new receptacle on a wall constructed of gypsum wallboard. Cut the channel along the bottom of the wall by removing the wallboard to expose the studs. Make the channel wide enough, so you can drill ¾-inch holes in the center of studs and work the cable through them. With the cable protected by the studs, nail the baseboard to the wall. You do not have to use adhesive.

Tapping Off an Existing Duplex Receptacle in an Adjacent Room

This option can be used only if the potential power source is an existing end-of-the-

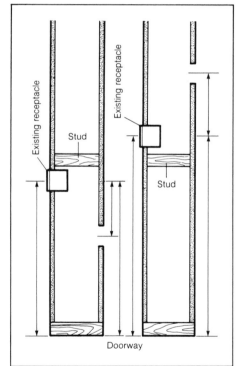

If the existing receptacle is on the opposite face of a wall, offset the new receptacle by 8 inches. Avoid any intervening studs.

run duplex receptacle. To determine if it is, deactivate the fuse or circuit breaker serving the existing live receptacle you have selected as the source of power (see Chapter 1). Remove the receptacle from its box. If two of the four terminals are unoccupied, the duplex receptacle is end-of-the-run.

The existing receptacle and the location of the new receptacle must fall opposite each other, aligned on either face of a wall. You must determine the spot for the new receptacle. Then run cable from the power source (existing receptacle) to the new box, as follows.

1. In the room housing the power source, measure the distance from a common doorway or corner to the power source.
2. In the room where the new receptacle is to go, measure an identical distance from the doorway or corner and draw a mark on the wall.
3. Remove the receptacle cover plate. Use a bent coat hanger to probe the open space between the studs to find which side of the existing box attaches to a stud. From the mark on the face of the wall that will hold the new receptacle, measure 8 inches away from the stud location, as shown, and make another mark. This is the new box location. In this way, there will be ample room for the new junction box, and you can fish cable easily between the old and the new box.
4. Prepare the cable as above. Push open the knockout hole in the existing receptacle box. Have a helper insert a fishtape into the wall through the knockout hole as you insert a fishtape through the opening you have made for the new box. Hook the ends of the two fishtapes together, and pull the tape held by your assistant into the room through the opening for the new box.
5. Attach cable to the end of the fishtape, and have your assistant pull the fishtape and cable back into the room housing the power source.
6. Install the new box, make the necessary wire connections, and patch the wall, as below.

STRINGING WIRES THROUGH CONDUIT

If your installation uses conduit, purchase color-coded, single-conductor wires in the standard colors: green for ground wire, black for hot and white for neutral wires. Some advanced projects require a second hot wire; this wire should be color-coded red.

For very short runs of several feet, you can simply push the wire through the conduit. For longer runs, you will have to fish the wire. Use the same techniques as described for fishing electrical cable: remove three inches of insulation from the wire ends, tape the wires securely to the fish-tape, and pull the wires through. As with a raceway installation, you can simplify the fishing process by coating the wires with a lubricant that has a wax base. This will help the wires slide through the conduit more easily.

HOOKING THE NEW CABLE TO THE EXISTING CIRCUIT

Once the wires are fished through, hook up the cable to the existing circuit. Almost every situation will require at least one wire splice. If you are uncertain about the acceptable splicing method, see Chapter 3. Any other method is not only unacceptable according to code, but creates a dangerous fire or shock hazard.

Wiring Procedures

End-of-run outlet. This is the easiest hookup to complete. Attach the black wire of the new cable to the unused brass screw. The white wire goes to the unused silver-colored screw. With a wire cap, splice the green ground wires together.

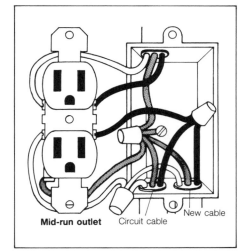

To hook up to a middle-of-the-run outlet, cut jumper wires from black, white and green wire. Cap the splices with wire nuts.

white jumper to the silver-colored screw. Finally splice the new ground wires together. The hookup is complete.

Middle-of-the-run switch. There are two sets of existing cable here. One set comes from the service box; the other runs to the fixture or outlet that the switch controls. Before you can hook up the new cable you

must find out which set comes from the service box. Otherwise, your new outlet will have power only when the switch is on.

To determine which cable comes from the service box, use the voltage tester. Disconnect the wires to the switch. Then, and only then, have an assistant turn on the circuit at the service box. Put one probe of the voltage tester against the metal junction box. With the other probe, touch one of the exposed black wires. If it is the feed wire (the one coming from

the service box), the bulb of the voltage tester will light. If the bulb does not light, test the other black wires. The one that lights the bulb is the one you want. Then turn off the circuit again before you continue.

Now you must have two 4-inch-long jumper wires—one black and one green. Splice together the black wire that lit the bulb, the new cable's black wire and the black jumper. Fasten the black jumper to the brass terminal on the switch. Fasten the black wire that didn't light the bulb to the other terminal of switch. Splice together the green wires with one end of the green jumper, and secure the other end of green jumper under the screw at the back of the box. Finally, splice the three white wires.

Middle-of-run ceiling fixture. Again you must find which of the black wires in the existing cables is live and is not controlled by the light switch. This black wire comes from the service box. Turn off the circuit at the service box. In the fixture will be at least two splices that connect black wires. The black wire coming from the

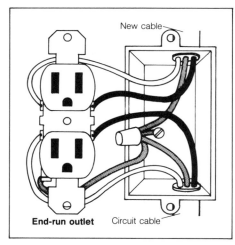

End-run outlet

To hook up to an end-of-the-run outlet, attach the black and white wires of the new cable to the unused brass and silver terminals.

Middle-of-run outlet. This hookup requires three wire nuts and two new jumper wires—one black and one white—each cut four inches long. Select a matching pair of black and white wires on the outlet. Detach these from their terminals. Splice together three wires: the black wire you just loosened, the black wire from your new cable and one end of a black jumper wire. Attach the free end of the black jumper wire to the brass terminal on the outlet. Now splice the two neutral cable wires and a white jumper. Fasten the

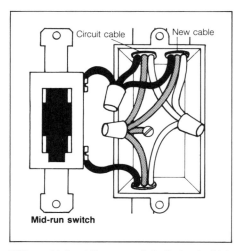

Mid-run switch

With a middle-of-the-run switch, find out which of the two existing cables is the incoming cable. That hooks up to the new cable.

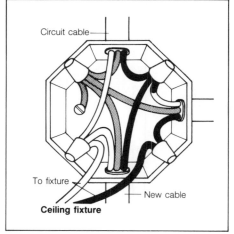

Ceiling fixture

To tap a middle-of-the-run ceiling fixture, first determine which cable is the incoming one. Hook the new cable to that set of wires.

service box will not be in the splice holding the black wire coming from the light fixture. Look for the former. Dismantle this splice and separate the wires so the bare ends do not touch anything. Turn on the circuit at the fuse box and use the voltage tester. The black wire that turns on the test light is the one to connect to the black wire of the new cable. Turn off the circuit. Splice together the black wire from the new cable and all black wires contained in the original splice. With the circuit still off, take apart the white wire splice and add the white wire from the new cable. Last, splice all green wires and one end of a 1½-2 inch green jumper. Fasten the other end of the green jumper under the box screw.

Major junction box. Several circuits may pass through this junction box. Have a helper turn off the circuits one by one, as you use the voltage tester to determine which cable controls the circuit you wish to tap.

Then splice together the wires—black to black, white to white, and ground to ground.

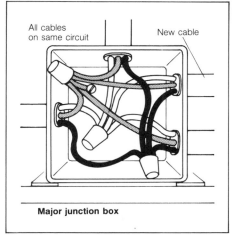

Major junction boxes are found beneath floors and in attics. Test the circuits to be sure you are tapping the right one.

Installing the New Receptacle

Once the cable is secured to the new junction box, insert the junction box into the wall, as described earlier. Then install the receptacle. The wiring will be that for an end-of-the-run receptacle.

CLOSING UP THE WALL

Once you have finished extending a circuit, you will need to repair the wall surface. The complexity of the repair will depend upon the size of the installation and the type of wall.

Nail Hole Repair, Plaster or Drywall

1. Mix a small amount of spackling compound with water. The spackling should be a stiff mixture, about the consistency of putty or stiff whipped cream.
2. Press the spackling into the hole and level it off with a putty knife. Let the material dry an hour or so.
3. Sand the area with medium or fine grit sandpaper.
4. If necessary, touch up the spot with paint. Try to feather out the paint into

Repair small holes in drywall and in plaster walls with spackling compound with the consistency of thick mud. Apply with a putty knife.

the surrounding area. Sometimes just a daub of paint on the spot works best. Try both and decide which looks better before the paint dries.

Patching Around Junction Boxes, Drywall or Plaster

1. Use a utility knife to create a clean edge that is hard and firm. Do not try to enlarge the hole; just cut away the loose material down to the firm inner core.
2. Mix up a large batch of spackling compound; prepare a stiff mixture.
3. Stuff the area between the wall and the box with mineral wool insulation. The fibers of the insulation will catch on the wall surface and hang in place.
4. Fill the open area with the spackling compound, but do not dislodge the in-

To repair large openings in drywall, apply spackling over the entire patch, especially the seams and nail dimples.

sulation, since it is the backing material for the spackling. When this initial job is finished, let the spackling dry for a day or so.

5. Once again, pack the opening full of spackling. Level the spackling with the putty knife so that the patch is slightly higher than the wall surface. This allows for normal shrinkage.
6. When the spackling is dry, sand the area lightly so it is level with the surrounding surface. Since the cover plate should conceal the patch, you need not paint over the surface.

Patching Large Openings in Drywall

If you have run the cable through the wall studs and must patch them over, follow these procedures.

1. Cut a patch piece from a piece of drywall: nail the patches to the studs with 8d nails.
2. Mix a batch of spackling compound so that it is fairly stiff. Using a wide-blade putty knife or wall scraper, spread the spackling into the seam and over the nailheads. Level the spackling to match the existing wall. Feather the edges so that the patch will not stand out.
3. Let the spackling sit for at least a day. Then sand the patch with fine grit sandpaper.
4. Cover the patch with paint to match the existing surface. Again, feather the paint to have an inconspicuous patch.

Let the spackling dry thoroughly. Then smooth the patch with fine sandpaper. The finished wall surface should be level and even.

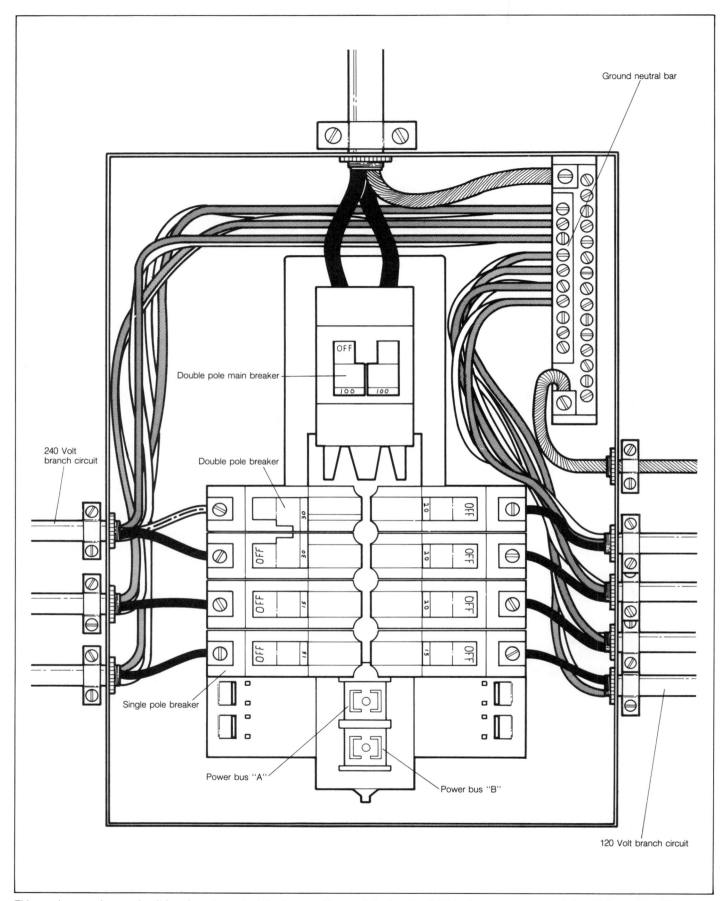

This service panel uses circuit breakers to protect the house wiring and the box itself. Note the arrangement at left, which provides 30 amps of power to a major appliance. The unused space at the bottom of the box can be used for new circuits at a later date.

The artificial lighting in your home falls into two categories: general lighting, which illuminates a room as a whole, and task lighting, which focuses on areas where you perform specific jobs. Task lighting, or local lighting, is needed over a kitchen sink, a chopping block, a range or cooktop, or above a desk or dining area. Both general and specific lighting contribute to or detract from the mood and convenience of a home.

GENERAL AND LOCAL LIGHTING
General Lighting

Ceiling fixtures most commonly supply the general lighting in a home. If you wish to increase general lighting, you can add a central ceiling fixture. This can be recessed, flush with the ceiling, or suspended from a canopy base on the ceiling. You may also select a hanging fixture designed in styles ranging from an elaborate chandelier to a simple industrial lamp.

Recessed fixtures. If you want to diffuse the light throughout the room, consider distributing several recessed multiple ceiling fixtures evenly throughout the room. (To do so, you will have to work around the joists in the ceiling.) Keep in mind, however, that multiple sources tend to be expensive to install and to operate. They require extra fixtures and supplies, and they consume more energy than a single fixture. In addition, because the lights are recessed, they do not direct any light upward. As a result, the light from the fixture is not supplemented with reflected ceiling light.

Ceiling grids. One innovative way to handle recessed ceiling lights is to create an egg-crate grid of criss-crossed strips of wood, metal or plastic. The bulbs are hidden in the grid openings. The openings can

An attractive decorating option is a ceiling fixture containing a fan and a light. This installation increases air circulation in a room to reduce heating costs in a home.

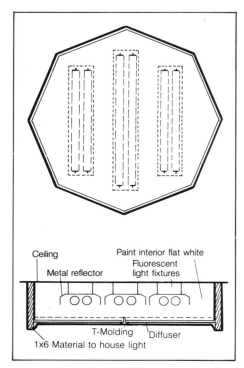

Create unusually shaped ceiling fixtures with 1x6s and diffusers. Have the shape mirror that of a table to integrate your decor.

be small enough to house only a single bulb or large enough to create perfect squares with the beams of a beamed ceiling.

Another way to increase general light is to transform part or all of the ceiling into a luminous light panel by suspending a ceiling of hanging translucent panels below a grid of fluorescent lights. The panels, usually made of acrylic, allow light to pass through but are not transparent. The installation is a fairly simple one. You can buy luminous ceiling kits, or you can construct your own. If you decide on such a plan, provide 40 watts for each 12 square feet of floor area.

Indirect light. A luminous ceiling is designed to create even lighting for an entire room. It needs no supplement. A central ceiling fixture, on the other hand, sometimes needs to be supplemented with installations that contribute to general illumination by means of indirect light, or light that is diffused into the room by bouncing off a reflective surface. Most indirect light installations depend upon fluorescent tubes for their light source, although some have long, tubular incandescent bulbs called linear filament lamps. The light is installed behind a baffle, an opaque shield that aims the light in the desired direction while hiding the bulb itself. There are two basic types of baffles: the valance and the cove.

You need not depend upon a single ceiling fixture in any room. Here recessed incandescents focus light; several fixtures set flush with the ceiling contribute general light.

Luminous ceiling panels are usually used in an office areas. However, small panels, such as those shown here, will fit into any room and can add illumination over work areas.

General lighting is as important as local lighting. Run a cable to above a bookcase, as here, and you can both highlight artwork and acquire reflected light for the rest of the room.

Valance. The valance is a single board, which is attached to a wall, cabinet or ceiling. When it concentrates the light downward, it accents such items as furniture, fireplaces or windows. When it directs the light upward, however, the light bounces

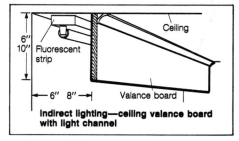

One method of indirect lighting utilizes a ceiling valance board. For the most effective installation, observe the distances noted.

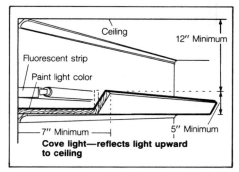

Cove light reflects light against the ceiling, which then reflects the light into a room. This is a subtle way of adding general light.

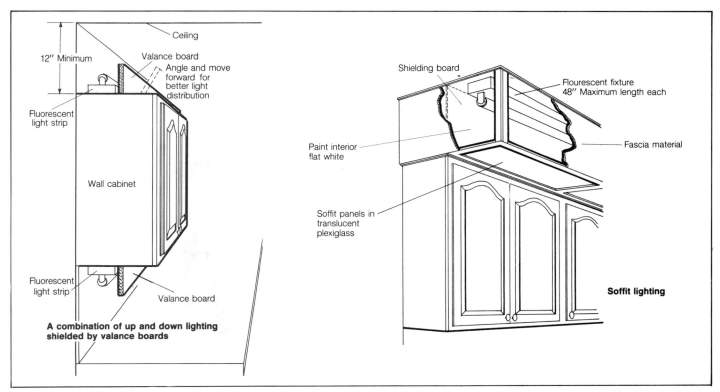

At left, fluorescent tubes are shielded by valance boards above and below the cabinets. Angle the boards for better light distribution. At right is an effective way of adding lighting to a work area. Placement in the soffit appears built-in; the diffuser creates even illumination.

off the ceiling and creates a soft, general light. In some settings, a valance directs light both up and down.

Cove. A cove baffle is especially constructed to create indirect general light. The base of the cove falls no less than 12 inches from the ceiling, is parallel to the ceiling and perpendicular to the wall. The light fastens to the cove base. A second board, no less than 5 inches in width, attaches to the outer edge of the cove base, at a 45 degree angle. The light is directed both up and out, away from the wall and into the room.

Local Lighting

Local lighting usually is not handled by ceiling fixtures. For specific tasks that demand good light, diffused light is never as satisfactory as direct, localized illumination focused on the job.

Reflector bulbs. One possibility is a reflector bulb installation. A reflector bulb has a coating designed to throw light in a desired direction. The bulbs are made with wide (flood) or narrow (spot) beams in many sizes and types and are excellent for task lighting. Because all their light is thrown exactly where it is wanted, bulbs

Areas such as this snack peninsula often are shadowy because of the soffit area above them. Track lights are an ideal way to illuminate the working and eating space below.

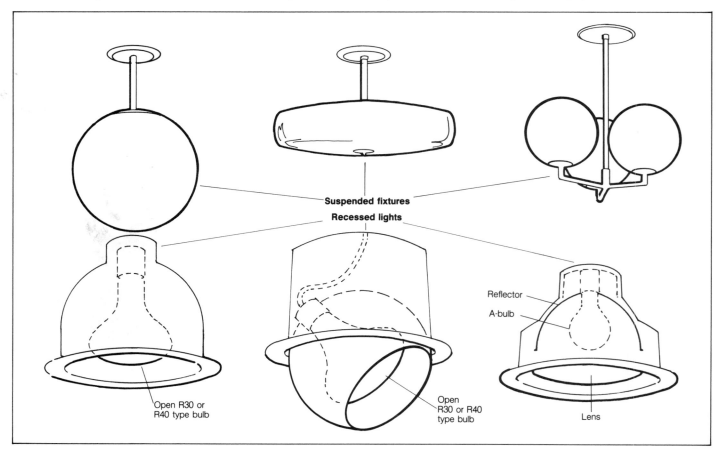

Incandescent bulbs may be used in suspended or recessed ceiling fixtures. Observe local requirements when housing recessed lights.

of lower wattage can achieve the same intensity as nonreflectors of higher wattage. Recessed spotlights in the ceiling can illuminate a kitchen work area or an oil painting in a dining room. Remember, however, that reflector lights also create heat as well as light. This can be an advantage during the winter, but the heat buildup also shortens the life of the bulb.

Track lighting. An attractive and functional option is track lighting. A track light has two parts. The first is a grooved metal strip through which electrical current passes. The strip connects to a power source, either directly through a ceiling junction box or indirectly through a cord adapter that plugs into an outlet. If you install one that attaches to a junction box, you will probably have to extend an existing circuit, since ceiling boxes often are not close enough to the track's location to provide a power source.

The second part of the system consists of lights or fixtures that plug directly into the track. Light from the track should hit the wall or work surface at a 35 degree or 40 degree angle for the best illumination. The location of the track on the ceiling is governed by the necessary angle of the light.

Tracks come in two types. Open channel tracks allow the fixtures or lights to plug in at any point you desire. Closed channel systems have specifically designated locations for fixtures and appliances. Although open tracks lend desirable flexibility, closed tracks are better for a kitchen setting because they do not become clogged with grease, as do the open ones.

Because you are able to aim the lights in a track system, and since the track itself can be as long as you wish, it is one way to light several areas at the same time. Also available are several adapters that give the system even more flexibility. Track lighting is sold in kits.

PLANNING CONSIDERATIONS
Fixture Placement

Several factors will affect the amount of general or local light given off by a given light fixture. One is its placement. If the fixture is high, it can light a wide area; if it is low, it lights a smaller area. A fixture installed behind a baffle will have its light directed to a given area.

Fixture Size and Intensity

Size also affects the brightness of a light

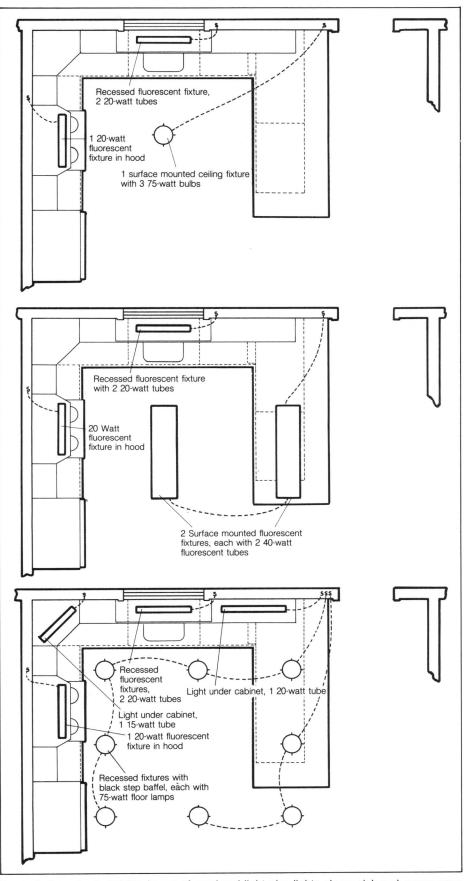

Top to bottom: basic lighting layout of overhead light plus lights above sink and range; more elaborate lighting layout with fluorescent fixtures; installation with recessed incandescent fixtures for general lighting, fluorescent strips above range and sink and under cabinets.

Select fixtures that complement the decor and the dimensions of your room. At left, suspended fixtures with opaque shades focus light in areas where it is needed. At right, a luminous ceiling panels add the amount of glare-free, shadow-free light needed in a dressing area.

fixture. The light intensity of a single ceiling fixture of high wattage is greater than several smaller wattage bulbs, even if their wattage when added together equals that of the large one. In other words, one 150-watt bulb gives off more illumination than three 50-watt bulbs working together. As important as wattage is the lumen rating of a given bulb. Although two 150-watt bulbs use the same amount of power, they do not necessarily give off identical amounts of light intensity, which is measured in lumens. For the greatest amount of illumination, select bulbs whose ratings, given on the package, are highest.

Fluorescent vs. Incandescent

The type of light you utilize—fluorescent or incandescent—affects lighting quality. You need not choose only one type—many remodelers use fluorescent lights above or below wall-hung cabinets and as a ceiling fixture, but place incandescent lights as spots for specific tasks. Each type of light has advantages.

Fluorescent light. Fluorescent light is even, glare-free and diffuse. A fluorescent tube has a life span of about four to five years, which is longer than an incandes-

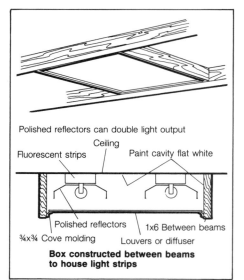

Polished reflectors can double light output
Ceiling
Fluorescent strips   Paint cavity flat white
Polished reflectors   1x6 Between beams
¾x¾ Cove molding   Louvers or diffuser
Box constructed between beams to house light strips

Use 1x6 wood strips to create a light box in a beamed ceiling. Paint the cavity flat white and install polished reflectors.

cent's, and it gives off more lumens. The bulb does not become hot, which is an aid in an area in which you have plants, as well as during hot summer months. However, the size and shape of a fluorescent limits design possibilities. In addition, the direction of the light from a fluorescent is difficult to control.

For years one of the criticisms of fluorescents was that their colors were too cold and added a greenish-purple cast to other colors in the room. This is still true with cool white fluorescent bulbs. However, the light quality of the cool white deluxe bulb is somewhat more acceptable. Manufacturers have come out with a warm white deluxe whose color is close to that of a white incandescent bulb. This development, paired with the research on fluorescents which is now in progress, may well make this energy-saving light source a desirable option in home remodeling.

Incandescent light. Even though incandescent bulbs are the usual source of lighting in the home, they can present problems. They create heat as well as light, although a new variety of cool beam bulbs creates only two-thirds the heat of standard incandescents. They do not last as long as fluorescents, and they are more expensive to operate. On the other hand, because of their wide-spread use they come in more shapes and types than do fluorescents. Their light, which is warm and pleasant, is easy to direct toward a given location—one reason why incandescents are used for local lighting.

Here the dark wood the walls and ceiling cause no problems because two skylights supplement the light. In most rooms, however, a flat white ceiling reflects the most light into a room.

STRUCTURAL CONSIDERATIONS
Attic Space
Once you have established the location for the new light fixture, you must determine whether you can work in the attic above the spot. If you can, adding a ceiling fixture is relatively simple. If you cannot work from the attic above, the fixture must be installed from inside the room. This procedure is more complex because you have to cut a hole in the ceiling in order to run cable and hang the fixture. You then must patch the ceiling. The methods used for these tasks will depend on whether the ceiling is composed of gypsum wallboard or of plaster and lath.

Switches
When installing a ceiling fixture where there was none previously, you also must decide the kind of switch that will control the fixture. Selecting a fixture that has a built-in switch simplifies the job, because you do not have to worry about routing cable to a switch location, installing the switch, and routing cable from the switch to the power source.

With a built-in switch, you simply mount the ceiling box, run cable between it and

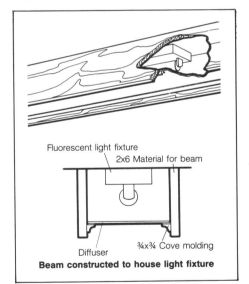

Fluorescent light fixture
2x6 Material for beam
Diffuser
¾x¾ Cove molding
Beam constructed to house light fixture

A fluorescent tube hidden in a beam uses cove moldings to hold a diffuser panel in palce. The beams will throw the light downward.

the power source, and connect the fixture to the ceiling box. The procedures involved will vary according to the structure of the fixture.

Power Source
The power source for a new ceiling fixture is usually a ceiling junction box to which

you have access in the attic. If there is no attic, power is normally drawn from an existing receptacle in the room in which the fixture is to hang.

INSTALLING A FIXTURE FROM INSIDE AN ATTIC
If Joists Are Exposed
Caution: Whether you are cutting through drywall or plaster, wear goggles to protect your eyes. You may also choose to wear an old hat or cap to keep material out of your hair. Follow these precautions for ceilings of gypsum wallboard or of plaster and lath.

Drilling a locating hole. In the room in which the new fixture is to hang, mark the spot where you want the fixture. At that spot, drill a ⅛-inch test hole through the ceiling. If the drill meets resistance, you are drilling into a joist. Withdraw the drill, move it 2 or 3 inches to either side of the hole, and drill another hole. After making sure nothing is blocking the way, drill a ¾-inch hole at the selected point in the ceiling. This hole is your locating hole.

Go into the attic. Lay several sturdy planks across the joists so you can walk to and work at the spot without accidentally putting your foot through the ceiling of the room below. Find the locating hole for the fixture.

Selecting a junction box. One of two types of boxes is used: one attached to an adjustable bar hanger or one attached to a flange. To determine which one to use, measure from the ¾-inch locating hole to the joists on each side of the hole. If the distance between the hole and the closest joist is 4 inches or more, use a box with an adjustable bar hanger and suspend the box between the joists. If the distance between the hole and closest joist is less than 4 inches, use a box with a flange. Attach the box to one of the joists by nailing down the flange.

Drawing in the ceiling opening.
Adjustable hanger bar. Place the box open end down, so the center of the box falls over the ¾-inch locating hole. Trace the outline of the box on the topside of the ceiling. Drill ⅜-inch holes at each corner of the outline. Position the bit so when holes are drilled, half the hole lies outside the outline.
Flanged box. Hold the flange against the joist, so the open end of the box faces down. Trace the outline of the box on the topside of the ceiling.

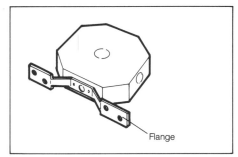

Use this style of box when you have access to the ceiling joists. The box is attached by means of screws or nails through the flange.

Cutting the ceiling opening. Go downstairs to the room in which the fixture is to be installed, and prepare to cut through the ceiling.

Drywall ceiling. If the ceiling is drywall, brace the ceiling with one hand. Insert a keyhole saw into one of the holes and cut out the opening for the box by sawing from one hole to another.

Plaster ceiling. If the ceiling is plaster and lath, use a utility knife to score the plaster along the lines going from hole to hole. Then, lay strips of masking tape along the outside of the outline to minimize plaster crumbling. Brace the ceiling by holding a piece of board against it. With your other hand, use a keyhole saw to cut the opening for the box.

Attaching the junction box. Back in the attic, run the cable to the new box (see below). Then, attach the box to the ceiling, as follows.

Adjustable bar hanger box. Attach the hanger to the box with a threaded metal box stud. Install the box in the hole in the ceiling and extend the adjustable bar hanger, so its ends are against the joists. Make marks through the screw holes. Then, retract the bar enough to drill pilot holes into the joists. Finally, screw the adjustable hanger bar to the joists with 1½-inch wood screws. This will supply more than adequate support for the weight of most fixtures.

Flanged box. To install a box that is held by a side flange, lower the box through the hole in the ceiling. Hold the flange against the joist and draw marks for the pilot holes. Remove the box, drill the pilot holes, reinstall the box, and screw the flange to the joist with 1½-inch wood screws.

If the Attic Has Rough Flooring
Drilling the locating hole. Drill the initial test hole and ¾-inch locating hole in

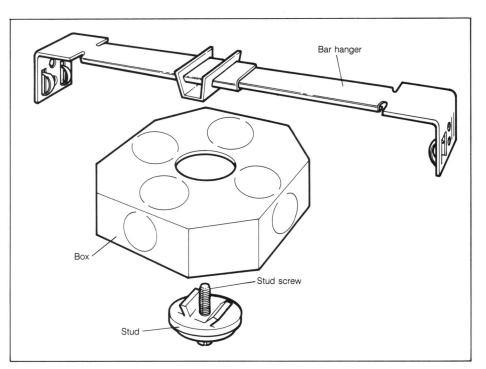

A ceiling box attached to a bar hanger suspends the box between the joists of a drywall ceiling. The stud shown screws into the center of the hanger to secure the box in position.

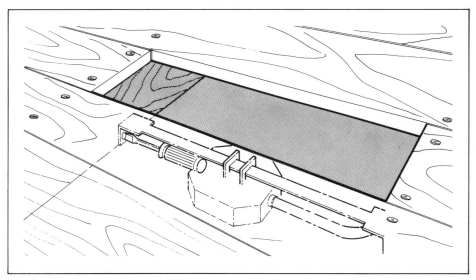

If the ceiling joists are covered with flooring, you must carefully remove a section to install the bar hanger. Attach the hanger to the joists with wood screws.

the ceiling as described above. Then perform one additional step to pinpoint the spot. Equip your drill with an 18-inch extension and a ⅛-inch bit. Insert the extension and bit through the ¾-inch locating hole and drill through the attic floor. Then push a piece of wire through the hole.

Opening the attic floor. Go to the attic and find the wire protruding through the floor. You now have to remove that part of the floor so that you can reach the joists to attach the junction box for the fixture. To do this, find the rows of nails holding

the floorboards to the joists on either side of the locating wire. Measure 1 inch in from the nails to allow for the width of the joist. Then cut through the flooring with a sabre saw and remove enough to permit you to insert and attach the junction box to the joists. If you do a neat job of cutting, the sections of floorboard will be in good enough shape to nail back into place when you are finished installing the box.

Finishing the installation. Cut the ceiling opening and install the box as described above. Then repair the attic floor-

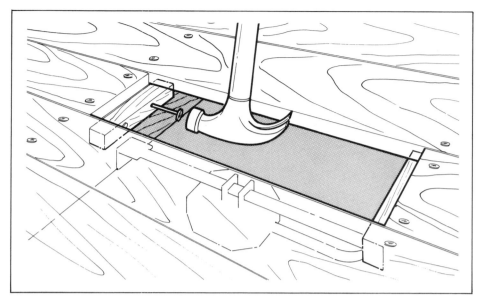

You must add supports before you replace the flooring. Cut small cleats and nail them to the joists on either side of the opening. Lay the flooring on top of the cleats and nail.

ing. To reinstall the pieces of floorboard that you removed, cut two 2x3-inch pieces of wood that are 2 inches longer than the width of the opening. These pieces will be used as cleats and will form supports for the pieces of floorboard that you removed. On the facing sides of the joists flanking the opening, use 10d nails to nail one cleat to one joist and the other to the other joist. Lay the pieces of floorboard across the cleats and nail the boards down, again with 10d nails.

INSTALLING A FIXTURE FROM WITHIN THE ROOM

To install a ceiling box for the new fixture when there is no attic, you must do all the work in the room that will house the fixture. The procedure you use, again, depends on whether the ceiling construction is gypsum wallboard or plaster and lath.

Drywall Ceiling

Caution: Wear goggles to protect your eyes when you do this job.

Tools and materials needed. This job requires a hammer and chisel, a junction box with an adjustable hanger bar, a drill and ½-inch bit, a piece of drywall at least 16x16 inches in size, a utility knife, carpenter's square, measuring tape, gypsumboard nails, perforated wallboard tape and spackling compound.

Locating the joists. Select the spot for the fixture and drill a ½-inch hole through the ceiling. Straighten out a wire coat hanger and, 6 inches from one end, bend the wire into a right angle. Insert the bent end

through the hole into the ceiling and circle it around to make sure there is no obstruction in the spot where you want to work. Move to another spot if there's an obstruction. If there is not, you can proceed.

Cutting the ceiling opening. To place the junction box, you must make a 16-inch x 16-inch square opening in the ceiling. The opening must extend from the center of one joist to the center of the next joist. To do this you must first locate the joists and then cut the opening.

If you must break an opening from below, draw a 16x16 in. square aligned with two joists. Break away the drywall with a hammer.

1. Often, a nail popping through the ceiling will locate a joist for you. If there is no nail, rap the ceiling with your knuckles until you hit a solid-sounding area. The solid sound indicates a joist. If this method does not prove successful, buy a tool called a stud-locator from a hardware or building supply store. Once you have located one joist

as a reference point, you can measure 16 inches to find the others.

2. Choose the two joists between which you want to locate the fixture. Mark each joist.
3. Using the two marks representing the two joists as reference points, draw a 16-inch square outline on the ceiling. Use a carpenter's square to assure that lines are straight.
4. With a utility knife, deeply score the ceiling along the lines of the square. Then, working diagonally, deeply score the ceiling from one corner of the outline to the other. Make another diagonal line between the other two corners. When you are done, the area to be cut out should be divided into four sections.
5. Using a hammer, shatter one section of the divided square at a time. Then, use a utility knife to cut away the remaining wallboard. When you are done, you should have an opening that extends from the center of one joist to the center of the other. The edges should be clean and straight. Pull out any nails that are protruding from the joists.

Installing the junction box. Run cable to the opening (see below). Then install the box as follows.

1. Measure the opening in the ceiling and draw the same size and shape, minus ⅛ inch from each side, onto the extra drywall panel. Cut the piece from the panel. It will be used to repair the ceiling.
2. Place the box for the new fixture, open end down, on the piece of new drywall, so that the center of the box falls on the center of the piece. Trace the outline of the box on the piece. Use the utility knife.
3. Cut out the opening for the box.
4. Using an adjustable hanger bar, hang the ceiling box between the joists.
5. Connect the cable to the box.

Repairing the ceiling. This is similar to closing up a wall (Chapter 9).

1. Hold repair piece in position against the joists. The opening should fit over the fixture box. Nail the repair piece to the joists with gypsumboard nails. Space the nails about three inches apart.
2. When the nailheads are flush with the panel, hit them one more time with the hammer. This creates a "dimple" in the surface of the piece and countersinks the nailheads below the surface of the

piece. These dimples will be filled later with spackling compound.

3. When the piece is in place, check the edges to make sure that they do not project above the surface of the surrounding ceiling. If the edges do project, you may be able to trim them down slightly with the razor knife.

4. Mix a stiff batch of spackling compound. With a putty knife or wall scraper, trowel on a thin layer of the spackling at the joints. Then embed the joint tape into the spackling compound. Run the wall scraper over the top of the tape, pressing it into the spackling.

5. With the tape embedded, fill all dimples with spackling compound, leveling the compound in these depressions using the wall scraper or putty knife.

6. Let the spackling dry one day. Apply a layer of spackling over the tape; let dry another 24 hours. Add a third coat. Once dry, sand the spackling lightly and prime the new panel with paint. Once the paint has dried, give the panel a light sanding and dust off the residue. Add a second coat of paint.

Plaster and Lath Ceiling

Caution: In order to protect your eyes, wear goggles when chiseling plaster.

Tools and materials. To complete this job, you will need these tools: a cold chisel, hammer, drill, ⅜-inch bit, ⅛-inch bit, small scrap lumber, keyhole saw, masking tape, 1½-inch wood screws, screwdriver, plaster, spackling compound, sandpaper and putty knife. You will also need a junction box with an offset bar hanger. This is a special piece of hardware used for hanging a box in a plaster ceiling when it is not possible to work inside an attic.

Opening up the ceiling. All you actually will cut out is a strip of ceiling, in which the box is centered.

1. Using a cold chisel and hammer, chisel out an opening in the ceiling at the spot where you want the fixture. Make the opening wide enough to expose a strip of lath. The lath lies at right angles to the ceiling joists.

2. If you see nails in the lath, the opening is beneath a joist. Chisel out the ceiling along the lath until you come to another row of nails, indicating an adjacent joist.

3. If there are no nails in the lath, chisel out along the lath in one direction from the opening until you come to nails, indicating a joist. Then, go back to the opening and chisel out in the other direction until you come to nails that indicate the adjacent joist.

4. Centered in the strip of exposed lath and between the two joists, trace the outline of the box on the ceiling and drill ⅜-inch holes into each corner of the outline. Apply strips of masking tape along the outside edge of the outline to minimize plaster crumbling. Then, using a utility knife, score the lines from hole to hole. Finally, brace the ceiling with a piece of board and use a keyhole saw to cut through the ceiling along the scored lines.

5. Now you must remove the strip of lath. Measure 1 inch in from the set of nailheads to account for the width of the joist. Saw through the lath on both sides. Then remove the remaining small pieces and the nails holding the lath. The nails are small, so they will not be difficult to remove.

Installing the junction box. Run the cable from the power source to the opening (see below). Then proceed as below.

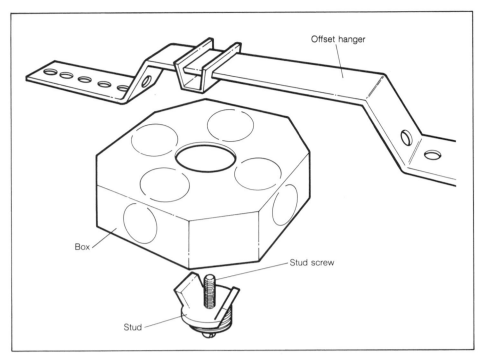

Because you will have very little work space in a plaster ceiling, you must use an offset hanger bar to support the ceiling junction box. Again, a stud secures the box to the bar.

To break through a plaster ceiling, use a chisel and hammer. (Use a hammer such as a ball peen hammer designed to strike metal.) Chisel the opening from one joist to the next.

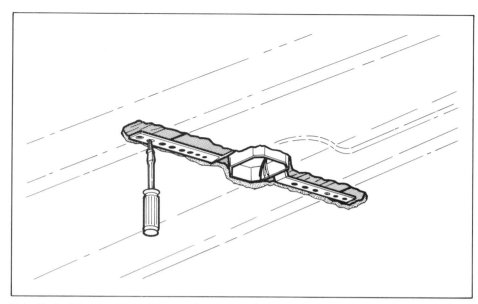

The offset of the special bar hanger allows you to fasten the bar to the lower edge of the joists. The ceiling box will be flush with the ceiling surface.

1. Equip the box for the new fixture with an offset hanger. Hold the box in the space in the ceiling you provided for it, and see that the ends of the offset hanger fall on the bottoms of both joists. Mark off the screw holes.
2. Withdraw the box and offset hanger, and, using the ⅛-inch bit, drill pilot holes in the joists.
3. Attach the cable to the box and secure the box to the joists with 1½-inch wood screws.

Repairing the ceiling. Patch the ceiling with plaster, but do not fill the entire depth. Leave a 1/16-inch depression. When the plaster dries, fill the depression with spackle or gypsum wallboard joint cement. Let this dry. Then, sand and paint the ceiling.

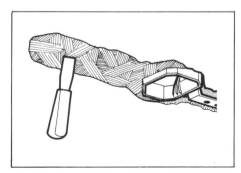

Once the cable has been fastened to the box, patch the opening with plaster patch. Once dry, fill and level with spackling.

TAPPING SOURCES OF POWER

There are three sources of power that can be tapped to serve a new fixture. They are a middle-of-the-run ceiling box, a wall switch, and an end-of-the-run receptacle.

Tapping a Middle-of-the-Run Ceiling Box

If a ceiling fixture has a built-in switch, the easiest way to get power to the fixture is to draw the power from an existing middle-of-the-run ceiling box. If you draw power from this source for a fixture requiring a switch, the fixture will be on at all times. For instructions on how to identify a middle-of-the-run ceiling box, see Chapter 9.

Laying the cable. If the cable can be run parallel to the joists, string the cable along the joist. Fasten the cable every four feet with cable staples. If the cable must run perpendicular to the joists, drill ¾-inch openings through the joists. Then string the cable from one junction box to the other.

Identifying the feed wire. When you are ready to hook up to the power source, use a voltage tester to find the hot wire that comes from the circuit breaker or fuse box—incoming or feed hot wire. With the help of an assistant, follow these steps.

Caution: Be careful! You are dealing with hot wires. Do not touch them or the ceiling box when power is on and don't accidentally push a bare wire into contact with the ceiling box.

1. Be sure the power is off.
2. Disconnect one of the existing fixture wires from one of the cable wires.
3. Turn on the power. Hold one probe of a voltage tester against the bare end of the cable wire; hold the other probe of the voltage tester against the metal box. If the voltage tester lights, you have found the power feed wire.
4. If the voltage tester does not light, *turn off the power,* reconnect the fixture and cable wires, and disconnect another set of wires. Follow this procedure until

The height of a ceiling fixture affects area it illuminates. Here hanging ceiling fixtures illuminate an eating area. The shades direct the light downward. These lights add little general lighting.

you uncover the power feed wire. Turn the power off. Then tag wire for future reference.

5. To test a system that has no ground wire system, touch the voltage tester probes to the black and the white wires.

Hooking up the power source. Insert the cable into the box through a knockout hole. Secure the cable to the existing junction box with a two-part clamp or a saddle clamp, as discussed in Chapter 9.

Now splice three hot wires together: the tagged feed wire, the black wire of the existing fixture, and the black wire of the new cable. Secure the splice of the three wires with a wire nut. Similarly, connect the white wire of the new cable to the two white wires already in the box you are tapping, and connect the ground wire of the new cable to the ground wires in the box.

Hooking up the new fixture. The final step is to connect the new fixture to the cable in the new ceiling box.

Tapping a Middle-of-the Run Wall Switch—Exposed Joists

If the fixture requires a separate wall switch, the best way to get power to it is by means of a middle-of-the-run wall switch in the room where the new fixture is to be hung. The fixture will light when the switch is flipped. To install the cable, you must fish wire across the ceiling and down the wall.

Fishing the cable. As always, first turn off power to the switch (see Chapter 1).

1. Drill a hole through the ceiling directly above the switch. Position a ⅛-inch hole as close as you can to the junction of the wall and ceiling.

2. Push a long wire through the hole. If the wire is blocked, drill another hole two or three inches from the first.

3. In the attic, find the protruding wire. It will be close to the top plate, which is a wood beam extending laterally to serve as the top support for the wall. Aligned with the wire, drill a ¾-inch hole down through the top plate. This should put you on line, more or less, with the existing switch box.

4. Remove the switch from the junction box, and open a knockout hole in the top of the box by punching out the knockout plug.

5. Have a helper drop a small chain down through the hole in the top plate as you push a fishtape into the wall space through the knockout hole. Catch the

chain with the fishtape hook and pull the chain out of the switch box.

6. Tape the chain and fishtape together as described in Chapter 9. Pull the chain and fishtape back into the attic.

7. Disengage the chain and fishtape, and attach the cable to the fishtape. Pull the fishtape and cable into the switch box and up to the ceiling.

8. Unhook the fishtape and cable, and use a saddle clamp to clamp the cable in the switch box.

9. Extend the other end of the cable across the attic and into the ceiling box for the new fixture. Fasten as necessary to the joists, or pass the cable through. Then, connect the cable to the fixture and hang the fixture.

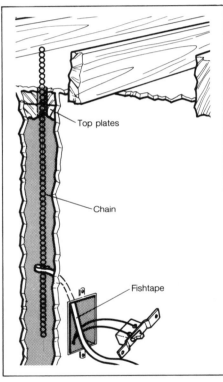

Drop a chain from the attic to the switch opening. Snag the chain with the fishtape; pull the tape up; draw the cable to the switch.

Hooking up to the switch. First, identify the hot feed wire, as above. Then, turn off the power to the circuit.

1. Cut a 4-inch black (hot) jumper wire. Working at the switch, connect one end of the jumper wire to a switch terminal screw.

2. Connect the other end to the outgoing wire and to the black wire entering the switch box from the ceiling box. In this way, the fixture will get power only when the switch is on.

3. While you are still at the switch, con-

nect the white wire entering the switch box from the ceiling box to the incoming cable white wire and the outgoing cable white wire.

4. Connect the ground wire entering the switch box from the ceiling box to the ground wire of the incoming cable and the ground wire of the outgoing cable.

Tapping a Middle-of-the-run Switch—Enclosed Joists

If the ceiling joists and top plate are inaccessible due to something such as finished flooring, you will have to cut access holes at the ceiling-wall juncture before you fish the cable from the fixture to the switch. The final hookups will be the same.

Cutting the plate holes. Shut off the current to the switch and to any other circuit, on either side of the wall or the ceiling, whose cables might run through the area in which you are working.

1. Following the joists, locate the place on the ceiling where the cable will turn to come down the wall.

2. At this spot on the ceiling, draw a rectangle that is 2 inches long and 1 inch wide; on the wall, draw a rectangle that is 4 inches long and 1 inch wide.

3. Cut away the ceiling and wall rectangles. The supporting boards behind form the top plate, and you have just cut a "wall plate hole" and a "ceiling plate hole."

4. If the wallboard is less than ½ inch thick, you will need to chisel a groove to hold the cable to the plates. Use a keyhole saw to make two cuts that are ¾ inch apart. Then chisel out the wood between the cuts.

Fishing the cable. The cable is fished in two steps: first, the cable is fed into and drawn down from the wall plate hole to the switch; then, the cable is drawn over to the ceiling opening. In greater detail, the steps are as follows.

1. Push the first fishtape upward through the appropriate opening in the switch junction box to the access hole at the top plates.

2. Insert the second fishtape through the wall plate hole and catch the first fishtape. Draw it through; fasten the cable to it with electrician's tape and then draw one end of the cable back down to the switch box.

3. Detach the cable from the tape and install it with a saddle clamp.

4. Move to the fixture hole. Insert a fish-

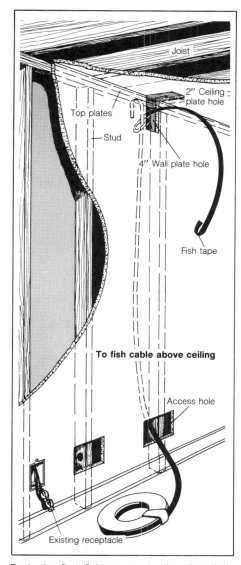

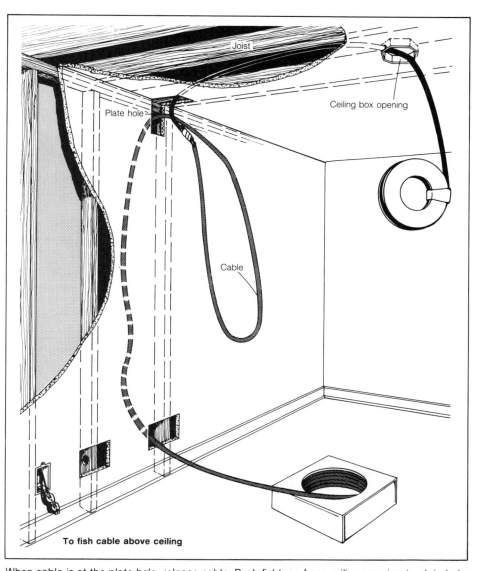

Push the first fishtape up to the plate hole opening; catch with a second; draw out.

When cable is at the plate hole, release cable. Push fishtape from ceiling opening to plate hole; snag the hook; draw it through. Attach cable; draw it to the ceiling opening.

tape again and push it across the ceiling toward the ceiling plate hole.

5. Insert the second fishtape through the ceiling plate hole.

6. Catch the first fishtape and draw it through the ceiling plate hole.

7. Attach the loose end of the new cable to the first fishtape and draw the cable across to the ceiling fixture hole.

8. Clamp the cable to the fixture junction box.

Finishing the installation. Complete the wiring as above. Then install the fixture.

Adding a New Fixture with a Switch Loop

In some situations you will have convenient access to a source of power, such as an existing ceiling fixture or an existing switch, but you will want a separate switch control for the new fixture. This is likely,

for instance, if you add a partition in a large room. In such a case, the best solution is to add a new fixture and a switch loop.

In this type of installation, you install a fixture and a switch. Cable carries the power to the fixture, but the power is routed through the housing and past the fixture to the switch. When the power is needed, the switch returns it to the fixture. It is from this circular path that this installation gets its name of switch loop.

The installation of a switch-loop ceiling fixture falls into three steps: running cable to the fixture from an existing power source, running cable from the new switch to the fixture, and hooking up the fixture wires.

Step one: running cable to the new fixture. The process here is the same as described earlier, until you are ready to hook

up the cable to the existing wiring.

1. Determine which of the incoming cable wires is the feed wire, as described above.

2. If you are tapping a ceiling fixture, add the new cable into the splice containing

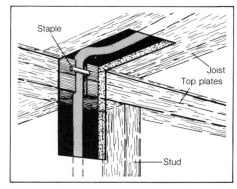

For a wall less than ½ in. thick, cut a groove ¾ in. wide and ½ in. deep into the top plate. Chisel out wood. Staple cable as shown.

the feed hot wire. If you are tapping a switch, cut a 4-inch black jumper wire. Splice together the jumper, the feed hot wire and the new cable wire. Attach the loose end of the jumper to the brass terminal on the switch.

3. Place the fixture, but do not hook up the wires.

Step two: running cable from the new switch to the new fixture. Fish the cable to the new switch just as you did above. Wire the switch as for an end-of-run switch. Finish with a cover plate.

Step three: setting up the switch loop.

1. To create the by-pass of the switch loop, attach the black wire of the cable coming from the power source to the white wire of the cable coming from the switch. Then recode the white wire to indicate that it now is a hot wire that carries power to the switch.

2. Attach the black wire of the cable coming from the switch to the black wire of the fixture so that the fixture can receive power from the switch.

3. Attach the white fixture wire to the white wire coming from the power source.

4. Cut a 4-inch green ground wire, splice it together with all other ground wires, and attach the loose end of the jumper to the fixture housing.

Tapping an End-of-the-run Receptacle

The wiring arrangement for this installation involves running cable from the fixture ceiling box to a new wall switch box, and from the wall switch box to an existing receptacle. The methods require far more wall repair than the above installations. Use this arrangement only if the following conditions exist:

(1) there is no way to tap power from an existing ceiling box;

(2) you want the fixture to be controlled by a remote switch, but there is no existing middle-of-the-run wall switch in the room that houses the new ceiling box.

Planning the project. Select the outlet you plan to tap. Then find a location for the new switch. If possible, it should be on the same wall as the receptacle from which power will be drawn, next to a doorway, and approximately 4 feet off the ground. Turn off *all* circuits that control power to the areas that you will be working on. Then, using the method appropriate to your home's construction, cut openings

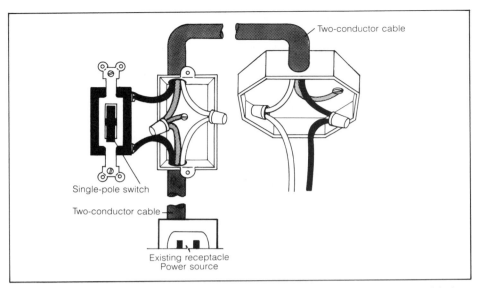

This shows wiring for a middle-of-the-run switch. Bring cable to the switch box; run cable from the switch to the fixture. Splice the white wires; fasten black wires to the switch.

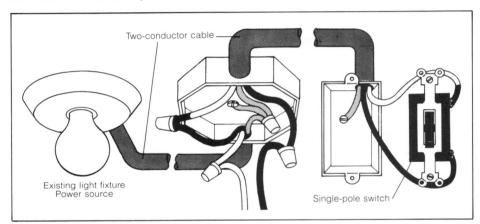

This illustrates the wiring arrangement for a switch loop. First run cable to the fixture, then to the switch. Be sure to recode the white wire to indicate that it carries power.

Run cable to the back of a cabinet overhang. Then install fixtures to illuminate the counter space below. This helps eliminate shadows that can render the counter space useless.

for the switch and for the ceiling fixture (see Chapter 9).

Fishing cable from the ceiling fixture to the switch. Follow the same fishing procedure as discussed earlier under "Tapping a Middle-of-the-run Switch." However, do not yet install the switch.

Fishing cable from the switch to the receptacle. Before you can fish the cable you must create access holes at the stud locations along the wall. Follow the procedure discussed in Chapter 9 for working from receptacle to receptacle through the wall studs. Install one final wall opening that is aligned with both the wall stud openings and the switch opening itself. Fish the cable over to this last access hole, as described in Chapter 9 for working from receptacle to receptacle.

Once the cable has been installed parallel to the floor, remove the cable from the fishtape. Insert the fishtape into the switch opening and push it down to the last access hole, which is below the opening. Catch it with the other fishtape and pull it through the access hole. Attach the cable and draw it up to and out through the switch.

Wiring the switch. This switch is a middle-of-the-run installation, since it falls between the fixture and the power source. Attach the two black wires to the two brass terminals on the switch. Splice the white wires together; splice the green wires with a green jumper wire. Fasten the free end of the jumper to the junction box with a metal screw.

ADDING A LUMINOUS CEILING

In some areas, such as a kitchen, a sewing room or a workshop, you may want a very high level of consistent general light. A luminous ceiling can give this kind of illumination.

Planning the Installation

The best size fluorescent for use in a luminous ceiling is a 4-foot length of 40-watt rapid-start lamp. (Rapid starters also come in other lengths.) To determine the number of lamps you need, sketch out the dimensions of the ceiling. Plan for the lamps to lie in parallel lines that are between 18 and 24 inches apart. (The narrower space gives a more even light, but it is also more expensive.) On both ends, allow about 8 inches between the end of the line of lights and the walls. Now figure the length of the lines in feet, and divide

One way to illuminate a wet bar is to install recessed fluorescent lights in the cabinet above the bar. This plan is feasible only if you have cabinet space to spare.

by four. If necessary, supplement the 4-foot lamps with shorter ones to obtain the coverage you desire.

Power source. A luminous ceiling is powered by a central, switch-controlled junction box in the ceiling. If you do not have one, you must install one. Remember to shut off the circuit that feeds the fixture before you begin work. If a box is already in place you need only remove the old fixture. Fasten a box extender to the junction box in the ceiling. (The extender will look just like the box in the ceiling, except it will have no back.) The extender will house the cable for the lines of lights. The lines themselves will be connected to each other with jumpers and then to the junction box. For a good, reflective surface,

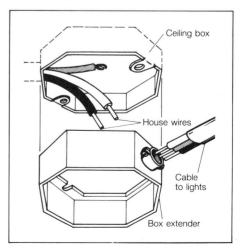

Install a box extender to the ceiling box. Use a two-part cable connector to attach the cable. Then hook up the like colored wires.

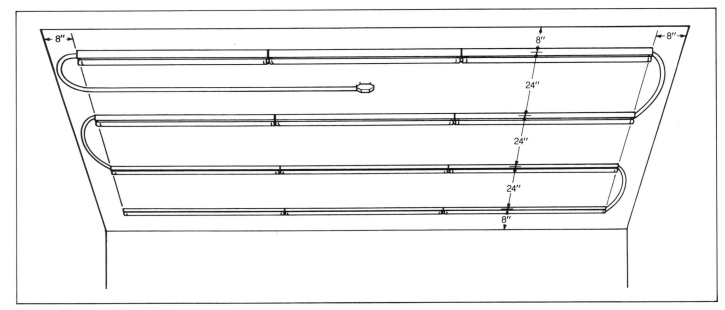

Rather than connect each individual row of lights to the central junction box, connect the rows to each other with jumper cables.

paint the ceiling with two coats of flat white ceiling paint.

Materials required. To connect the channels to each other you will need single conductor wires (black, white, and green) equal to at least one and one-quarter times the total planned length of your lines. You also will need wire nuts, electrician's tape, a wire cutter, a wire stripper, and two-part cable connectors to secure the cable to the junction box.

Finally, you will need cable that has a temperature rating compatible with that listed on the lights (usually 75° F). To determine the amount, multiply the number of lines of lights you have by the distance between each line. Then select one end of an outermost line of lights. Measure the path that a cable will have to take from that corner in order to connect with the ceiling junction box. Add this to the above total; divide by 12 to convert from inches to feet. To allow for connections and for the fact that the cable will never lie completely flat and straight, purchase fifty percent more cable than your plan requires.

Installing the Lights

Step one: installing the channels. To fasten the channels to the ceiling, you will need a screwdriver, screw anchors (to ensure the stability of the installation), and channel connectors to hold adjoining channels together.

1. Starting at either end, hold the channel against any of the lines on the ceiling. Draw in the position of the screw holes.

Continue on; remember that the channels in an individual line will butt right against each other.
2. Install the screw anchors.
3. Before you secure the channels in place, remove the knockout holes at the ends of the individual channels that will butt against each other.
4. Fasten the channels to the ceiling, butting the ends as you go.
5. To secure the butted ends of the two channels, use the channel connector sleeves that come with the channels. Run the sleeve through and fasten as directed. The connector is called a chase coupling.

Step two: connecting the lights in each line. To wire the adjoining fixtures in a line of lights together, you will need to use jumper wires. Begin with the first fixture in an outermost row.

1. Measure the distance between its black wire and the black wire in the next fixture. Cut a jumper equal to this length plus 2 inches for splicing.
2. Splice together the black wire of channel one and the black jumper wire with a wire nut.
3. Do the same with the white wire and a white jumper.
4. Pass the two jumper wires through the channel connector between channel one and channel two.
5. Cut jumpers to connect the black and the white wires of the second channel to the black and white wires of the third.
6. Splice the black jumper from channel

one, the black jumper from channel two and the black wire of channel two.
7. Do the same with the white wires.
8. Pass the channel two jumpers through the channel connector to channel three.
9. Continue this process until the entire line of lights is connected.
10. Do the same for all the lines.

Step three: connecting the lines together. When you have wired all the lines, you are ready to connect the lines to each other and then to the junction box.

1. Move to the end of an outermost line. Remove the knockout at the end of the last channel.
2. Then remove the knockout at the end of the last channel in the next line. (The two knockouts will be directly across from each other.)
3. Cut 30 to 32 inches of cable, or as much as you require to connect the two ends plus 4 inches for splicing.
4. Strip 2 inches of sheathing from both ends of the cable, exposing the black, white and green wires inside; strip about an inch of insulation from those wires.
5. Using a 2-part cable connector, fasten one end of the cable through the knockout in the outermost line.
6. Splice black to black, and white to white.
7. With a metal screw, fasten the green ground wire to the channel.
8. Now move to the next line and fasten the other end of the cable to the knockout you prepared earlier. The first and second row are now con-

nected to each other at one end.

9. Move to the opposite end of the second line. It must be connected to the third line, in the same manner as above.

10. Once completed, connect the third and fourth. Continue until all the lines are connected. The result will look like a continuous zig-zag pattern.

Step four: hooking up to the junction box. When the lines are all joined, you are ready to connect the final lines to the junction box.

1. Strip 2 inches of casing from one end of the remaining cable.

2. Run the cable from the channel to the junction box. Attach the cable to the ceiling with cable staples as you go. Be careful so that you do not pierce the cable sheathing.

3. Strip about 8 inches of sheathing from the cable end and then an inch of insulation from the wires.

4. Connect the cable through the opening in the extender box, using a two-part cable connector.

5. Splice the black fixture wire and the black circuit wire; do the same with the white wires; fasten the two green ground wires to the base of the junction box.

6. Attach the protective lids to the channels, insert the fluorescent lamps into the lamp sockets, turn on the circuit, and test to make sure that everything works properly.

7. Then turn off the circuit.

Step five: installing the panels. The panels will be suspended in a metal grid, which should be installed 10 to 12 inches away from the lights. The distance between the grid and the floor should be no less than 7½ feet. The grid includes these components: an L-shaped metal framing, which fastens to the wall; main L-shaped runners, which hang from the ceiling by means of eye screws and hanger wires; and

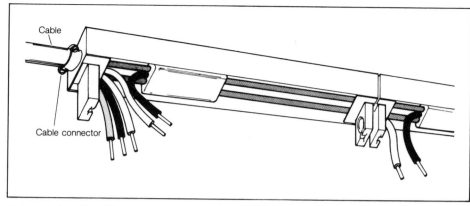

Butt each individual fluorescent channel in a row of lights. Remove all the channel knockouts. Then extend the cable through the knockout at the end of the initial channel. Connect like-colored wires; attach the ground wire with a screw to the channel.

T-bars, which span the main runners.

1. Decide on the height of the luminous ceiling and draw a corresponding line on the walls all the way around the room. Using a carpenter's level, check that the line is completely level. Then nail the edge framing along the line.

2. The manufacturer's instructions will tell you how far from the edge framing the first main runner should be (usually 2 to 4 feet). Measure out, and draw a line along the ceiling, parallel to the wall. Measure every so often to be sure that the line is straight.

3. Install the screw eyes every two feet along the ceiling line. If your ceiling is of wallboard, you should first install screw anchors and then insert the eye-screws. If the ceiling is plaster, you will have to drill holes first, using a bit size slightly smaller than the eye screws. You can then install the eye screws directly into the ceiling.

4. Now cut the hanger wires; their lengths should be twice the distance from the ceiling to the runner. Pass a fourth of the hanger wires through the eye screw; fold the end back against the wire itself; twist the end around the wire.

5. Lift the runner into position—have a helper for this. Pass the free end of the hanger wire through the opening provided in the main runner. Check the runner's height to be sure that it is the same as the distance between the ceiling and the edge frame.

6. Hook the wire so it will support the runner. Your helper probably will have to hold the runner for a while, until you have hooked several wires. Go on to the next screw eye and repeat.

7. Once you have completed the hangers for a runner, check to be sure the runner is level. Make any necessary adjustments.

8. Bend the hooks closed and twist the ends firmly around the wires. Place all the runners in the same manner. The distance between them will be determined by the size of the plastic panels you are using.

9. Once the main runners are in, install the T-bars. These will fit into special slots built into the main runner. The size of the plastic panel determines the distance between the T-bars. Once the T-bars are in place, you need only to slide the panels in to cover the ceiling.

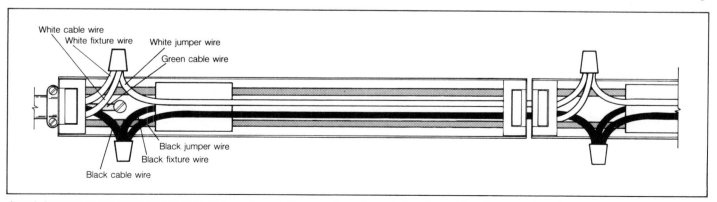

Attach jumpers to the like colored wires of one channel; then run them through the channel knockouts to the adjacent fixture.

ADDING A RECESSED LIGHT FIXTURE OR A FAN

Heat builds up around a recessed fixture; therefore you must follow NEC regulations on placement. The enclosure sides must be at least ½ inch from combustible material and 3 inches from any insulation. Allow for a constant flow of air around the fixture for safety.

Supporting the Fixture Junction Box

The weight of a heavy fixture, such as a chandelier or a ceiling fan, requires extra bracing between the joists in a ceiling. Recessed lights come with casings that are set into the ceiling, and these casings can benefit from the added support.

If you have access to the attic area, nail two 2x4s between the joists to support the fixture. Space them so the fixture housing will fit snugly between the 2x4s.

If the joists are enclosed, it is difficult to add extra support, but it can be done by following these steps.

1. Cut two 2x4s for a snug fit between the joists. Tape them into place.
2. Mark the inside edges of the joists at the ends of each 2x4. Remove the 2x4s.
3. Cut 2x4 blocks (cleats) about 4 inches long, and drive two 8d nails partially (a little over halfway) through each one.
4. Put them next to the marks on the joists and finish nailing the blocks to the joists.

5. Tap the longer 2x4s into position against the blocks and toenail the headers to the cleat.
6. After connecting the wires, nail or screw the fixture to the 2x4s.

ADDING TRACK LIGHTING

Another way to add local lighting is to use a track light. In many ways, a track light is similar to a raceway, for it is a piece of surface wiring that extends a circuit. Because of its flexibility it can find a place in almost any room in your home. The track comes with various adapters, which enable you to add outlets or, in some cases, even a chandelier.

This apartment is located in an old loft. Power is brought to the track through metal conduit. The track lights direct the light downward, so the illumination is not lost in the open beams.

A recessed fixture or an attic fan will require extra bracing between the joists in order to support the weight of the installation.

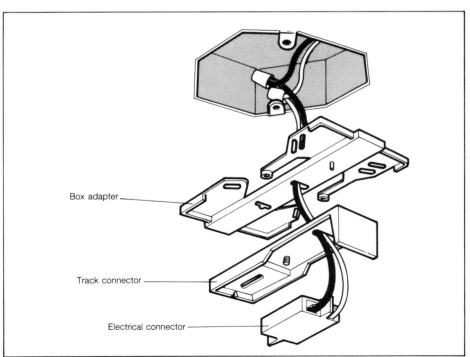

Box adapter

Track connector

Electrical connector

To install a track light that attaches directly to the house wiring, utilize a metal adapter plate. Then attach the track connector, which holds the electrical connector in place.

Power Sources

Track lighting comes in two styles. The first has a line cord and plug that can be hidden behind curtains or other features in your home. To power the track, simply plug the track to an outlet. The second style is wired into the house wiring, like any other ceiling fixture. As pointed out earlier, you probably will have to add a ceiling junction box to install this style of raceway, since the existing boxes will not be close enough to the track to be useful.

Suggestions for a Plug-in Track

Track light installation procedures will vary according to the manufacturer and model, so read all instructions carefully. If the channel is attached to the ceiling, you should use expansion shields or masonry anchors to ensure the stability of the installation. Use insulating washers between all screws and the metal channel.

Installing a Powered Track Light

Installing the power source. Turn off the circuit on which you will be working. Roughly plot the position of the track on the ceiling. Install a ceiling junction box at one end of the track's location, and fish cable to the box.

1. The track will come with an adapter plate, which covers the junction box and holds the track connector and the electrical housing. Assemble these pieces.
2. Splicing like-colored wires together, hook up the track wires to the cable wires.
3. Fasten the adapter assembly to the junction box ears. Screws will be provided.
4. Working from the mounting slot of the track connector, draw a line along the ceiling. This line will pinpoint the track's location.
5. The track itself is held in place by special clips spaced evenly along the length of the track. Hold the clips in place, and mark for pilot holes.
6. Drill the holes and install anchors, if necessary. Install the clips.
7. Connect the track channel solidly to the electrical connector; slip the channel into the track connector.
8. Snap the track channels into the clips. Then tighten the set screws along the sides of the clips to hold the channels firmly in place.
9. Install the raceway cover to finish the installation.

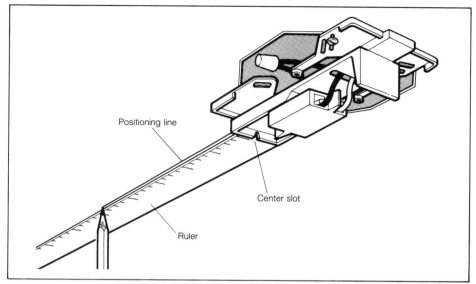

To plot the line for the track itself, align a ruler with the center slot on the track connector. Draw the line across the ceiling to the location of the opposite end of the track.

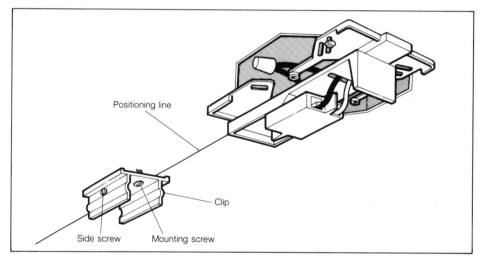

The track will be held along the line by plastic clips. Center the clip on the line; draw a mark for the screw hole. Then install the clip. Use screw anchors if necessary.

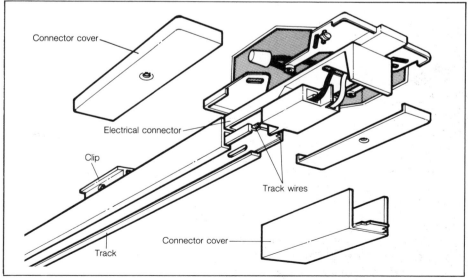

The wiring that powers the track is built right into the track itself. Push the track sections firmly into the electrical connector. Finish off with the cover plates.

There are several reasons why you may want to install electricity outside the home. You may wish to have a post light on the front lawn to greet visitors. Or you may want to hang spotlights on the corner of the home to light the way from a detached garage. It is always a good idea to illuminate a patio or pool area—for both aesthetic and safety reasons. Maybe you want to place outdoor receptacles at convenient locations to accommodate small appliances or an extension cord for an electric lawnmower. You may even want to run cable to a detached garage or utility shed to turn it into a home workshop.

LOCAL CODES

First, contact your municipal building inspector to determine the requirements that have been established for your community concerning outdoor wiring. In some areas, only a professional electrician can make the final hookup. In other areas, the work must be inspected before it can be put into operation. You will have to find out whether the municipal electrical code permits the use of Type UF cable, or if it specifies Type TW wire and conduit. Generally, local codes require that outdoor wiring be protected by conduit in any instance in which outdoor wiring is installed above ground. If the wiring is to be buried, most codes allow Type UF cable. However, some require that Type TW wire and conduit be used.

TYPES OF OUTDOOR LIGHTING

Exterior or outdoor lighting falls into two general categories: functional and decorative. Functional lighting illuminates high-use areas such as steps, stairs, gates, walkways and outdoor grills. Because of its importance as a safety feature, lay out this

Use outdoor lighting to create mood, highlight landscaping and safeguard those who use the patio area. Outdoor receptacles also increase the utility of a patio area.

type of lighting first when you draw up your plan. Once you have decided on the functional requirements of the area you wish to light, you can introduce decorative lighting, which adds dimension and mood to exterior space. In some cases you will

find that, with slight modification, your functional lighting can also be decorative.

BASIC LIGHTING RULES

Whether you plan to light the walkways or paths for safety, spotlight an important

Outdoor light can serve many functions. Here low floodlights camouflaged by garden plantings highlight the foliage overhead and the low stone garden wall. Because of the floodlight attached to the roof above the patio, the patio appears to be an extension of the family room inside.

site feature or provide overall illumination for nighttime entertainment, follow these basic rules.

1. Provide enough light to meet the needs of a given location, but do not overlight. Too much light can ruin the atmosphere of an exterior space and can cause surface glare. Instead of one or two powerful lights, always use several strategically placed small ones. You will have more flexibility in your lighting options and will avoid giving the area a "whitewashed" look.

2. Try to arrange the lighting so that only the light is seen, not the source. A bare spotlight is unsightly, so where possible, allow for indirect lighting. It casts a uniform level of illumination without accentuating the fixtures' locations. There can be a magical quality to night lighting; if the source is visible, that quality is lost.

3. To achieve a visual effect that is seldom available in any area even in the daylight, backlight architectural or landscaping features. At night, this technique creates shadow and depth, dramatically transforming commonplace plants or shrubs.

4. Position lighting with efficiency in mind. In some cases, a well-placed series of light can extend the interior lights bordering a backyard or patio. Exterior lighting should complement your interior lighting.

5. Try to keep the distance between lights to a minimum. Remember that all the lights must be connected to a power source. The more spread out the lighting, the more costly the installation.

6. Provide at least 5 lumens of light at all walkways, ramps and stairways.

7. Light on stairways should be cast down toward the risers so that the treads will not be in shadow.

DRAWING A PLAN

Map out exactly where the lighting will be installed. If you have electrical circuits to the front of the house as well as the back, you might want to separate circuits, one for each area. Make a sketch of the home and outdoor area to show the prospective locations of the electrical components you want to install. Indicate what the components are, such as receptacles, post lights or floodlights, and determine the best route for bringing power to them.

If you plan on exterior switches, note their positions also.

Cable and Conduit Paths

As you plan, try to place all fixtures and receptacles so that they are easily accessible for both installation and for future maintenance. Try to keep the total distance between fixtures to a minimum. In plotting the route for cable or conduit trenches, avoid underground electrical or telephone wires, sprinkler systems and drain fields. It is also a good idea to avoid rocky areas, which make digging a trench difficult. By laying out a plan of circuits and fixtures, you will be able to estimate quantities of materials and will know which tools are required to accomplish each task. Careful planning will save you extra work later on.

Exterior Receptacles

In considering the location of exterior power receptacles, try to place them in an area where you will be using the greatest number of appliances for outdoor entertaining, or where the outdoor lighting source will be. It is possible to purchase exterior lighting fixtures with a power outlet or receptacle already installed. If at all possible, all exterior electrical power circuits should be controlled from the interior of the house.

Exterior Lighting

Types of exterior lighting. There are primarily two types of exterior electrical lighting available to you: standard voltage (120 volts) or low voltage (12 volts). Before you install either system, verify which is acceptable through the building inspector's office. The low-voltage system may be more suitable for a very small garden space, but a standard 120-volt system with interior control is recommended for a normal-sized garden area and patio or deck.

There are many different styles of outdoor lighting fixtures. Some are used only for in-ground application, while others are only wall-mounted. In choosing lighting fixtures, select a type that is specified for exterior usage. If you use any model that is designed for interior use, a breakdown can occur.

Control of exterior lighting. If you have a master control unit or an automatic time switch to power the lighting, you must have an override feature from a remote location. Most devices have this provision

Small "mushroom" lights around the edge of a patio define its outline and warn pedestrians of the raised edges and the step treads.

already incorporated into the design. We suggest that all lighting circuits be separate from other exterior power circuits. This allows flexibility in the control of power and lighting. It is also recommended that you use three-way switches, so that you can control the lights from inside the house. (See Chapter 12 for a discussion of three-way switches.)

Ground Fault Interruptors

Ground fault circuit interruptors (GFI) are now required by the NEC in all outdoor locations. A GFI is an electronic device that supplements conventional circuit breakers or fuses. The device electronically compares amperage flowing through the hot wire to amperage flowing through the neutral wire. If the circuit is not leaking current, amperages will be equal. But if there is a difference of as little as 1/200 of an ampere, the GFI detects the loss of current and automatically cuts off power within 1/40 of a second. Such a current leak can injure or kill someone coming in contact with it. For installation instructions for a GFI, see Chapter 4.

Types of Cable

Type UF cable. Type UF cable is covered by a heavy plastic sheathing. The cable is designed for placement in the ground without being encased in protective metal conduit.

Type TW wire. Type TW wire has a thin thermoplastic insulation that provides the wire with some measure of moisture resistance. However, for maximum protection, the wire has to be encased in conduit.

Types of Conduit

If local codes call for conduit, first find out which kind the local electrical code requires. It can be one of three varieties: thin wall thermwall conduit, which is referred to as electrical metallic tubing (EMT); rigid plastic conduit; or rigid metal conduit. Where no requirements are set by the local code, consider these facts before making your choice.

1. EMT is the easiest type of conduit to work with. It is also the least expensive. However, if you use EMT, it should be buried in a trench that is at least 12 inches deep. Rigid plastic conduit also requires a 12 inch deep trench.
2. Rigid metal conduit requires a trench that is only 6 inches deep. Both it and rigid plastic conduit are hard to bend. Furthermore they cost more than EMT.

While it is true that EMT is easier to use than other types of conduit, be aware that its use in underground installations is not approved by Underwriter's Laboratories, so it is best avoided.

Existing Power Source

Check your power source. Can you get power from an existing outdoor circuit, or must you draw from inside the home? If there is electricity already out-of-doors, you can generally draw from it. Investigate this possibility by judging the reserve capacity of outdoor lighting fixtures and receptacles. Follow the same procedures as you did earlier for creating a circuit map of your home.

A ground fault circuit interrupter is a requirement for all outside receptacles. The heavy cast metal box, the gasket covering and the door all ensure a watertight, safe fixture.

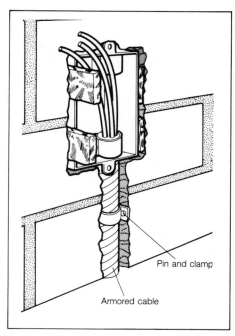

To install a junction box in a masonry wall, chip out the opening with a cold chisel and ball peen hammer. Wedge the box sides.

If you must draw from an indoor source, try using a basement receptacle or junction box. It is more convenient to extend power from the basement than from the living quarters of the home.

If you have to get power from a source other than the basement, try the attic. You may be able to run cable through an exit point, down the side of the home, and then underground to the point where electricity is needed.

EQUIPMENT FOR OUTDOOR USE

The basic rules for extending electricity to the outdoors are the same as those used for extending electricity indoors. The major difference between the two jobs lies with the equipment requirements. Equipment you use outdoors must be able to withstand the effects of weather.

The following is a rundown of the most common pieces of outdoor electrical equipment.

Equipment Used for Housing Receptacles

The receptacles used outdoors are the same duplex type you use indoors. However, the equipment that houses the receptacles is different. Outdoor receptacle boxes, which are the same size and shape as indoor receptacle boxes, are made of heavy metal. Instead of knockout plugs, outdoor receptacle boxes have threaded

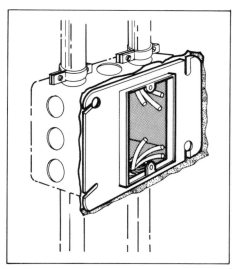

To mount a junction box in a masonry wall so that the box is flush, install what is called a plaster ring over the face of the box.

openings into which conduit is screwed. If conduit is not used, UF cable passes through a thick plug that is screwed into the threaded opening.

Cover plates for outdoor receptacles are made of heavy-gauge metal. They are outfitted with spring-action doors that close tightly over the outlets when they are not in use. The joint between the receptacle box and box cover plate is fitted with a thick gasket to prevent moisture from seeping into the box. In addition to the safety hazard that moisture presents, it also would attack the parts in the box, such

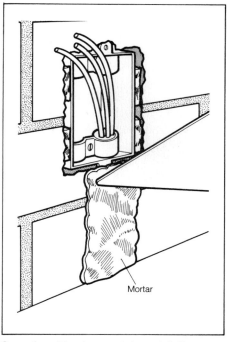

Once the wiring is complete, patch the opening around the cable with cement mortar mix that is tinted to blend with the wall.

as receptacle terminal screws, causing them to corrode.

Equipment for Outdoor Light Fixtures

Outdoor light fixture boxes possess the same characteristics as boxes for outdoor receptacles. To inhibit moisture, there is a gasket made of the same material as the gasket in an outdoor receptacle installa-

Have several heights for your lighting fixtures. The diffuser on this lamppost is designed to give broad overall illumination.

Adjustable floodlights such as these can illuminate a walkway or a patio deck. Place them so they do not cast glare into peoples' eyes. If possible, disguise them with shrubbery.

tion. This seals the joint between the fixture box and the fixture box cover plate.

Electrically, the fixture is set up the same as an indoor fixture (see Chapters 6 and 10). Conductors connect the fixture to wires coming from the power source. Ground wire connections are also the same.

Note: Be sure to use weatherproof bulbs in outdoor fixtures. These resist shattering when the temperature drops.

Outdoor Switches

Heavy cast metal is used for the construction of switch boxes that will be mounted outdoors. Cover plates for the boxes are also made of the same material and are outfitted with weatherproof gaskets. An outdoor switch is an ordinary toggle type (see Chapter 4). However, it is completely encased in the box. Even the toggle is covered. A lever on the outside of the cover extends into the box to engage the toggle. You manipulate the lever to turn the switch on and off.

Connectors and Fittings

LB fitting. This piece of equipment is a right-angle connector that is used with conduit to bring cable through the wall of a home. The fitting routes cable toward a trench that has been dug from the home to the area where the electricity is needed. LB fittings are threaded on both ends. Conduit passing through the house wall to the outside is screwed to one end. Con-

duit leading down the side of the home to the trench is screwed to the other end. Thus, cable is enclosed in metal to provide an efficient seal from the time it leaves the home to the time it enters the ground. LB connectors are outfitted with thick gaskets and metal cover plates, so that they are impervious to moisture.

Box extender. You will use this piece of equipment when tapping an existing outdoor receptacle or fixture junction box for power. The extender can be outfitted with a nipple and 90-degree elbow so that wires may be brought from the fixture, through conduit, to the point where power is wanted.

As an example of how all these components work together, let us suppose you wish to bring power from an existing receptacle to a lamppost. First, turn off power to the existing receptacle (see Chapter 1). Then, disassemble it (see Chapter 4). Screw a nipple to the box extender. If the place where you wish power is not in line with the existing receptacle, screw a 90-degree elbow to the nipple. Then, screw the conduit to the 90-degree elbow. If the point where you want power is in line with your power source, do not use a 90-degree elbow. Attach the conduit directly to the nipple.

Fasten the box extender to the existing receptacle box. Use conduit straps to attach the nipple and the conduit to the side of the home. Caulk to fill the joint between the box extender and siding.

All About Conduit

Three kinds of conduit are made for outdoor use. Rigid aluminum and rigid steel conduit provide equivalent protection to the wires that pass through them. Rigid aluminum is easier to work with, but if it is going to be buried in concrete, first coat it with bituminous paint to prevent the conduit from corroding. Although each type of conduit is available in a variety of diameters, conduit that is ½ inch in diameter will usually suffice around the home. This is wide enough to accept one AWG No. 14/3UF cable or nine individual AWG No. 14 wires.

Each type of conduit comes with a variety of fittings, including elbows, offsets, bushings, couplings and connectors. If offsets and elbows do not provide the necessary turns in rigid metal or EMT conduit, you will need a bending tool called a hickey. Discuss your particular task with the electrical supply dealer, who can advise you which items to purchase. A hickey sometimes can be rented.

Rigid metal conduit. Rigid metal conduit is made of either aluminum or steel.

Rigid aluminum conduit. This is available in 10-foot lengths and in diameters of ½, ¾, 1, 1¼, 2, 2½, 3, 3½, 4, 5 and 6 inches. Both ends are threaded. One end is usually equipped with a coupling that acts to protect the end of the conduit and the adjoining piece of conduit from moisture. If moisture were allowed to attack the ends, they would rust.

Rigid steel conduit. This also is available in 10-foot lengths and in diameters of ½, ¾, 1, 1¼, 1½, 2, 2½, 3, 3½, 4, 5 and 6 inches. It is threaded on both ends. Each length of conduit is outfitted with a coupling at one end that fits over the end of the conduit and the end of the adjoining conduit to protect the threads.

Thin-wall steel conduit (EMT). Thin-wall steel conduit is made from galvanized lightweight metal that comes in 10-foot lengths and in diameters of ⅜, ½, ¾, 1, 1¼, 1½, 2, 2½, 3 and 4 inches. The material is easy to bend and handle. However, because of the thinness of its walls, the tubing is not threaded. Instead, special pressure fittings have to be used to join lengths and to connect conduit to receptacles, fixtures, and switch boxes.

Rigid plastic conduit. Rigid plastic conduit is made from either polyvinyl chloride (PCV), which is normally used above ground, or high-density polyethylene, which is suitable for burial. If PCV is going to be exposed to direct sunlight, cover it with two coats of latex paint to prevent deterioration.

Plastic conduit is available in 10- and 20-foot lengths and in diameters of ½, ¾, 1, 1¼, 1½, 2, 2½, 3 and 4 inches. Unthreaded ends are joined with an adhesive. Of the different types of conduit, plastic conduit is the easiest with which to work.

EXTENDING POWER TO A REMOTE LOCATION

If you want to install a post light, garden lights or receptacles in an area away from the home, there are three steps involved in bringing electricity from inside the home to the location:
(1) bringing electricity from the power source in the basement or attic to outside the home,
(2) digging a trench from the place where the power exits the home to the place where the power is wanted,
(3) installing the new outlets and making connections.

Bringing Electricity from a Basement to the Outside of a Home

To bring electricity through a basement wall, follow these guidelines:
1. Select a reference point on an exterior wall that is identifiable on both the inside and outside of the house. One such point is a water pipe that extends through the wall. As an alternative, you might start at a corner.
2. Inside the basement, measure from the reference point to a spot on the wall through which electricity can be brought. This spot should be at least 3 inches from a joist, sill plate or floor. The clearance is necessary to allow for the junction box you have to install.

3. Outside the home, measure from the common reference point to the spot you have selected for the exit. Many times, this spot will be on the foundation. If it is, be sure the location does not fall on a seam between cinder blocks. If it is not, be sure it does not fall at a place where two pieces of siding join together. The spot has to provide a firm base to hold the LB fitting.
4. Outside the home, drill a ⅛-inch pilot hole through the wall to verify that the path is clear. If you are making a hole in a concrete block wall, do not drill the hole through the top row. The center of the blocks in the top row of a foundation generally are filled with solid concrete. Blocks below the top row usually have hollow centers and are easier to penetrate.
5. To cut the opening for the extender, use a ⅞-inch star drill, which is a hand-held hardened metal tool made to penetrate concrete block. As you hit the drill with the hammer, turn the bit ⅛ of a turn. Or, you may use a carbide-tipped bit in a power drill. Be sure to make the hole in the center of the block, so you hit the hollow area.
6. Inside the basement, open one of the knockout holes from the back plate of a junction box, and mount the junction box so the knockout hole coin-

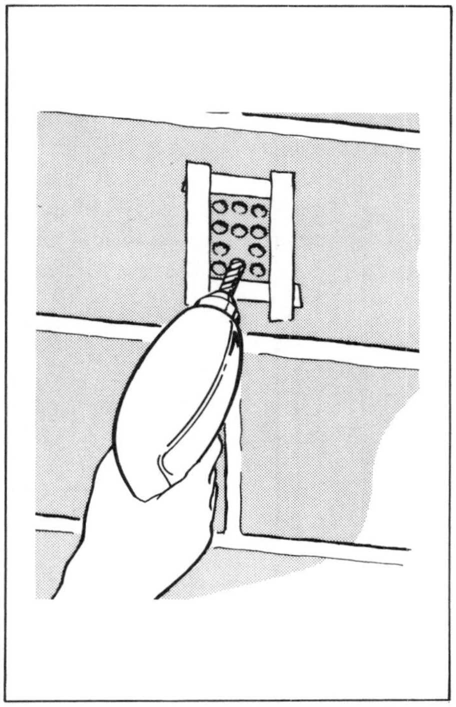

Outline the box area with tape. Drill holes through the block with a ⅜-in. masonry bit. Tap out any material left between the holes.

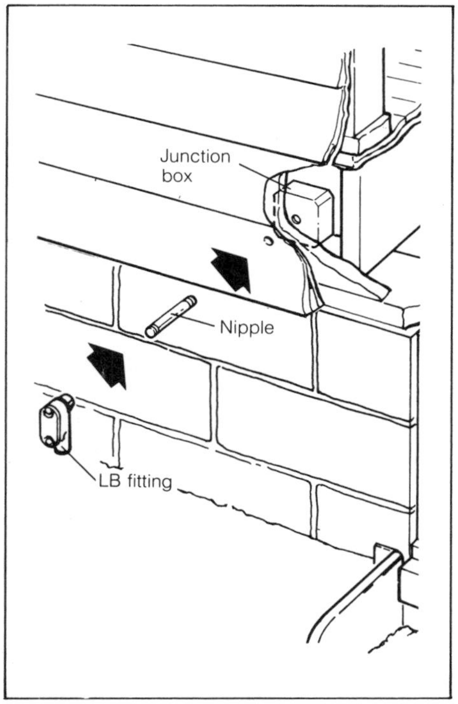

Locate the hole by a point accessible from both sides of the wall. Space the hole at least 3 in. from joists, sill plate and flooring.

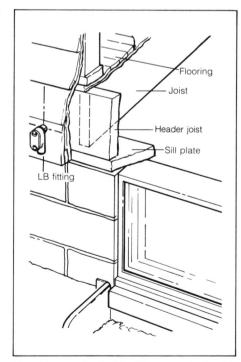

Mount box on the inside. Choose a nipple able to reach through the wall and into the junction box; screw on the LB fitting.

cides with the hole through the wall. To mount the box to the cinder block, first hold it against the wall and mark the location for fasteners. Then, using a masonry bit, drill into the cinder block at the marks. Tap plastic or lead screw anchors into the drilled holes, and screw the junction box to the wall by inserting screws through the holes in the box into the plastic or lead anchors.

7. Outside the house, dig the trench (see below).

8. Onto an LB fitting, screw a nipple long enough to extend from inside the junction box through the hole in the wall to the outside.

9. Outside the home, attach conduit to the LB fitting and run the conduit down the side of the home to the trench. Secure the conduit to the side of the home with a conduit strap.

10. Seal the joint around the LB fitting with a caulking compound.

11. Inside the home, secure the nipple to the junction box with a connector. Install a plastic bushing over the connector to protect the wires or cable from the metal edge of the conduit.

Bringing Electricity from an Attic to the Outside of the Home

To bring electricity through an eave, you require these fittings: an outdoor outlet box, a nipple, a 90-degree corner elbow, and a length of conduit long enough to extend down the side of the home to the trench. Assemble the pieces together. Then install them as follows:

1. Turn off the power to the circuit you plan to tap.

2. Hold the assembly against the overhang (soffit), so the box and nipple are against the soffit and the conduit is against the wall of the home. To make the conduit as inconspicuous as possible, run it down the side of the home close to a downspout.

3. Make a mark on the soffit where the cable from the electrical source in the attic will pass through the soffit into the outdoor outlet box. Using a 1⅛ inch bit, drill the hole in the soffit for the cable opening. Then, with a 3/32-inch bit, drill holes to accept No. 8 wood screws to hold the outdoor outlet box to the soffit.

4. Run cable from the power source in the attic and out the hole in the soffit. Fasten the cable to the box with a two-part cable connector; attach the box to the soffit.

5. Using conduit straps, strap the nipple and conduit into position and complete the installation by running conduit down the side of the home to the trench.

6. Once the cable has been laid to the new junction box, hook up the wiring to the existing power feed wire of an existing switch or outlet; otherwise, the outlet circuit will have power only when the switch or fixture is on.

Installing Roofing Heating Cables

Once you have a receptacle installed in the eave of your home, it is a simple matter to install heating cables in the gutters in a zigzag pattern on the lower section of your roof. These cables can prevent damage to a home in those areas in the country that are subject to heavy accumulations of snow and ice. The cables are available in kit form. Purchase 2 sets. One should measure only slightly longer than the gutter, in which it will lie. The other will form the zigzag on the roof. If you want the zigzag to be 1 foot high, multiply the gutter length by 1.8. For a 2-foot zigzag, multiply by 2.6; for a 3-foot zigzag, multiply by 3.5. Included in the kit will be special fasteners that are installed so that they protrude from beneath the edges of the roof shingles.

Lay the cable according to the manufacturer's directions. It is most important that the roof cable be looped down so that it extends down into the gutter at the point of each intersection. The cables must not cross each other, or they can short each other out. When you plug the cables into the eave's receptacle, they must hang down below the receptacle. In this way water will run down the cable and drip off to the ground rather than run into the receptacle itself.

Digging the Trench

When you lay out the path from the house try to make the path straight. If you cannot avoid bends in the path, make the bends gradual curves, not sharp turns.

1. Outline both sides of the trench with stakes and strings. No matter whether you are using cable or conduit, the trench should be 4 inches wide.

2. To a depth of 2 to 3 inches, cut along the outline with a squared-off shovel such as a garden spade. Dig out the sod, and lay it carefully on plastic sheets. Until you are ready to replace the sod, dampen it often with a gentle spray of water after the first half hour.

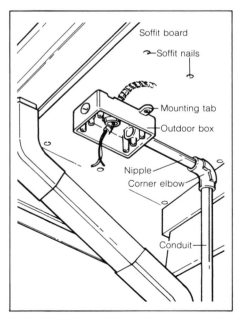

Assemble the junction box, pipe and elbow. Position the box between rows of soffit nails; the conduit must rest against the siding.

Run heating cables in the gutter and in a zigzag pattern at the bottom edge of your roof to melt away built-up snow and ice. The low point of the zigzag must hang in the gutter.

Do not soak the sod—there should not be standing water on the plastic, or the grass will drown.

3. Now dig the trench. (If you are doing a long trench, rent a trencher for this task.) If you are using EMT conduit or UF cable, the trench should be 12 inches deep; rigid metal or plastic conduit requires only 6 inches of depth. To get the conduit from one side of a walk to the other, use a short-handled hammer called a maul. This has a three-pound head on it and is ideal for the job. Dig the trench right up to the sidewalk. Then, continue digging the trench on the other side of the sidewalk. Then, measure and cut a piece of conduit that is at least 10 inches longer than the width of the sidewalk. Hammer one end of the conduit to a sharp point. Lay this in the trench, the point facing the edge of the sidewalk. Hammer the conduit under the sidewalk until the sharp point extends into the trench on the other side. Using a hacksaw, cut the sharp end off the conduit. You can now join this piece to pieces of conduit on either side.

INSTALLING AN OUTDOOR, FREE-STANDING RECEPTACLE

An outdoor receptacle should be at least 12 inches above ground level and must be securely anchored underground. This is accomplished by laying the cable or conduit either through the center opening of a cinder block or through a coffee can in which you then place concrete.

Fastening the Receptacle to the Conduit

Bend a piece of conduit connector so that the 90-degree angle falls at least 13 inches away from one of the ends. Then attach the free end to the conduit in the trench. If you are using UF cable, run the cable through the length of conduit and attach the conduit and the cable to the receptacle.

Creating a Concrete Anchor

1. Cut both ends from a two-pound coffee can. Widen the trench enough so that it will accommodate the can; slip the can over the receptacle.
2. The can and the conduit must be braced in position while the concrete is placed around the conduit. In the ground on each side of the trench, pound 2x4 stakes. Run wire from the

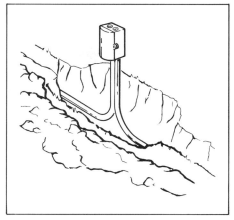

For a middle-of-the-run receptacle, use a box with two conduit openings. Fasten the conduit with a threadless connector.

Lower a cinder block over the box. Fill in the core with gravel. Fish wiring through the conduit and then install the receptacle.

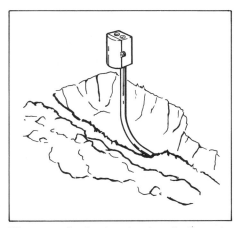

When you dig the trench, also dig the extra space to hold the cinder block anchor. Extend the conduit 8 in. above the ground surface.

conduit, below the receptacle to the stakes from both sides. Pound in 1x2 stakes around the outside of the can to keep it from sliding.

3. Mix up a batch of concrete mix according to the manufacturer's directions. Use a trowel to fill the can with concrete. Work carefully from all sides

so that there are no air pockets. When the can is full, push the trowel up and down along the sides of the can to be sure that the can is filled. Level the concrete; let it cure (harden) for as long as the manufacturer recommends.

Using a Cinder-Block Anchor

Widen the trench to accommodate the block. Attach the receptacle to the conduit as above. Then slip the block over the receptacle and seat the block firmly in the ground. To support the conduit, fill the openings in the block with gravel. Tamp the material with the head of a hammer; refill as necessary. Add sand to fill in the spaces between the gravel. A tight fill now will prevent the earth above the block from settling later and creating depressions in your lawn.

ATTACHING A RECEPTACLE TO THE EXTERIOR OF THE HOUSE

Steps involved in installing a new receptacle on the outside of a home are:

    (1) cut a hole in the siding;
    (2) run cable from the power source to the new receptacle;
    (3) make connections;
    (4) patch the wall.

This project is relatively easy to carry out if the house siding is wood, aluminum, or polyvinyl chloride (PVC).

After measuring the opening for the new receptacle box, drill ⅜-inch holes at each corner to provide starting points for a cut-

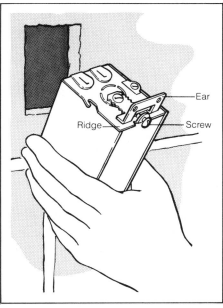

Loosely insert screws into the box's mounting tabs so mortar will not fill the screw holes. Have the edge protrude about 1/16 in.

ting tool. Cut the opening so the receptacle can be recessed in the wall. The procedure is handled in much the same manner as making an opening in a wall inside the home for a new receptacle.

Run cable from the interior power source to the box according to the provisions of the local electrical code. In other words, if the local code says to use conduit in the basement where the power source is located, use it. If the local code allows the use of plastic-sheathed cable, do so, since cable is easier to handle.

Finish the job by sealing the space between the receptacle box and the siding with caulking compound.

INSTALLING A LAMPPOST

An outdoor lamppost must be buried at least two feet deep to give the installation stability and add protection from frost heave. Some types of posts are adjustable. They come with an opening for UF cable; if you are using conduit, you must extend the opening in the post.

1. Mark your guidelines, 18 inches long and ⅞ inch apart, onto the post. To cut out the outlined strip, use a hacksaw that grips the blade at the handle end and at the center. The blade extension cuts through the post.

2. Once the sides are cut, bend out the ⅞-inch strip and saw it off. Use a file to smooth the edges' sharp corners or burrs. If the lamppost will be in the middle of a conduit run, cut another slot on the opposite side of the post.

3. If you are using conduit, measure and cut a piece that will extend from the already-positioned conduit to the top of the locknut of an adjustable post or the top of a nonadjustable one. Bend the conduit so that the 90-degree angle falls above the posthole.

4. Once the hole is dug, attach the conduit and cap the conduit with a plastic bushing to protect the cable.

5. Dig a post hole that is 2 feet deep and about 8 inches wide. Place the conduit, if needed, as described above. Position the post over the conduit, or thread UF cable through the cable opening. Place the post.

6. Lay alternating layers of dirt and large gravel around the post. Tamp and compact the fill with a 2x4 after every addition. Fill the hole only to the bottom of the trench. Fill in the rest of the hole when you backfill the rest of the trench.

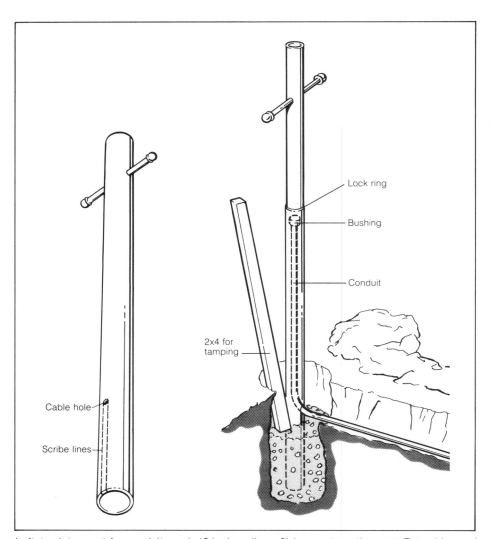

Left: to slot a post for conduit, mark 18-in. long lines, ⅞ in. apart, on the post. Extend beyond the opening for UF cable. Cut along the lines with a special hacksaw. *Right:* to anchor the post, dig the hole 2 ft. deep and 8 in. wide. Bend the conduit to come up in the middle of the hole, almost to an adjustable post's lock ring or a fixed post's full height.

FISHING CABLE AND HOOKING IT UP

Once all the receptacles, lights and other features are in place, fish the wire through the conduit as discussed in Chapter 9. Hook up all wiring as you would for conventional systems. Then fill in the trenches you have dug. Tamp the earth firmly over the conduit or cable; water generously before replacing the sod. This will help with the soil around the pipe, thus preventing depressions from forming later. Lay the sod; tamp and water as necessary.

LIGHTING AND POWER FOR A SWIMMING POOL

In most climates, exterior lighting can extend the hours that you can use a swimming pool. As you plan outdoor lighting around a pool, try to achieve a well-lit exterior area while still treating the space as a stage set. The lighting can perform

many functions. Use it to accent structures, contribute to the landscaping, illuminate the water in the pool and assure the security and safety of the pool surround.

The lighting directly around the pool, installed primarily for safety and security purposes, is probably the most important form. Several spotlights located above the pool level can serve as local lighting. However, this type of installation, although inexpensive, can detract from the visual and spatial qualities of the pool. Lights installed in the coping of the swimming pool are quite effective. Along with the pool lights, plan a series of small garden lights that throw light over the pool surround area. This maintains security and safety and at the same time enhances the visual impact of the pool.

No matter what type of lighting you may desire or require, consult a licensed

Light a pool to achieve the maximum use, beauty and safety. Light the surround for the benefit of both onlookers and bathers. Do not create glare that might momentarily blind a diver.

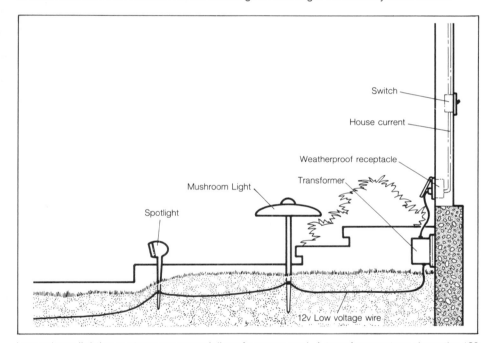

Low-voltage lighting systems are especially safe near a pool. A transformer steps down the 120 volts of a circuit to the 12 volts needed by the lights. The switch is inside the home.

or trip over floats or other objects. The most effective type of fixture is the Malibu light, or a similar low-voltage light, which sheds indirect light on the surround surface. This provides illumination that is free of glare and harsh shadows. The bulbs should not be visible to the viewer. Backlighting for fences, hedges and other prominent features will accent the three-dimensional quality of the landscaped area and provide visual warning to bathers, who may be oblivious to potential hazards.

Light can make the surround visually pleasing. Avoid the use of colored lights; they often make the area appear distorted or warped. Balanced light intensity creates a pleasing setting. If you require intense light in one area, provide a lower light level elsewhere. This can be accomplished with dimmers.

Using Underwater Lighting

Underwater lights are a wonderful addition to an in-ground pool. They make swimming at night easier and safer. The lights are by far easier to install during the construction of the pool than afterwards. Most in-pool lighting, whether it is above or under the water, must conform to the National Electrical Code requirements for fixture safety. The NEC states that all installations must be grounded and watertight, that waterproof wiring must be used, and that all electrical connections must be located above the surface of the water.

Determining the number of lights. The first consideration in the selection of in-pool illumination should be the type and number of lights that are needed. A rule of thumb is to have one light for each 24 to 30 linear feet of pool side. A 16x32 foot pool, which has 96 linear feet of pool side, should have at least three lights. You might also consider the addition of a light in the area of the pool stairs. It is a good idea to place one light on each side and one under the diving board or at the deep end of the pool.

Voltage level options. Once you know the number of lights that you need, then select the voltage system to be used. You can choose from two types: the normal 115-volt system or a low-voltage system carrying only 12 volts. In the 12-volt system, the full 115 volts of the circuit are fed to a transformer that in turn feeds the underwater light. The low-voltage light is available in 300 watt lamps. The primary

electrician. We do not recommend that you attempt to work on lighting fixtures or power outlets in or around your pool area. The consequences of any problems are too great. In addition, any work in this area is heavily regulated. A professional electrician is the best course.

Lighting the Surround for Accent and Safety

Accent lighting. Many pool owners prefer to position the deep end of the pool away from the house in order to see the divers and swimmers move towards the shallow end. However, at night a light that highlights the diving area can also shine into the house. To avoid this problem, position the fixture high enough above the pool so that the light does not shine in the diver's face, nor into the house itself. Illuminate physical features such as a diving board so that you highlight the feature but eliminate any possible glare. The ideal position is above the feature, rather than beside it.

Surround lighting. The pool surround should also be well lit so that children or adults moving around the pool will not slip

advantage of the low voltage system is that the pool is still safe if a short develops. A swimmer will not even be aware of a shock. However, if a 115-volt line develops a short, the shock could be lethal. The low voltage system is recommended for almost all installations around a pool and is equal in cost to the 115-volt system.

Lamp assemblies. The lighting lamps are placed either in a "wet" or a "dry" niche. A niche is the housing that accommodates the lamp assembly. A wet niche is a waterproof housing with a chrome-plated face plate that will fit in all in-ground pools, whether the walls be made of fiberglass, vinyl, steel, aluminum or structural polymer. The lamp assembly of a wet niche is sealed, so the lamp can be changed underwater. In fact, the sealed lamp will function only under water. The dry niche does not have a sealed assembly; as a result, you must drop the level of the water in the pool in order to change the lamp. Both systems are available in 115 volt and 12 volt systems. Be aware that any lights you purchase must be sealed and must meet NEC requirements for underwater operation.

Lens options. Colored lenses are available for underwater lamp assemblies. The lenses can easily be changed without changing the lamp.

Portable underwater lights. Several manufacturers offer a portable underwater lamp that can open up a whole new world of after-dark beauty for those pools built without underwater lighting. This lamp is safe. It operates on a low-voltage, rechargeable battery. The lamp assembly hangs below the water and illuminates a pool up to 20x30 feet in size. Since a portable lamp is quite economical, it is often chosen as an alternative to permanent pool lighting.

Decorative pool lights. There are several types of pool lights, commonly called floating blossom lights, that add decorative ambience rather than serve a functional purpose. These are designed solely to enhance the beauty of the pool and should not be used when bathers are swimming.

Other Power Needs for the Pool

Plan for electrical needs ahead of time, rather than adding circuits after everything is completed. Running power lines and lighting circuits is critical to the operation of the pool. All power outlets must be at least 18 inches above the level of the

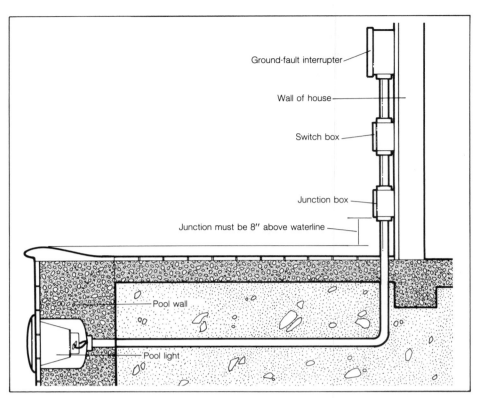

When you plan the electrical needs of a pool, include underwater lights. These are housed in special watertight niches. The power connections are above the waterline.

surround and must be fully grounded. Install GFI receptacles for further safety. The circuit for power outlets must be separate from the lighting circuits. The electrical service to the pump and the filtration equipment also must be on its own circuit. It is recommended that you check with an electrician or swimming pool contractor to make sure that the amperage level for the present circuits is adequate for the size of the pump in your pool.

Filtration system requirements. Keep in mind that the size of the pump in your pool is dependent upon the size and type of pool you select. The motor size on most filtration systems varies between ½ to 2½ horsepower. The general ratings based on approximate pool size are given in the accompanying chart.

The pump horsepower is determined by the number of gallons per minute (gpm) passing through the pump. The gpm is in turn determined by the filtration cycle. A

PUMP CAPACITIES

Motor Size (hp)	Pool Size	Voltage Requirements
1/2	16 x 32	115 volts
3/4	18 x 36	115/230 volts
1.0	20 x 40	115/230 volts
1.5	20 x 45	115/230 volts
2.0	24 x 46	115/230 volts
2.5	25 x 40	230 volts

three-wire connection to the motor junction box and the disconnect switch permits a 230-volt system for future use, if you so desire. All wiring should be grounded and, in most localities, codes will require the installation be done by a licensed electrician.

When you figure out your power requirements, take into account the installation of a pool heater or any additional pumps for other parts of your recreational area. If you want an electric water heater, check your current electrical service before making the final selection. Electric water heaters can service pools having from 4,800 to 42,000 gallons of capacity. Their power demand can run as high as 71 amperes on a three-phase, 480-volt connection. This type of service is not found in most residential installations.

Entertainment areas. Entertainment areas around the pool call for a number of outlets. Install underground conduit or cable connected to a series of carefully placed outlets. If you plan to build a gazebo or cabana, make some provision for lighting or outlets. Also consider including an electrical insect control device, which requires an outlet to operate. Examine the many ways that you will use the outdoor area when you are designing your power requirements.

The principles for wiring work throughout your house remain basically the same, no matter how complex the project you attempt. If you have understood and can put into practice the principles presented so far, there are many electrical projects you can do in addition to those already discussed. Twelve projects are outlined in this chapter. You will note that many of the basic steps and operations (fishing cable, opening walls, splicing and connecting wires) are the same. If you want to do a job that is not explained in this book, you can put together your own procedures list based upon the projects here and in earlier chapters. Usually all you need to do is find an equivalent situation and manipulate the steps; no new techniques are required.

DOING AWAY WITH PULL CHAINS

Do you have a fixture in a closet, basement, attic, or laundry room that is operated by a pull chain? Do you find it a nuisance, especially in the dark, groping for the chain? You obviously need to replace the chain with a wall-mounted switch. Here is how.

Caution: While working with the circuit on, do not touch any metal part with your body. Be sure to stand on a wooden ladder or nonmetallic stool.

Instead of replacing the chain in a basement light, install a switch, then run conduit or cable to the light, and hook up the wiring.

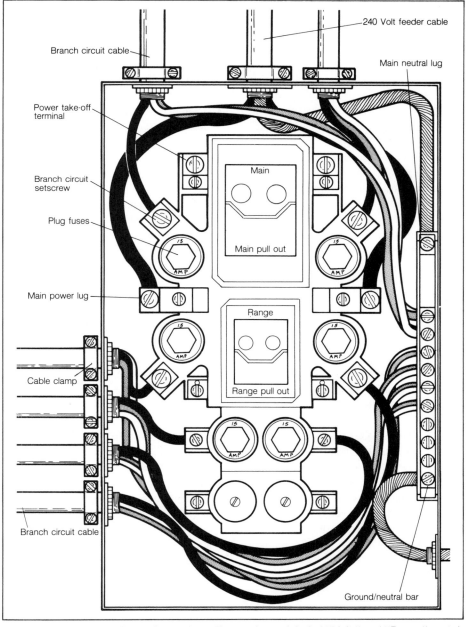

This service box is based upon fuses alone. The two boxes labeled "Main" and "Range" contain cartridge fuses. Pull both from the panel to turn off all power to the box. The unoccupied terminals along the bus bar can hold ground wires for heavy workshop tools or new circuits.

Tools and Materials

To complete this task you will need cable to run from the fixture to a new switch, a new switch, wire nuts, electrician's tape, a fishtape, single-conductor ground wire, wire cutter-stripper, and needlenosed pliers. You also may require a voltage tester if your house wiring is old and lacks color-coded wires.

1. Turn off the current to the fixture (see Chapter 1).

2. Disconnect the fixture from the ceiling box as outlined in Chapter 6. If the fixture is heavy, be sure to hang it using a hook you have fashioned from a wire coat hanger. This, too, is discussed in Chapter 6.

3. Identify the fixture wires, determining which is hot and which is neutral. If your home is fairly new, wires are probably color-coded, so that the black or red conductor indicates the hot wire and the white conductor indicates neutral.

4. If your home is older, both wires may be colored the same. In this case, you will have to test to identify the wires. If the wires from the power source are connected to wires of the fixture, unscrew the wire nuts to reveal the bare ends of the conductors before you apply the voltage tester. Wires from the power source may, instead, be connected to fixture terminal screws; do not loosen these before using the voltage tester.

5. Hold one probe of a voltage tester against a metal part of the fixture or fixture box. Touch the other probe of the voltage tester to the bare ends of one of the wire connections or to one of the fixture terminal screws.

6. Have someone at the fuse or circuit breaker box restore power to the circuit. If the voltage tester glows, you have located the hot wire. If it does not glow, touch the probe of the voltage tester to the bare ends of the other wire connection, or to the other fixture terminal screw, to verify that it is hot.

7. Have your assistant turn off the power.

8. Color code the hot wire by dabbing the insulation with black or red paint, or by wrapping a strip of black electrician's tape around it.

9. Install a wall switch at a convenient location. Then, run cable from the switch into the fixture junction box (see Chapter 9).

10. Disconnect the fixture wires from the power source wires, or detach them from the fixture terminal screws. Remove the fixture.

11. Use a wire nut to connect the neutral wire from the power source to the white wire of the fixture. If the fixture has terminal screws, connect the neutral wire from the power source to the silver-colored terminal screw.

12. Use a wire nut to connect the black hot wire coming from the new switch to the black hot wire from the power source.

13. Use a wire nut to connect the white wire coming from the new switch to the black wire of the fixture (or the brass-colored terminal screw). On this white wire, at the end near the switch and the end near the fixture, recode the wire to indicate it is part of a switch loop and that it now carries power.

14. Connect the ground wire from the power source to the ground wire coming from the new switch. Attach a 4-inch green jumper wire to the ends of these wires and secure the splice with a wire nut.

15. Now, use a machine screw to connect the unsecured end of the length of bare copper wire to the metal fixture box. This completes the ground connection.

16. Reattach the fixture to the ceiling box and restore the power.

INSTALLING A SMOKE DETECTOR

Important: Before installing a detector, read the manufacturer's suggestions for installation. You can also get information concerning smoke detectors by writing to the National Fire Protection Association, 470 Atlantic Ave., Boston, MA 02210, and by consulting the fire department in your municipality.

A smoke detector receives electrical energy from one of three sources: from a self-contained battery, from an existing receptacle (the detector comes equipped with a power cord, which plugs into a receptacle), or directly from the household wiring. Installation of battery-operated smoke detectors, or those that have power cords, does not need detailed instructions. Although they are easier to install than wired-in detectors, they have disadvantages. In the case of a battery-operated instrument, the battery becomes weak and

has to be replaced. Furthermore, the detector requires frequent testing to assure that the battery is in good condition.

In the case of a smoke detector equipped with a line cord, you may object to the appearance. A cord running from the detector to the wall, then down the wall to the receptacle is not particularly attractive.

Here are the procedures for installing a wired-in smoke detector, which we feel is the best of the three models.

1. Decide where you want to position the smoke detector. The best locations are the center of a ceiling area or on a wall 10 inches down from the ceiling.

2. Make a hole in the ceiling or wall for the smoke detector and install the mounting plate.

3. Select a junction box to tap for power. Turn off power to that particular circuit (see Chapter 1).

4. Run a length of cable from the power source to the spot for the smoke detector. Connect the cable to the power source.

5. Connect the other end of the cable to the detector. Join black wire to black wire, and white wire to white wire.

6. Screw the detector to the mounting plate and snap on the cover.

7. Turn on power and test the detector by using the test button, if there is one, or by blowing smoke on the detector.

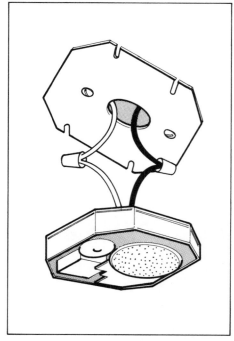

A cable-powered smoke detector is easy to install once you fish cable to the detector. Splice like-colored wires; cap with wire nuts.

GROUNDING AN APPLIANCE

There is only one way to be sure that major appliances are grounded. You must remove the cover from a service panel and trace conductors from the receptacle serving the appliance to the service panel to see if the neutral and ground wires in the cable are connected to the neutral/ground bus bar terminals in the panel. If they are not, you could have a problem. If a short circuit were to occur in the appliance motor, and the fuse or circuit failed to shut down the circuit, the body of the appliance would become electrified and present a serious shock hazard. To prevent this situation, you should ground each motorized appliance in your home by connecting the appliance to a metal water or gas pipe near the appliance. Follow these steps.

Caution: The cold water pipe must be metal. Grounding cannot be achieved by connecting the ground wire to plastic pipe.

1. Find the grounding screw on the chassis of the particular appliance. If there is no screw designated for the job, use any screw inserted in the metal housing.
2. Select green wire that is of the same amperage level as the appliance. Cut a piece long enough to extend from the appliance to a cold water pipe. This is the ground wire.
3. Remove insulation from both ends of the ground wire. Attach one end tightly to the screw on the appliance. Wrap the other end around the cold water pipe and secure the wire with a *metal* clamp that is screwed over the pipe. Be sure that the clamp, the ground wire, and the pipe all touch one another.

Position lights on either side of a mirror to prevent shadows and harsh glare.

LIGHTING A DRESSING AREA

If lighting in a dressing area is inadequate, you can either install an overhead incandescent or fluorescent fixture to give the entire area more lighting (see Chapters 6 and 10), or you can concentrate the light on a mirror that occupies a wall over a vanity by installing an incandescent or fluorescent wall-mounted fixture above the mirror or one on each side. Some fixtures possess receptacles that give the additional benefit of allowing you to plug in personal care appliances, such as a hair dryer, electric razor, and electric toothbrush. If you install a new receptacle in a bathroom, it must contain a GFI.

Guidelines for Placement of Lighting Fixtures Near Mirrors

If you follow a few general guidelines, you will be able to locate lighting fixtures in a dressing area where they will be most helpful for such tasks as shaving or applying makeup.

Wraparound lighting. So that there will be no shadows under eyes, nose, cheeks or chin, illuminate both sides of the face, the top of the head and below the chin. To achieve this ideal you need fixtures that can supply light across the top and down both sides of the grooming mirror well below chin level. Install strips of lights around the mirror. These can either feature opaque individual bulbs of low wattage or enclosed and covered single fixtures. Either will prevent glare and shadow. The side fixtures should be placed from 28 to 36 inches apart and should extend up 60 inches or more off the floor if the mirror is one at which people stand; above

Several lights installed above a mirror can provide adequate shadow-free light.

a dressing table the strips should be at least 45 inches above the floor.

Side lighting. Side lighting can be just as effective as wrap-around lighting if the illumination extends high enough to include the top of the head and low enough to fall shadow-free under the chin. Swag lights hung on either side of the mirror are easier to install than wall-mounted fixtures. Any hanging lights however, require a large amount of room for a balance layout. When space is restricted, use wall-mounted side lighting.

If you cannot use side fixtures, over-mirror lighting stretches and improves the lighting field. For best results, the ends of the fixture should align with the vertical sides of the mirror, or with the mirror's frame, if one is included. The best over-mirror lighting should extend 78 inches across.

For a quick and simple installation, buy one of the framed fluorescent fixtures with a wooden box fitted with a panel of translucent plastic. This fixture can be suspended by chains from the ceiling, or attached directly to the ceiling or to the underside of a soffit.

Light diffusion. Diffused light spreads illumination over a range of angles to produce a soft light that does not fall in a single beam. Fixtures at a mirror should direct light toward the person and not into the mirror. On the other hand, the directed light also should not contain pinpoints or spots of glare, both of which can cause eyestrain and discomfort. Grooming lights must have either built-in or attachable diffuser shields.

Providing Recessed Soffit and Canopy Lighting

If the design of a room includes long mirror expanses over vanities or countertops, consider wide-field overhead illumination. Incandescent or fluorescent light sources that are recessed inside a soffit or canopy can provide local lighting for grooming and a general illumination throughout a room as well.

The reflection from the mirror and the countertop will augment the light radiating downward from the fixture. Countertops that are done in white or in light shades are good reflectors; dark countertops are more absorptive. Select bulbs or fluorescent tubes that are a step or two higher in output than you would ordinarily choose, in order to assure full illumination.

Building a Soffit or Canopy Box

Construction guidelines. Both a soffit and a canopy box are basically boxes on the ceiling with open bottoms into which sheets of translucent plastic are fitted. The arbitrary difference between a canopy and a soffit is that a canopy does not necessarily go clear to the ceiling, while a soffit always does. To remove and replace the lamps, either the diffuser surface should be removable, or you should be able to reach over the top of the canopy.

To make the lights accessible, construct the box so that the panels can be lifted, turned and removed out of the way. An alternative is to make a narrow wooden frame around the bottom. This frame will be hinged on one side and held in place on the other side with magnetic latches. Around the inside edges, the frame is rabbeted to hold the plastic panels. A third method, appropriate for a soffit with a deep frame, is to create a deep enough box that one panel can be lifted up and slid on top of another. In this way, you can replace one section of lights at a time.

Dimensions. When you design a canopy or a soffit light, the illuminated field should be 16 inches from front to back, 8 inches deep from top to bottom edge. The box itself should extend the full width of the mirror. The translucent shield, or bottom diffuser can be made of sheets of frosted glass, acrylic panels, or eggcrate baffles of metal or plastic. The bottom edge of the soffit or canopy should be within ½ inch of the top of the mirror, which should itself be 78 inches above floor level.

Supporting the framework. If the enclosure box is fitted between two walls, then the walls can provide support for the ends of the framework. If the enclosure will be free-hanging, you must attach the framework to the ceiling. With a closed-in soffit, this presents no problems, since the ceiling cleats to which the box is attached will be hidden inside the ceiling itself. A canopy open at the top does present some problems, since any cleats will be exposed. One method of disguising the cleats is to recess them so they are flush with the ceiling. For example, you can use ½-inch lumber that will be flush with ½-inch plaster. If

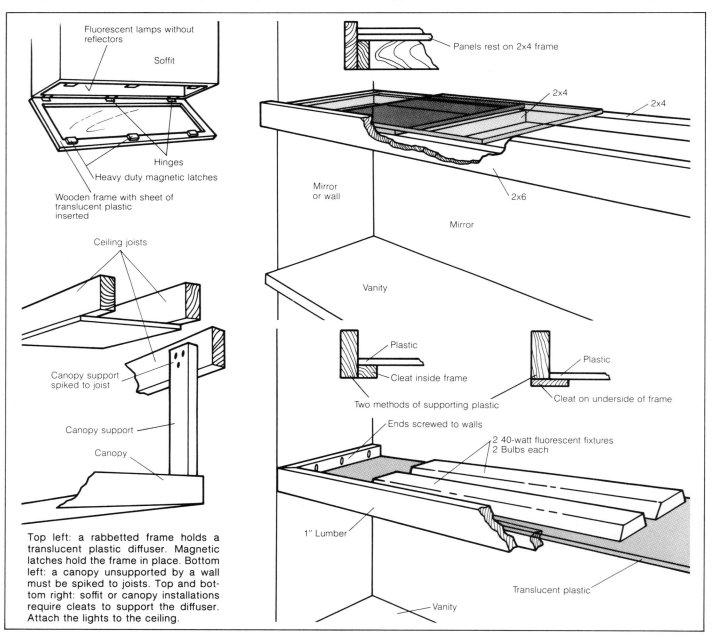

Top left: a rabbetted frame holds a translucent plastic diffuser. Magnetic latches hold the frame in place. Bottom left: a canopy unsupported by a wall must be spiked to joists. Top and bottom right: soffit or canopy installations require cleats to support the diffuser. Attach the lights to the ceiling.

the ceiling joists are spaced so that they correspond to the size of the framework, cut holes in the ceiling and attach the supports for the canopy directly to the joists. This will require some taping and plastering on the ceiling around the supports.

Using chains or hooks. For a decorative and strong support for a canopy, use fancy metal chains, such as those used to hang swag lamps. The fancy hooks can be fastened to the ceiling with Molly or drywall wall anchors. The hooks can also be driven directly into the ceiling joists through the ceiling material.

INSTALLING A RANGE HOOD

Once you have learned how to extend a circuit, you can install a range hood in your kitchen with much less expense than if you had hired a professional. Place the hood high enough that its front edge does not impair the cook's view of the rear burners. If the depth of the hood is under 18 inches, the bottom edge should stand no less than 56 inches above the floor. If the hood's depth is 18 inches or over, the bottom edge should stand no less than 60 inches above the floor.

Hood Styles

Hoods come in two styles, ducted and ductless. After passing the air through a filter to remove grease and odors, a ductless hood pushes the air back into the room. The filter must be changed quite often, and the hood does not remove heat or moisture.

A ducted hood removes the heated air from the room. If you install a ducted hood, plan as short and straight a path as possible for the exhaust ducting, in order to get the best performance from the hood and to ease installation of the ductwork. Always vent ductwork to the outside of your home. Never vent into an attic or unused house space; the resulting grease buildup creates both fire and health hazards.

CFM Rating

The size of the hood you purchase will depend upon the size of your kitchen and the type of cooking that is done there. You must also consider the length of the ducting itself. A long duct will require a larger fan in order to function properly. As you select the hood, note its "CFM rating."

The abbreviation means "cubic feet per minute," and the number preceding the abbreviation indicates the amount of air that the fan in the hood can move. The recommended rating for a range hood is at least 200 CFM for minimum ventilation, according to kitchen experts.

The rating of an average sized hood can range from 400 to as high as 600 CFM. Anything rated above 400 requires larger ducting than fans with lower ratings. A barbecue fan, which often is rated as high as 1000 CFM, requires a round duct that is 10 inches in diameter.

The steps for installing a range hood vary from manufacturer to manufacturer. Specific instructions are given in each manufacturer's package. However, options regarding duct planning and placement can be generalized.

Installing a Range Hood

Step one: removing an old hood. A range hood is fairly large and can be heavy, so do not attempt this job without a helper. Before removing the existing hood, turn off the power to the circuit that feeds the hood. Then disconnect the wiring that powers the exhaust fan and the hood light. This is usually housed in a junction box behind a metal pan covering. Loosen the terminal screws and remove the wires. Separate the cable wires and completely wrap each wire end with electrical tape.

Step two: choosing the ductwork. Ductwork is the series of rectangular or round pipes that lead from the hood's vent to the outside of your home. The pieces come in several sizes and shapes to accommodate a variety of pathways. Either wall or roof caps finish off the outside openings. To prevent fire hazards, be sure to purchase metal rather than plastic ducting.

Although most ducting is made of standard sheet metal, flexible metal duct

A range hood is a valuable addition to a kitchen. It removes humidity, heat, grease and odor from the room. This particular hood also adds illumination over the cooking area.

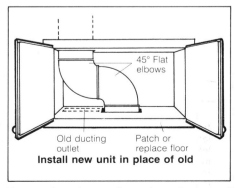

Install new unit in place of old

You may have to use elbow pieces to connect the new opening to old ductwork.

is also available. Since this type comes in only round duct, install a rectangular-to-round converter to connect the duct with the hood. Flexible duct is quite easily dented or crushed, more so than conventional ducting. On the other hand, it is light and goes around corners without requiring elbows or other adapters.

Step three: connecting up to the old ductwork. You will save yourself a great deal of time and frustration if the duct opening in the new hood is in the same position as (or similar to) the duct opening already in existence. If this is not the case, you may be able to use two pieces of elbow ducting to angle the channel over to the old vent. Then patch the old cabinet opening. If this procedure is not feasible, you must abandon the old duct and install an entirely new run.

Sometimes new ducting is the best course, especially if the old duct is too grease-laden for safe use. If you do install a new duct, there are two ways to deal with the old duct:

(1) remove the old ductwork and patch the holes that remain (however, in the case of a house made with brick or aluminum siding, such repairs could be prohibitive); or,

(2) screw down the damper in the exterior wall and caulk it closed securely—then fill the duct with insulation and repair only the cabinet or wall opening.

Step four: planning the ductwork. The pathway you choose will depend upon your home's construction and the hood's location. If the stove sits against an exterior wall, the shortest path is straight out

through the back of the hood. Once this installation is complete, be sure that the damper in the hood's duct and the one in the wall cap do not interfere with each other. If they do, either the hood exhaust will be impeded, or air will blow in from the outside. If this situation does exist, you can remove the hood damper. Another satisfactory method is to install a short vertical pipe from the top of the hood, then angle through the wall. In most homes this duct path travels up through the cabinet or soffit above the hood, rather than through the insulation between the kitchen wall and the exterior shell.

If the hood is on an interior wall, your options depend upon home construction. Avoid extremely lengthy and twisted paths. Go straight up through the wall space to the roof, if you can. If this path is ob-

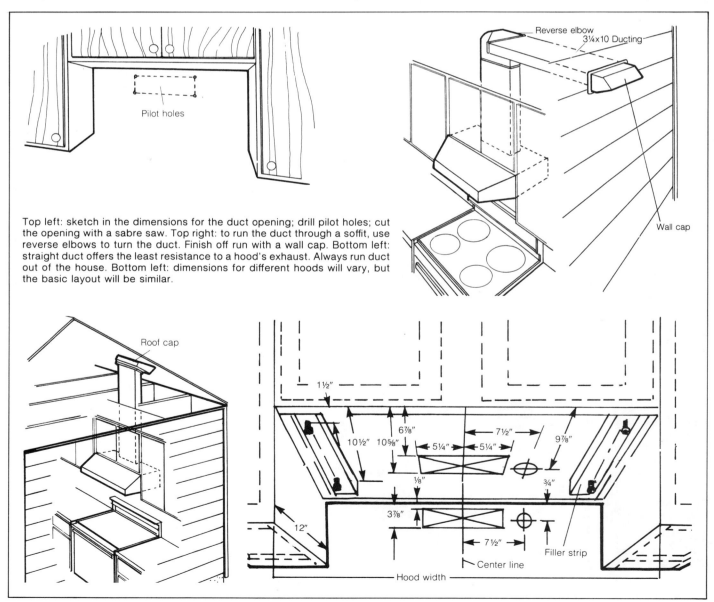

Top left: sketch in the dimensions for the duct opening; drill pilot holes; cut the opening with a sabre saw. Top right: to run the duct through a soffit, use reverse elbows to turn the duct. Finish off run with a wall cap. Bottom left: straight duct offers the least resistance to a hood's exhaust. Always run duct out of the house. Bottom left: dimensions for different hoods will vary, but the basic layout will be similar.

structed by a second story, you will have to pass the ducting through the soffit to an outside wall.

Step five: inserting the duct. As you work with ducting, keep one thing in mind. Although its primary purpose is to provide a passage for exhaust fumes and residue, unfortunately it sometimes also provides a passage for the flames of a grease fire. To be certain that any fire is enclosed in the metal ducting, as you connect sections of ducting together, tape the joints very securely with duct tape.

First cut the opening in the exterior of the house with a sabre saw or a keyhole saw. If you own a saw that has a blade that projects from the front, such as the Milwaukee Saws-All, your job will be much easier. This opening should be slightly larger than the ducting. (If local codes require, install casing strips around a wall opening in a wood house.) Then insert the ductwork.

The difficulties of this task will depend upon the complexity of the duct's path. A straight path will present few problems. Taping one section to the next, one at a time, lower the duct from above. If your path has a center angle, insert the section from the outside, and push the vertical section to meet it. If they meet inside a cabinet or above an unfinished attic, the junction will pose few problems. The same is true of a path through the soffit channel, provided that the soffit has not been finished off. In paths where the junction is enclosed, however, you will have to cut a small access hole at the junction point in order to tape the junction as securely as all other joints.

Step six: capping and sealing the duct. If the duct comes through an exterior wall, trim the duct even with the siding and attach a wall cap to the duct according to instructions. Then fasten the wall cap to the wall and caulk the opening well. If the duct comes through the roof, it should extend at least ¾ inch above the high side of the roof. Using plastic roof cement, completely seal the opening between the duct and the roof. Be generous so you prevent later water seepage. Then install the roof cap. Insert the high-side edge under the shingles and apply plastic roof cement all around the cap.

Step seven: making the final hookup. The power must be off to make this connection. Fasten the cable to the hood with the connecter locknut. Now use wire nuts to splice

the black cable wire to the black hood wire. Do the same with all white wires. Finally, using the green ground screw, attach the cable ground wire to the grounding bracket built into the hood. Comply with all local codes. Regulations may vary. Then replace the wiring box cover and screw. Be careful not to pinch any of the wires.

REPAIRING A FAULTY DOORBELL

A circuit must be a complete circuit. If there is a break in a doorbell circuit, the sounding device will not work. A break in the circuit may be in the form of a broken wire, corroded door button contacts, a burned-out transformer, or a defective signal device.

If your home has two door buttons—one serving the front door and the other serving a rear door—and one sounding device serving both doors, there are two complete circuits. If the contacts of one of the door buttons corrodes or a wire from the door button to the transformer breaks, the sounding device will not work when that door button is pressed. However, the device will work when the other door button is pressed. A system with two buttons and two signal devices has two complete circuits. A system with three door buttons and one signal device has three circuits. In other words, every door button has its own circuit, which, when it fails, will not affect the other circuits. The only malfunction that will cause an entire door sig-

A doorbell installation needs less than 120 volts of power. Therefore you must install a transformer to step down the circuit voltage.

nal system not to work is a burned-out transformer. Usually all door signal circuits attach to a common transformer. Keep this in mind in case the entire signaling system in your home fails.

The following discussion is based on one door button. However, the same principles apply to homes having any combination of door buttons, sounding devices and circuits. Turn off the circuit while you work on the wiring.

If the doorbell does not sound. Follow the steps given below for testing the installation of a new doorbell.

If the Door Signal Device is Not Loud Enough

1. If a sounding device suddenly becomes barely audible, check all terminals for cleanliness and tightness. These include the terminals on the door button(s), transformer, and sounding device. Disconnect the wires and clean the terminals with sandpaper. Then, wipe the terminals with a cotton swab that you have dipped in alcohol. Secure the wires to the terminals. If sound is not restored, the push button, transformer, or sounding device is failing. Test as described below.

2. If a new bell, buzzer, or set of chimes you have just installed is barely audible or gives a dull sound, it and the transformer are not of comparable voltage. Older signal devices require less voltage to operate than more modern chimes and bells. Check the data on the new sounding device and on the transformer. The voltage output marked on the transformer should be within two volts either way of the voltage requirement marked on the sounding device. In the case of a mismatch, replace the transformer.

If the Door Signal Device Keeps on Sounding

A signal device that won't shut off means the door button has shorted, probably because of corrosion on the terminals. Clean the terminals with sandpaper and a cotton swab saturated with alcohol. If this does not fix the trouble, replace the door button.

INSTALLING A DOORBELL

Electric doorbells that ring, chime, buzz or play songs are perhaps one of the simplet and easiest of electrical devices to install; however, a proper installation does require planning, preparation and attention to safety. The devices have one thing in common. They are operated with a low-voltage power source. The low-voltage power source is a small transformer that steps down the normal house voltage of 120 volts in a circuit cable to 24 volts or less to power the doorbell device.

Planning the Job

The first step in a doorbell installation is to select a location for the doorbell sounding device. It should be placed near the center of the home and mounted approximately six feet above the floor. The devices cannot be mounted above a heat source or on a door. The second step is to locate a 120-volt source to tap for the transformer. The source cannot be switch-controlled. The transformer may be wired directly into a junction box in a basement or attic or above a dropped ceiling. Once the doorbell and transformer locations are determined, you can estimate the amount of low voltage wire you need. Measure the entire distance in feet from the transformer to the sounding device and then from the device to each door button. Add an additional 15 feet to allow for connections and turns in the wires' pathways.

Purchasing the Equipment

The equipment you purchase will depend upon the doorbell. Its power requirements determine the size of the transformer in amperes, and reduced voltage. If the doorbell does not include the transformer and door buttons, they all must be purchased separately. Purchase low voltage wire that is a 300 volt rated wire. It will be designated as thermostat wire, a Number 20 or larger AGW, or equivalent bell wire. Your electrical supplier will be able to assist you in the selecting of the equipment.

Installing the Transformer

Determine which circuit feeds the outlet that the transformer will be mounted on, and turn off that circuit. Test the circuit with the voltage tester, as discussed earlier, to verify that it is off. Remove one of the knockouts in the junction box, and mount the transformer according to its instructions. In most cases, there will be two terminals on the outside of the transformer and two wires extending out from the transformer. The terminals are for bell wire; the wires are for connection to the higher voltage circuit wires. Pass the wires, which are not color-coded, through the knockout. Connect one of the high voltage wires to the black cable wire in the outlet box and the other high voltage wire tc the white cable wire. The order makes no difference. Secure the transformer and replace the box cover.

Making the Low Voltage Connections

The instructions for wiring the bell may vary; follow them carefully. In essence, you will have three places from which you must run wire—the door buttons (front and back) and the sounding device. From one terminal screw on the transformer you run wire to the sounding device; from the other terminal you will run wire to the door buttons. At each door button there will be two terminals. One holds the wire from the transformer, the other holds the wire that leads to the sounding device.

Step one: creating the openings. Drill a ½-inch hole in the wall. This will hold the sounding device. Then drill a ¾-inch entry hole in the plate in order to run the low voltage wire to the transformer.

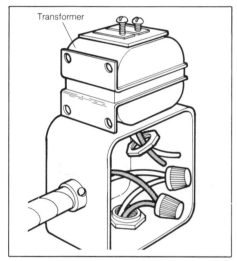

Pass the transformer wire leads through the knockout; secure with a locknut.

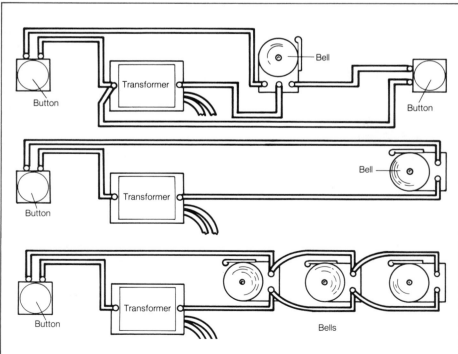

A connection must exist between transformer and signal, transformer and button, and button and signal. Above, two buttons operate the same signal; below, one button operates three bells.

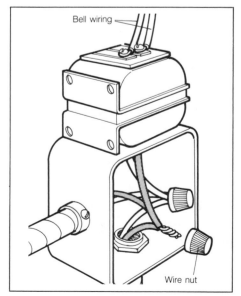

Connect the wire leads to the splices containing the circuit wiring; run the bell wires.

Now create the openings for the door buttons. These should stand at waist-height, about 4½ feet above the ground. Measure

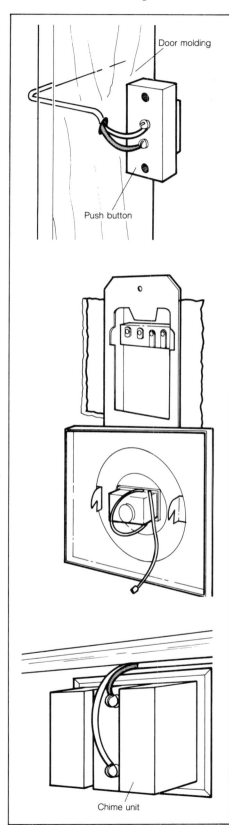

Fish the wire to the door buttons and to the door signal. The signal will have labeled terminals to indicate the order of wiring.

in about 4 inches to mark the opening; otherwise, you will drill into the studs at the side of the door frame. Drill ½-inch hole at the mark, or the size required for your particular door button. In the sill plate directly below the first hole, drill a ¾-inch hole.

Step two: fishing the wire. Using the fishing techniques discussed in Chapter 9 and 10, extend low-voltage wire from the transformer to the sounding device, from the sounding device to the door buttons, and from the door buttons to the transformer. Use cable staples to staple the wires to the joists approximately every 4 feet.

Step three: hooking up to the transformer. Strip approximately ½ inch of insulation from the wires. Connect the wires to the transformer terminals as marked, and tighten the terminals. Do the same for the wires at the door button and sounding device locations.

Step four: finishing the installation. Mount the sounding device with the appropriate type of wall anchors. Mount the door buttons with the wood screws that come included in the package.

Testing the Installation

Once the installation is complete, turn the circuit on. Then check both door buttons, to make sure they both function. If the sounding device responds to both buttons, your installation is fine. If there is a problem, either both buttons will not work or one or the other will not function.

If neither doorbell signal works, the trouble is probably in the transformer or in the wire from the transformer to the sounding device. Work through the following list until you determine the source of the problem.

1. Have someone test the door button while you listen for a hum at the transformer. If no hum occurs, the problem is either a faulty transformer or a dead circuit. Check to be sure that the fuse or circuit breaker controlling the circuit is on.
2. Open the box containing the transformer and release the wire nuts connecting the transformer wires to the circuit wires.
3. Hold the probes of the voltage tester to the ends of the circuit wires (always hold the probes by the insulated parts) and have a helper turn on the circuit. The bulb should light. If it does, replace

the transformer. If it does not, call in an electrician; there are problems with the circuit wiring.

4. If the device does not work, replace it.
5. If the transformer does hum, disconnect the low-voltage wire connections at the transformer and from the sounding device. Twist the sounding device wires together and use a continuity tester to see if the sounding device is working. Then untwist the wires and run the test again on the separated wires. If the device fails either test, replace the device.
6. If the bell still does not sound, there is a break in the wire between the device and the transformer. Replace the wire.

Testing the door buttons. If one button functions correctly but the other does not, the problem is either with the button itself or with the wires connecting the button to the transformer and the sounding device.

1. Test the button with the continuity tester. If the bulb lights, the button is working. If the bulb does not light, replace the button.
2. Turn off the circuit controlling the doorbell.
3. At the doorbutton, release the connection to the wire coming from the transformer.
4. Hold one low voltage tester probe against the incoming circuit wire, the other against the outgoing wire.
5. Turn the circuit on. If the tester lights, the wire from the transformer to the button is not broken; replace the wire running from the button to the sounding device.
6. If the tester does not light, the wire between the transformer and the button is broken; replace the wire.

Finishing the Installation

Install all cover plates. Caulk and seal the outside wire entrance if the sillplate was penetrated. Also caulk around the door button openings.

Installing Three-Way Switches

Three-way switches are valuable in any home. As discussed in Chapter 4, the switches themselves have three terminal screws: one called "Common," which holds the incoming hot wire; one holding the traveller wire, which connects the one switch to the other so that both have power available to them; and one that carries power to the fixture.

Three conditions affect the wiring procedure for a three-way system.

1. What junction box will you tap for power? This can be any of the sources discussed in Chapters 9 and 10.
2. Which junction box will hold the incoming circuit cable? As in Chapter 10, the power-carrying cable can feed into the switch junction box or the ceiling fixture junction box.
3. What is the pathway of the cables connecting the switches to the fixture and to each other? (The answer to this depends largely upon the answers to No. 1 and No. 2.) The three possible combinations are switch-fixture-switch, switch-switch-fixture, or fixture-switch-switch. Select the path that will give you the convenience you desire and that will cost the least in amount of materials required.

Power Feeds for the Ceiling Fixture

If the power cable feeds into the ceiling fixture junction box, the power must be routed through to the switches that will control the light, just as in the Switch Loop discussed in Chapter 10. Depending upon your particular installation, you will either install one long switch loop that includes both switches or two shorter switch loops, one to each switch.

For example, suppose that the fixture is in the center of a family room and that you want a switch beside a door that leads from the living room, with another one leading to the garage at the opposite end of the room. In this case, you need two switch loops, one for each switch.

However, with a different layout, where the two switches are both on the same side of the fixture rather than on each side of the fixture, two switch loops are not necessary. In this case, one long switch loop that includes both switches is the best choice.

Wiring two switch loops. This installation requires two kinds of cable. Use two-conductor cable, which contains one hot wire and one neutral wire, to connect the power source to the fixture. Use three-conductor cable, which contains two hot wires and one neutral wire, to connect the fixture to each of the switches. (As always, be sure to purchase cable containing a ground wire.)

1. Turn off the power to the circuit you are going to tap (see Chapter 1).
2. Cut the openings for the fixture and the switches (see Chapters 9 and 10).

3. Connect the fixture to the power source with two-conductor cable (see Chapters 9 and 10).
4. Fish three-conductor cable from each switch to the fixture (see Chapter 10).
5. Install the switch and ceiling junction boxes (see Chapters 9 and 10).
6. Find the Common terminal on one of the switches. This either will be labeled or will be darker in color than the other terminals. Attach the black wire to this terminal.
7. Attach the red wire to one of the light-colored terminals. This is the traveler wire.
8. Then attach the white wire to the other light-colored terminal. This wire will carry power to the fixture; you must code the white wire black. Use paint or electrician's tape.
9. Now wire up the fixture. Splice the red wires together.
10. Find the white wire coming from the power source. Splice this wire to the white wire coming from the fixture.
11. Find the black wire coming from the power source. Splice this wire to the black wire leading to one of the switches.
12. Find the black wire coming from the fixture. Splice this to the loose black wire leading to the other switch.
13. There should be two loose white wires left, one from each of the three-conductor cables. Splice the two together.
14. Make all the connections necessary to hook up the ground wires in the ceiling junction box and the two switch junction boxes, as shown.
15. Finish off the installation.

Wiring one long switch loop. To wire a long switch loop, you will use two-conductor cable to connect the power cable to the ceiling junction box. Two-conductor cable also connects the ceiling junction box to the closest switch. Three-conductor cable then connects the two switches. The installation is as follows.

1. Turn off the power to the circuit you are tapping (see Chapter 1).
2. Cut the wall and ceiling openings.
3. Fish two-conductor cable from the power source to the ceiling opening (see Chapter 10).
4. Fish two-conductor cable from the closest switch opening to the ceiling opening.
5. Fish three-conductor cable between the two switch openings.

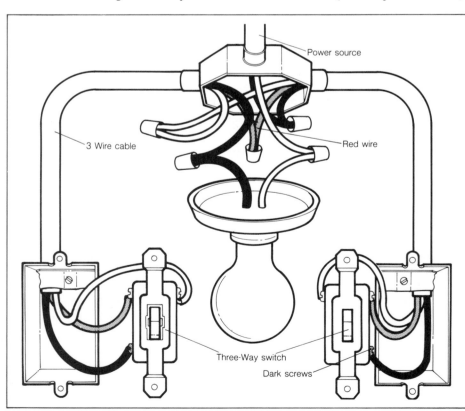

Power source

3 Wire cable

Red wire

Three-Way switch

Dark screws

If the ceiling fixture falls between the two switches, and if the power source feeds into the fixture, run a switch loop to each of the switches with three-conductor cable. Attach the black hot wire to the Common terminal.

6. Install the junction boxes at all three locations.

7. Wire up the farthest switch: black wire to the Common terminal, red and white wires to the remaining light-colored terminals. Recode the white wire to show that it carries power to the fixture.

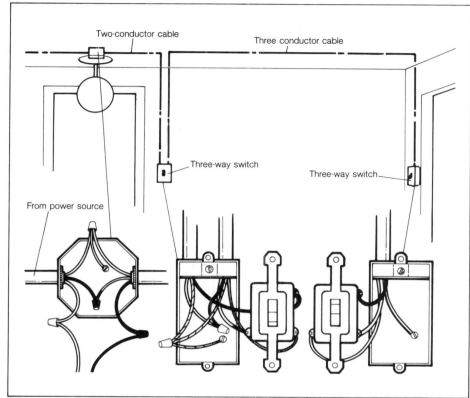

If the ceiling fixture falls in front of the two switches, and if the power source feeds into the fixture, run two-conductor cable to the first switch and three-conductor cable to the second one. Note the necessary splicing techniques.

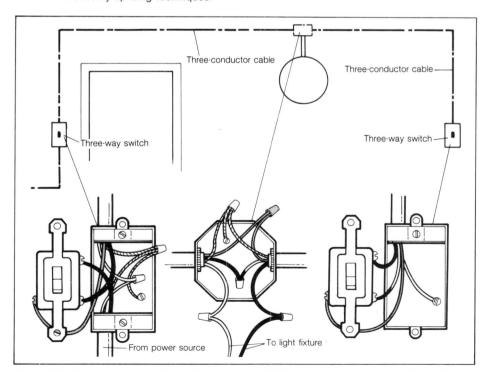

If a switch falls on each side of the ceiling fixture, and if the power feeds into one of the switches, you must run three-conductor cable between the fixture and the switches. Be sure to recode the white wire in the fixture as shown.

8. Wire up the closest switch. Hook the black wire of the two conductor cable to the Common terminal. Hook the red and the white wires of the three-conductor cable to the light-colored screws. Recode the white wire to indicate that it carries power.

9. There should be two loose wires left: the white wire of the two-conductor cable and the black wire of the three-conductor cable. Splice these two together; recode the white wire.

10. Move to the fixture. Splice the two black cable wires together.

11. Find the white wire that connects to the power cable. Splice this with the white wire on the fixture.

12. Find the white wire coming from the switch; recode this wire black; splice this with the black wire from the fixture.

13. Make all the connections necessary to hook up the ground wires in the ceiling junction box and the two switch junction boxes, as shown.

14. Finish off the installation.

Power to the Farthest Switch

If the power cable feeds into the farthest switch, you must route power to the other switch and to the ceiling fixture. The complexity of the installation depends upon whether the ceiling fixture is centered between the two switches or it is at the end of the run.

Wiring a centered fixture. In this installation, use two-conductor cable to connect the switch to the power source. Use three-conductor cable between the fixture and each switch.

1. Turn off the circuit you are tapping (see Chapter 1).

2. Cut the wall and ceiling openings, fish the cable through, and install the junction boxes (see Chapters 9 and 10).

3. Start with the switch attached to the power cable. Splice together the white wires.

4. Hook up the black wire from the power cable to the Common terminal.

5. Hook up the black and red wires to the light-colored terminals.

6. Hook up the farthest switch next. Attach the black wire to the common terminal; attach the red and the white wires to the light-colored terminals. Recode the white wire to indicate that it carries power.

7. Finally, hook up the fixture. Splice the two red wires.

8. Identify the black wire coming from the farthest switch. Splice with the black fixture wire.

9. Identify the white wire coming from the farthest switch. Recode it black and splice it with the black wire from the other cable. (This will be the only loose black wire left.)

10. There should be one loose wire left—the white wire of the cable from the nearest switch. Splice this with the white wire of the fixture.

11. Make all the connections necessary to hook up the ground wires in the ceiling junction box and the two switch junction boxes, as shown.

12. Finish off the installation.

Wiring an end-of-the-run fixture. In this installation, use two-conductor cable to connect up to the power source, three-conductor cable between the two switches and two-conductor cable between the nearest switch and the fixture.

1. Turn off the circuit you are tapping (see Chapter 1).

2. Cut the wall and ceiling openings, fish the cable, and install the junction boxes (see Chapters 9 and 10).

3. Hook up the fixture by splicing like-colored cable and fixture wires.

4. Hook up the middle switch. Splice the white wires.

5. Hook the black wire of the two-conductor cable to the Common terminal.

6. Hook up the black and the red wires of the three-conductor cable to the two light-colored terminals.

7. Now hook up the other switch to the three-conductor cable and the two-conductor power cable. Splice the white wires together.

8. Hook the black wire from the power cable to the Common terminal.

9. Hook the black and the red wires of the three-conductor cable to the two light-colored terminal screws.

10. Make all the connections necessary to hook up the ground wires in the ceiling junction box and the two switch junction boxes.

11. Finish off the installation.

LOW VOLTAGE REMOTE CONTROL SWITCHING

Three- and four-way switches are a convenience in any home, but this type of system requires a great deal of work to install. It has other problems, too; power must be present at every switch at all times; long runs of cable result in a drop in the voltage level; the pathway of the circuit can become awkward and difficult to route; and,

no matter how carefully you plan, there still comes a day when you wish you had one more switch.

A form of switching called low-voltage remote control provides an alternative that does not have these disadvantages. Power cable runs only to the outlet or fixture itself. A switching device called a relay turns power off or on. Connected to the relay are any number of sets of low-voltage wires that lead to a corresponding number of wall switches. When you push a switch, an electrical pulse is sent to the relay, which then turns on the power to the fixture or outlet. The same thing happens when the switch is pushed to turn the fixture off. The switch sends a signal to the relay, which then turns off the power.

There are several advantages to a low-voltage system. The wire connecting a switch to a relay is thin because it only needs to carry 24 volts of power, the amount required to signal the relay. The wire size is less expensive than two- and three-conductor cable and is much easier to work with. You can run the wires over a longer distance than cable because of the wires' size and flexibility. More switches can control a fixture because bulky cable connections and long cable runs are no problem. Nor do the smaller wires result in dropped voltage when run over long distances. Finally, the low voltage level is safe; the shock danger of conventional switches is gone. Full voltage exists only at the location where it is being used.

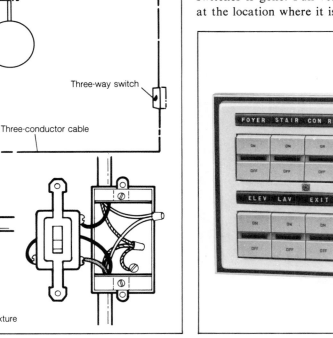

If the fixture falls after the two switches and the power feeds into the first switch, run three-conductor cable between the switches and two-conductor cable between the nearest switch and the fixture. There are no recoded wires in this setup.

Low voltage remote control switches are usually rocker-arm style switches. The larger panels contain controls for all over a home.

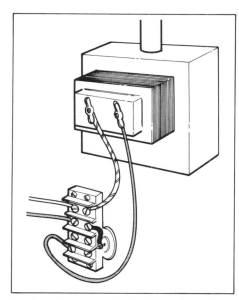

The transformer is attached to a circuit junction box. Then a white wire and a blue-and-white striped wire attach the transformer to the terminal board.

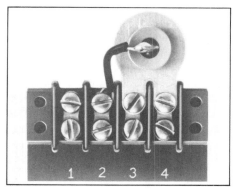

A rectifier is a special device designed to protect the relays.

A relay is an electrically run switch. The wire leads shown here attach to the wires coming from the special switch.

The following discussion is based upon General Electric's system. Other manufacturers may vary.

System Components

The low-voltage system has three basic parts: a transformer, similar to the one used for a doorbell; the wires, which either are specially made for a low-voltage system or are No. 18 gauge AWG, depending on local code and NEC requirements; and the relays, which switch a fixture or outlet on or off.

The transformer. Since the relays require a signal of only 24 volts, you must install a transformer that steps down the normal voltage level of a circuit to the 24-volt level. Transformers come in at least two sizes, one that is powered by a 115-volt line and one that is powered by a 240-volt line. The smaller size is usually adequate for a residence, but discuss your needs with an electrical dealer before you begin your installation. The transformer needs a circuit of its own; this should be handled by a professional electrician.

Leading from the transformer is a white neutral wire and a blue-and-white striped power wire. These attach to a terminal board, to which you attach the wiring for the switches throughout the house. The size of the board you require depends upon the number of switches and relays you want. Also attached to the board is rectifier, which is designed to protect the system by supplying what is called "half-wave rectified current" to the relay for better operation.

Relays. Basically, a relay is a switch that operates by electricity rather than by manual control as do normal switches. There are two ways to handle the placement of the relays. If you are remodeling or adding on to an existing home, and thus can install the wiring before the paneling is in place, install a components box. This holds the transformer, the terminal board and the relays. Have an electrician run the cable for the new circuits from the components box, where it hooks up to the relays, to the fixtures and outlets being controlled.

The most efficient system is one in which both terminals and relays are housed in a component box such as the one shown here, which can house nine relays.

This system is not recommended, however, if you are adding the wiring to a finished room. The amount of rerouting of cable that must be done would be too great and would entail too much wall repair to be worthwhile. Instead, insert the relays into the junction boxes you wish to control. Run the two sets of low voltage wires, one from the switches in the walls to the relays in the junction boxes, another from the switches to the terminal board in the basement.

Wires and switches. The third element of the low-voltage system is the wires that lead from the transformer to the switches and then on to the relay. The switches come in two styles. The most often used are rocker-arm switches that come with or without pilot lights. If you prefer, you can select toggle-style switches that are designed for low-voltage systems.

The main low-voltage wires come in two colors, white and blue. White wires connect all switches to the terminal board; blue wires connect the board to all relays. Black and red wires feed into the relay from the switch. Power is made available to the switches through the white wire. When the switch is pushed on, a pulse is sent to the relay through the red wire; when the switch is pushed off, a pulse is sent to the relay through the black wire. Return current is sent through the blue wire to the terminal board to complete the circuit.

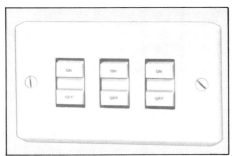

The low-voltage switches are rocker-arm devices. Each side sends a pulse to the relay either to switch off or on.

Tools and Materials

You will require a transformer, a terminal board and rectifier, and a relay for each fixture or outlet you wish to control. You also will need sets of two-conductor wires, one blue and one white to connect to each relay to the terminal bar. Finally, you need sets of three-conductor wires (colored black, red and white) to connect each switch to the relay. To determine how

much wire you need, add 6 inches for each connection to allow for any splicing you may do and to give yourself ample working room. To complete the splices you will need wire caps and electrician's tape. You will need a fishtape for routing the wires and cable staples to secure the wires along the joists.

If you want a pilot light switch, purchase four-conductor sets for the switches; this set contains a yellow wire to power the pilot light. The relay you purchase must have four terminal wires also. A non-pilot light relay has only three terminal wires.

Installing the Transformer

Turn off the power to the circuit you are tapping. The transformer fits over either an octagonal junction box that is 3¼-, 3½- or 4-inch size or a standard 4-inch rectangular box. Attached to the transformer are lead wires. Splice the wires with the cable wires feeding into the junction box. Then screw the transformer into position at the cover plate over the junction box. On top of the box are two wing screws, one for the white wire and one for the blue-and-white wire. These connect the transformer to the terminal board. The rectifier fits onto the terminal board as shown.

Installing a Relay System

Turn off all power to the conventional circuits in the area in which you are working, especially circuits controlling switches you are replacing. Never splice high voltage

(120 v) wires with low voltage (24 v) wires.

1. Fish a set of blue and white wires between the terminal board and the fixture you wish to control. Staple the wires to joists every 4 feet or so. (See Chapters 9 and 10 for fishing techniques.)
2. Fish three-conductor wires from the switch location to the fixture.
3. At the fixture, splice the white low-voltage wires together.
4. Splice the color-coded relay terminal wires to like-colored low voltage wires.
5. Turn back the setscrews built into the relay. Insert the black cable wire into one of the openings provided. Tighten the setscrew to secure the wire.
6. Insert the black wire of the fixture into the other opening. Tighten the screw to secure the wire. (If the fixture wire is too short, cut a jumper wire to con-

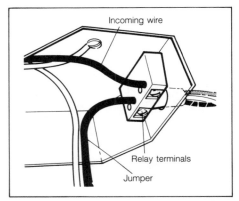

Slide the low-voltage wires back through the knockout; slide the barrel into the knockout.

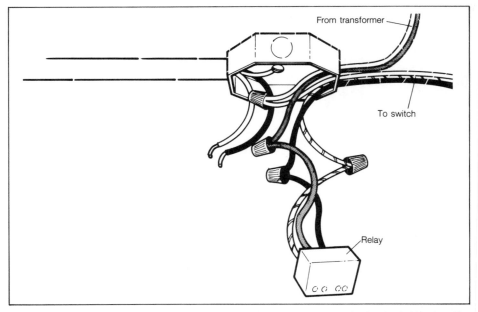

The house wires in the junction box will fit into the spring openings at the back of the relay. The low voltage wires from the switches splice together with the relay's wire leads.

nect the fixture to the relay. Be sure that the jumper is made of 120-volt wire, not 24 volt).

7. Go to the switch location. If you are replacing an existing switch, splice the black power wires attached to the switch, since you will not use these wires for the low voltage switch.

8. Install the switch plate mounting bracket in place. This screws into position along the sides, unlike the mounting arrangement for a conventional switch. Splice the red terminal wire to the red low-voltage wire; do the same with the black and the white wires.

9. Install a switch in the mounting bracket and finish off with a cover plate.

10. Go to the terminal board. Attach the white wire to the terminals marked for switches. Attach the blue wire to the terminals marked for relays.

Installing Several Switches to One Relay

The set of wires connecting one of a series of switches to a given relay can hook up to the relay either directly at the relay or indirectly at another switch. No elaborate wiring procedures are involved. Choose the pathway that is most convenient and requires the least amount of materials.

1. To make the connection at the relay, splice all the red relay wire, and red wires together. Then splice the black relay with the black switch wires. Splice all the white low-voltage wires together.

2. To make the connection at a switch, splice the red wires, then the black, then the white.

Installing a Switch-Controlled Outlet

A switch-controlled outlet will enable you to turn on or off a radio in another room or an outdoor electrical facility. The installation is fairly simple, since you will work only with the black power cable wires. However, you probably will have to gang a junction box to make room for the relay.

1. Turn off the circuit controlling the outlet you wish to control. Pull the receptacle from the box and release it from the wiring.

2. If the receptacle is end-of-the-run, cut a 4-inch jumper. Insert one end in the relay. Insert the black cable wire into the other opening. Attach the loose

end of the jumper to the receptacle.

3. If the installation is middle-of-the-run, you can control the upper or the lower outlet. Look on the side of the receptacle. There should be a brass tab connecting the upper and lower brass terminals. Use a needlenose pliers to snap the tab connection. (If no tab is present, purchase a new receptacle that has this feature.)

4. Gang the junction box to make space for the relay.

5. Cut two 4-inch jumper wires of single-conductor, 120-volt black wire. Splice these with the black wires of the two cables.

6. Connect the loose end of one jumper to the bottom brass terminal on the receptacle.

7. Connect the loose end of the other jumper to one of the relay terminals. Tighten the setscrew to secure the wire.

8. Cut another 4-inch jumper wire. Attach one end to the top brass terminal screw; insert the other end into the empty opening on the relay.

9. Fish the set of low-voltage switch wires and the set of low-voltage transformer wires to the center knockout in the junction box. Splice the white wires. Then splice the like-colored wires to their respective color-coded wires on the relay.

10. Push the relay through the knockout until it snaps into position.

Adding a Master Control Panel

A master control panel can give you control over eight or twelve switches from one location in your home. The panel can be located in an entryway near the front door, in a master bedroom, or in any other location in your home that you wish. The eight-switch panel contains eight low-voltage switches. The twelve-switch panel has two numbered, circular dials, one controlling the On signal, the other controlling the Off signal. Both panels have pro-

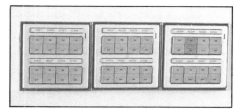

A master control panel in a convenient area can give you control over all the low-voltage circuits.

visions for a directory to the switches and pilot-light indicators. The circular dials are so constructed that you can turn all the fixtures on or off by pressing the dial inward and rotating it. To control only one fixture, dial its number, then press the dial. Be sure to purchase relays with pilot light terminal wires.

1. Select the location for the master panel. Install a ganged junction box that is at least three inches deep.

2. Run sets of four-conductor wires between the relays and the master control. Label each set of wires as you bring it into the control junction box.

3. Run a set of blue and white wires between the transformer and the master control location.

4. Splice the blue transformer wire to the master control blue wire.

5. Splice the white transformer wire with the white wire on the master control and the pilot light panel (if included).

6. Working in order, splice the red wires to the red wires of the master control On terminals. Then splice the black wires to the master control Off terminals. Finally, splice all the pilot light wires to the pilot wire terminals.

7. If you have unused positions on the master panel, splice the like-colored wires together; these you can utilize later if you wish.

8. Push all the wires gently into the box. Install the cover plates as necessary.

INSTALLING REMOTE CONTROL HIGH FIDELITY

Remote control can supply music in a room above, below or beside a record player. This can add pleasure for members of the household, especially if the record

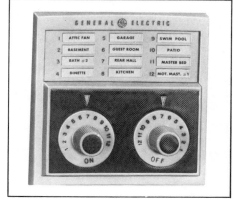

A master switch such as this one also gives you control of remote fixtures. The system has dials for on and off. Dial the area; then push the button.

player and television share the same room, since neither appliance disrupts the other. You can even run speaker lines outside to a patio and enjoy music at a poolside without subjecting your recording system to the effects of temperature, humidity and weather.

Installing Speakers in Another Room

With a length of two-conductor cable you can add two speakers in another room to a standard high-fidelity amplifier and suffer no loss in sound quality. Select No. 18 wire if the run will be less than 60 feet; use No. 16 wire if the run is 60 feet or more. Some speakers and amplifiers will require soldered connections; others will not. Follow the directions given by the manufacturer of the amplifier. Do not work with the amplifier on; you can ruin the amplifier.

1. Select the speaker location. Drill ½-inch holes at baseboard level behind each speaker.
2. Drill a 1-inch opening behind the amplifier at baseboard level.
3. Examine the back of the amplifier. You will find two sets of terminals, one right and one left, under a heading of Remote. Each set of terminals probably will be labeled plus (+) or minus (−). Some setups use a color-coding system, in which red means positive and black means negative. The terminals will be either screw-type or spring clamp-type.
4. Examine the back of the speakers. Here too will be a set of terminals labeled positive and negative.
5. Determine what color-coding system is used in your cable. Here grey is positive and white is negative. Strip ½ inch of insulation from each end of the cable,

and fish the cables between the amplifier and each of the speakers (see Chapters 9 and 10 for instructions.)
6. If your amplifier has screw terminals, attach the positive wire to the plus terminal and the negative wire to the minus terminal.
7. If your amplifier has spring-clamp terminals you must tin the wires before you insert them in the clamps. Twist the strands in each wire tightly together. Heat the wire with a soldering iron; then touch the solder to the wire. If you have heated the wire sufficiently, the solder will melt and cover over the wire. Then insert the wires into the clamp.
8. Hook up the wires to the individual speakers.

Installing a Remote Volume Control

A remote volume control can add to the utility of remote speakers, since the sound can be heard only in the room in which you desire it. This installation requires three-conductor cable, which connects the volume control to the amplifier, and two-conductor cable, which connects the volume control to each speaker. You also need an autotransformer type volume control that is compatible with the amplifier and small wire nuts.

1. Cut a rectangular opening to house the volume control device. The dimensions

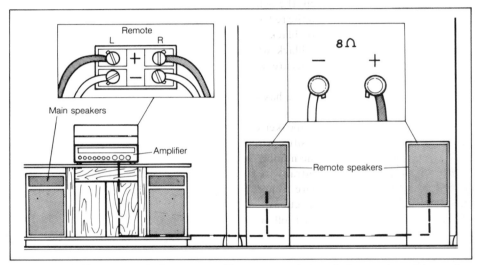

By utilizing the Remote terminals on an amplifier, you can pipe music from a stereo into another room.

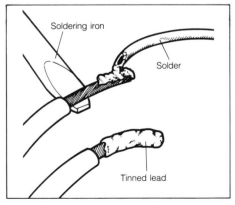

To tin a wire, heat the wire with a soldering iron. Then touch the iron with rosin-cored solder. It will melt and cover the wire end.

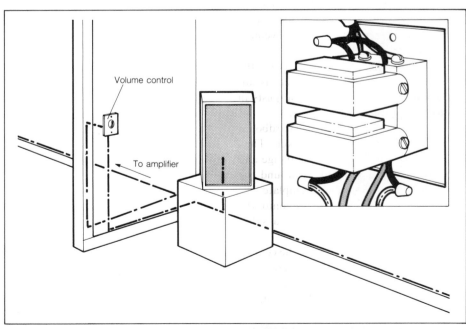

To hook up a volume control in another room, attach the white wire to Input 1, and the red wire to Input 2. Splice the black amplifier wires with the black volume wire.

should be 2x2½ in. Drill 1 inch access holes at baseboard level behind the amplifier and the speakers.

2. Fish three-conductor cable between the amplifier and the volume control opening. Fish two-conductor cables, one to each speaker, from the volume control location.

3. Make the amplifier hookup. The three-conductor cable will have a red, a black, and a white wire. The black wire attaches to the left negative terminal; the white wire attaches to the left positive terminal; the red wire attaches to the right positive terminal.

4. Find the side of the volume control that is labeled Input. The amplifier wires are attached here. Fasten the white wire to Input 1, then fasten the red wire to Input 2. Splice the two black amplifier wires with the two black wires coming from the control; secure with a wire nut.

5. The output side of the volume has the same layout as the top. Remove ½ inch of insulation from the two speaker cables. Work first with the positive wires, attaching one to each of the numbered terminals. Match each neutral wire to the corresponding black wire from the control. Splice these connections; secure with a wire cap. Finish off with the control's cover plate.

Installing a Ceiling-Mounted Speaker

In a den, a family room or a location which has limited amount of floor space, a ceiling-mounted speaker can be a convenient installation.

1. Determine the desired position for the speaker. Then make sure there is adequate clearance between the joists in the ceiling (see Chapter 10).

2. Lay the speaker on a piece of cardboard and draw around the speaker. Then measure in the width of the flange and draw a second circle. Cut around the second circle to create a template.

3. Draw around the template onto the ceiling; cut the opening with a sabre saw.

4. Next position the speaker in the ceiling. Mark the position of the screw openings. Drill pilot holes. You must install screw anchors to ensure the installation.

5. Fish two-conductor cable between the opening and the amplifier.

6. Install the speaker housing, pulling the cable through a center knockout.

7. Strip ¼-inch of insulation from each wire in the cable. Install what is called a solderless crimp connector to each end. The connector slips over the ends of the wire strands. Squeeze the base tightly to secure the connection.

8. Slide the positive wire onto the positive connection. This connection will be indicated either by a plus sign or a red dot. Slip the negative wire onto the remaining connection.

9. Install the speaker in its housing with the screws provided.

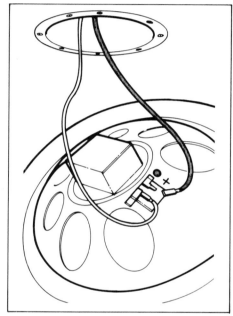

A ceiling speaker is a convenience when there is no room for a conventional speaker. Attach the silver wire to the terminal coded either with a red dot or a plus sign.

Installing a Speaker Jack

If you do not want a speaker to have to be in a given spot, or if you only occasionally listen to music in a given room, attach jacks to the speakers and install speaker outlets in the locations you desire. This will give your system the flexibility you want.

Attaching the jack. Purchase ¼-inch phone plugs for the speakers, and the desired length of No. 18 two-conductor cable. This will be color-coded.

1. Remove the jacket from the plug and slip it over the cable ends.

2. Split the cable for about two inches. Find the copper wire—it usually is encased in gold-colored insulation. Cut this wire ½ inch shorter than the silver-colored wire.

3. Remove ¼ inch of insulation from each wire. Tin the ends.

4. The two connections in the plug will be of different sizes. Attach the copper wire to the longer connection. Attach the silver-colored wire to the shorter connection.

5. Slip the jacket over the connections. Then hook up the speakers to the cable.

Installing the outlet. To hook up the outlet, you will need a soldering iron, rosin-cored solder, a 1-inch drill bit, a drill and needlenosed pliers.

1. The outlet requires a 1-inch hole in the wall. Drill this opening; fish cable between it and the amplifier.

2. Split the cable up to about 2 inches. Strip ¼ to ½ inch of insulation from the wires.

3. The back of the outlet has a spring contact and a sleeve contact. Loop the silver-colored wire through the spring contact. Hold the wire in place and

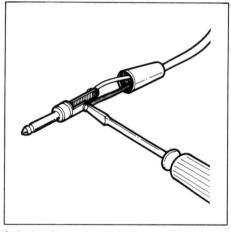

Split the zip cord, attach the silver side to the short terminal, the gold side to the long terminal.

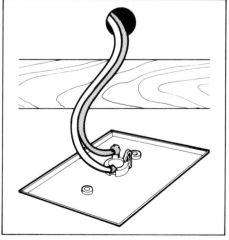

Solder the gold side to the sleeve contact and the silver side to the spring contact.

heat it and the spring contact with the soldering iron. Touch the connection with the solder. It will melt to cover the contact with melted metal. The solder coating should be smooth. If it is not, heat the solder some more. It should even out.

4. Solder the copper-colored wire and the sleeve contact in a similar manner.

5. Fit the outlet into the opening; fasten in place with screws.

The opening for the jack and the control knob are attached to the cover plate with a locknut.

Installing an Earphone Hookup

An earphone outlet is a convenient installation in a family room or living room where space is limited.

Materials and tools. This installation requires a 4-inch square standard blank double gang plate for a switch, an L-pad volume control (be sure you ask for stereo), a three-conductor stereo headphone jack, a soldering iron, rosin-cored solder, a continuity tester, a three-conductor cable that is 18 inches longer than the distance between the jack and the amplifier wire nuts and two 330-ohm, two-wall resistors. You also will need a ⅜-inch carbide-tipped drill bit, a drill and a sabre saw.

1. On the switch plate center two marks, one between each pair of screw holes already present. Drill ⅜-inch openings at the marks.

2. Insert the volume control shaft through one of the holes. Slide the volume indicator plate over the shaft; secure the volume control with a locknut.

3. Install the jack receptacle in the other opening.

4. The volume control mechanism has two sets of three terminals, one at the base and one at the center of the con-

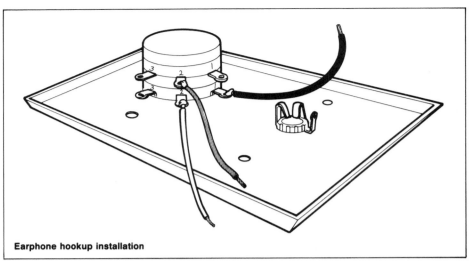

Earphone hookup installation

Attach the jumper wires to the terminals of the two levels of the control in the order shown.

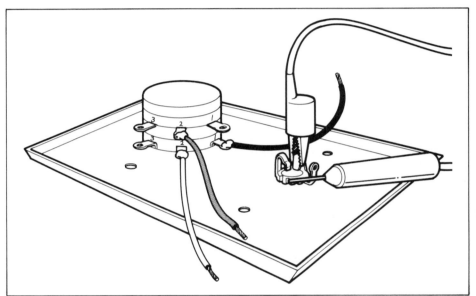

Test the contacts and the terminals of the speaker opening with a continuity tester in order to find the mating parts.

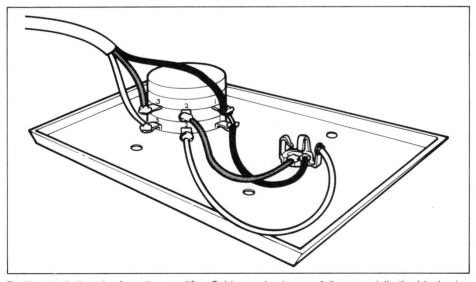

Finally attach the wire from the amplifier. Solder each wire carefully, especially the black wire, which must hook to the lower terminal as well.

trol body. Cut three 4-inch jumper wires of red, white and black. Each will be soldered to a terminal. The black wire goes on base terminal 1; the white goes on base terminal 2; the red goes on center terminal 2.

5. The jack base has three terminals and three contacts: a spring contact, a sleeve contact and a short spring contact. Attach the continuity tester to one of the contacts. Touch the ter-

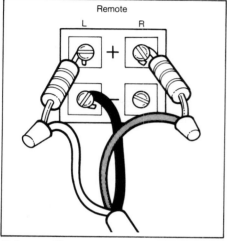

At the amplifier, you must install resistors if you are going to use an earphone jack.

The housing for an outdoor speaker outlet is the same as the one for an outdoor receptacle. Protect it as you hammer the post into the ground.

minals, one by one, with the probe until the bulb in the tester lights up. Make a mark on the plate, indicating what the terminal matches up with. Do this for each contact.

6. Now make a solder connection with the loose jumper ends. Connect the black jumper to the terminal that matches the sleeve contact; connect the white jumper to the terminal that matches the long spring contact; connect the red jumper to the terminal that matches the short spring contact.

7. Cut a 12-inch length of three-conductor cable. Strip away 3 inches of the outer casing; strip ¼ inch insulation from the red and the white wires and 1½ inch from the black wire.

8. Work with the black wire first. Be careful, however, or you will break away the black jumper. In the center 1 terminal on the volume control there is a hole. Pass the end of the wire through that hole, down to the base 1 terminal. Pass the end under and around the base 1 terminal, so the wire hooks the terminal. Secure the wire at both terminals with solder.

9. Solder the other two cable wires. The white wire fastens to the base 3 terminal; the red wire fastens to the center 3 terminal.

10. Drill a pilot hole in the wall where you want the earphone installation. Probe the wall as described in Chapter 9 to locate any joists or other obstructions. Then cut a 2½x4 inch opening with the sabre saw. Fish the remaining cable between the opening and the amplifier.

11. Splice the amplifier cable wires to the like-colored wires of the earphone plate. Secure the splices with wire nuts.

12. Attach a resistor to the left and right terminals of the amplifier's remote terminals. Then connect the white, red and black wires as shown.

Installing an Outdoor Hookup

An outdoor hookup for a speaker can add enjoyment to a patio or a pool area. Select three-conductor cable that is approved for outdoor use, and follow all local codes regarding cable and conduit.

Tools and materials. An outdoor hookup is housed in an outdoor receptacle box. You will also need three pieces of ½-inch steel pipe—a 6 and a 12-inch length and

on T connector. In the receptacle box will be a switch plate, cut to fit, and two jacks. The final hookup requires three wire nuts and electrician's tape. You also will need a ⅜-inch carbide-tipped drill bit, a drill, a metal cutter and a hammer.

Installing the housing.

1. Connect the 6-inch and the 12-inch pipe with the T connector. Screw the other end of the 6-inch pipe into the receptacle housing.

2. Dig a hole 4 inches deep at the spot where you want the receptacle.

3. Using a piece of scrap lumber to protect the receptacle housing, pound the pipe into the ground, as shown, up to the base of the T connector.

4. Run the cable to the box in a trench as discussed in Chapter 11. (If code requires conduit, however, use it instead.)

Creating the plate. Use a metal cutter to cut the size of the switch plate to measure 2x4 inches. Measure ⅞ inch in from the mounting openings. At these points, drill ⅜-inch openings for the jacks, as shown. Use a carbide-tipped drill bit for this job.

Installing the jacks. Insert the jacks into the plate and secure with the locknuts provided. Cut 6-inch jumpers, one red, one white, and two black. Solder the black jumpers to the right hand terminals on each jack; then solder the red and the white jumpers to the left hand terminals, as shown.

Installing the plate. In the gasket, there will already be some mounting openings,

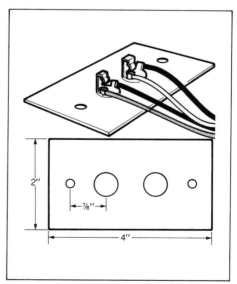

Use a metal bit in a power drill to cut the necessary openings in a blank switch plate. Then hook up the amplifier wires to the jack.

but they will not align with the openings in the adapter plate. Use the plate to mark the positions on the gasket; drill the openings with a ⅜-inch bit.

Use wire nuts to splice the cable wires to the like-colored wires of the jacks. Insert the plate in the box, then the gasket. Fasten the receptacle cover in place, using 1-inch, No. 6/32 screws. Finish by hooking up the amplifier wires.

INSTALLING A ROOF-MOUNTED ATTIC FAN
Placement and Planning

A roof-mounted attic fan should be positioned as near as possible to the center of the attic; place it on the back side of the roof so it is not seen from the front of the house. Assemble the fan and carry it to the roof near one of the gables. Using a straightedge or a piece of wood as a guide, set the fan assembly so the top of the fan is level with the roof ridge. Measure this distance from the ridge to the center of the fan.

In the attic, locate the central part and measure down from the roof peak (on the back side of the roof) a point that corresponds to the desired location of the fan. Locate this point halfway between the rafters. Drive a nail up through the roof at this point so it can be located from the top of the roof.

Cutting the Opening

1. On the outside of the roof, locate the marker nail. Using it as a center, draw a circle about four inches wider than the size of the hole specified in the instructions provided by the fan's manufacturer.
2. With a utility knife, remove the shingles and underlayment down to the plywood sheathing underneath.
3. Using the nail as a center point, draw another circle that is the size specified in the instructions. Cut a hole in the sheathing or battens along this circle, using a sabre saw or a keyhole. The specified hole size may be larger in diameter than the distance between the rafters. If so, do not cut the rafters; saw along their inner edges.

Installing the Housing

About 6 inches above and below where the fan flashing will cover the roof, hammer four nails into the roof to mark the location of the rafters. You can then install the housing.

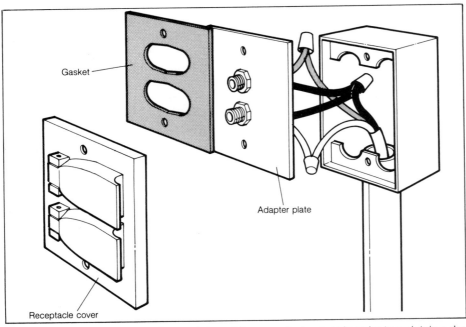

The gasket falls between the adapter plate and the receptacle cover in order to maintain a dry, safe installation.

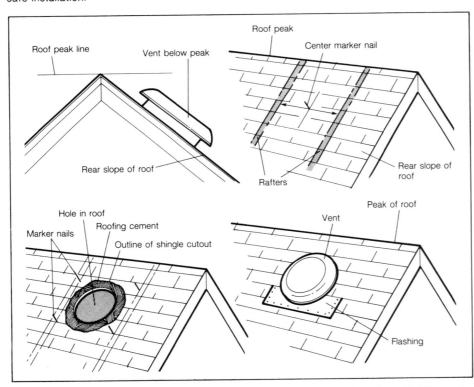

Position the fan so that it will not be seen from the front of the house. Pound a nail at the center of the proposed site. This should fall between the rafters. Marker nails will remind you of the rafters' positions. Cut the opening. Fit the flashing on the high side underneath the shingles; the flashing below the fan falls on top of the shingles.

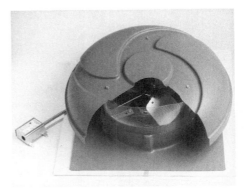

An attic fan can help keep your home cool during the warmest weather. As a result it can save you money in air conditioning costs.

1. Remove any shingle nails within the area above the hole that may prevent insertion of the fan flashing underneath the shingles.
2. Apply a liberal amount of roofing cement to the exposed sheathing and the underside of the fan flashing. Slip the fan housing sheathing underneath the shingles above the hole.
3. Line up the opening of the fan housing with the hole cut in the roof. Using the rafter marks as a guide, drive galvanized roofing nails through the flashing at the top and along the sides at 4- to 6-inch intervals.
4. Place a tab of roofing cement under any shingles that have been lifted; seal any cut edges and exposed nail heads. Do not seal the bottom edge of the flashing.

Ensuring Ventilation
To achieve the kind of ventilation that will most benefit your home, you must add vents to the soffits.

Figuring needs. To determine the amount of venting you require, first figure the square feet of attic space. The recommended ratio for every 150 square feet of attic space is 1 square foot of what is called "net free vent area." Net free vent area does not include any screening or louvers designed to keep out rain or insects. You must convert the net free vent figure to a gross vent area figure that takes into account any screening you install. Use the table given here to make your conversion.

CONVERSION TABLE

Protective material	Net:Gross
Hardware cloth (¼-in. mesh)	1:1
Screening (⅛-in. mesh)	1:1¼
Insect screen (1/16-in. mesh)	1:1½

If you have an attic that has 1500 square feet, divide 1500 by 150 to find the amount of net free area you require, in this case, 10 square feet. Then turn to the table. It tells you that if you install hardware cloth, the requirement is 1 times the net free area, or still 10 square feet. If you use insect screening, however, the requirement is 1½ times the net free area, or 15 square feet. This is due to the fact that the screening impedes the free flow of air through the venting.

Installing the vents. Soffit vents are sold as trim vents, either 4 or 8 inches wide and 16 inches long, or as continuous vents, 4 and 8 feet long.

Calculate the vent area and the number of vents required. Plan for vents at regular intervals in all eaves. Locate the vents midway between the edge of the eave and the outside wall, and halfway between the lookouts that support the soffit.

Outline the screened area of the vent on the soffit, and cut out the outlined area with a sabre saw. Place the vent in or over the hole and screw it to the soffit through the holes in the vent flange.

Continuous vents. Continuous vents are installed in a similar manner. Cut out the outlined area between the lookouts. Use a hand saw to cut the soffit where it attaches to the lookout. Some vents are recessed into the soffit, which means you may have to cut a notch in the soffit. As an alternative, place 1x2 cleats on either side of the cutout, and nail the vents to the cleats.

Baffles. One problem encountered with vents placed under the eaves is that insulation from the attic can cover the vents and reduce their effectiveness. Baffles can prevent this, but they can reduce the thickness of the insulation at the point between the edge of the roof and the top of the wall. Careful workmanship is important here. Install baffles or ducts that are high enough so that a full thickness of insulation does not restrict air flow through the vent.

Connecting the Wiring for the Fan
In the attic, fasten the fan thermostat to a rafter so that the dial is easily accessible and the temperature-sensing element is exposed to the air. Make sure the element is not in the fan's direct air stream when the fan is operating. A 120 volt circuit using a junction box in the attic powers the fan. If there is no junction box available, run a No. 14 AWG cable through a wall to a junction box in a room on the floor below.

Turn off electrical house current at the service entrance before doing any wiring.

1. Drill a ¾-inch hole in the top plate above an inside wall and directly above the receptacle junction box you wish to tap.
2. Be sure the power is off; then remove the receptacle from the box and fish cable from the attic to the junction box, and clamp the cable in the box.
3. In the attic, run the cable along the side of a ceiling joist, up the side of a rafter, and connect the cable to the thermostat. Secure the cable with cable staples or clamps.
4. Hook up the wires at the receptacle junction box as you would for any cable run (see Chapter 9).

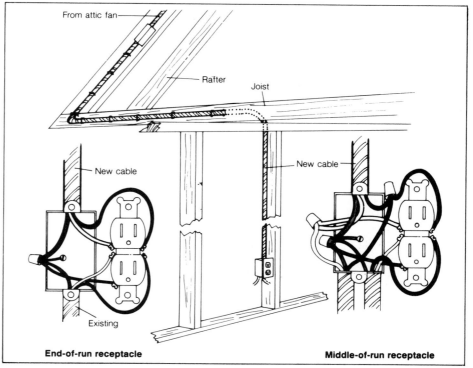

End-of-run receptacle   **Middle-of-run receptacle**

Run cable from an existing receptacle to the attic. Then run it along the joists to the rafters and then to the attic fan box. Hook up to the power source as shown.

Connecting the Fan Thermostat

After you have extended cable up to the fan, connect the two wire leads in the thermostat wiring box to the two cable wires, matching wire color and fastening with wire nuts. Fasten the cable ground wire to the ground screw on the thermostat. You may wish to be able to turn the power on or off manually in order to bypass the thermostat, to turn the fan on or off manually, or wire in a humidistat. With the last installation, you have the capability of automatic operation triggered by temperature and humidity, or manual operation bypassing the thermostat and humidistat, and the convenience of easily turning the fan on or off.

INSTALLING SURFACE-MOUNTED RECEPTACLES TO SERVE HEAVY HOME WORKSHOP TOOLS

Each heavy stationary workshop tool, such as a drill press and lathe, should be accommodated by its own individual circuit. To bring electricity to areas where tools are to be installed, begin by tapping into the service panel. Let a professional electrician do this phase of the job unless you have had experience with this operation or feel confident that you can tackle it after reviewing the steps which are outlined below.

The following instructions for installing receptacles for heavy home tools assume that the workshop is in the basement.

Thus, surface-mounted cables and receptacles will suffice. However, if a home workshop is in another part of the home where concealing wires is desirable, refer to Chapters 9 and 10 for instructions on fishing wires through walls. Another alternative is to use raceway (see Chapter 7).

To begin the operation, turn off the main power switch or pull the main fuse (see Chapter 1). Remove the cover from the fuse or circuit breaker box to determine if there is room for a new circuit. If you find a blank space in a circuit breaker box, you can add a new breaker. In some cases, a spare circuit breaker may have been installed by the contractor who built your home, but it may not be hooked up. So, don't be fooled by the fact that a breaker is in position. Look to see if wires are connected to the terminals at the side of the circuit breaker.

In a fuse box, look to see if any fuse sockets and terminals are unoccupied. If all sockets and terminals are being used, you need to have an electrician install a sub-panel. This is a smaller fuse box which is installed adjacent to the main fuse box and connected to the main fuse box terminal lugs.

Working at the Service Panel

When you work at the service panel, make sure power is off. Even though you may have killed the power to all circuits, current may still be entering the panel. In this situation if you touch the wrong terminals, you could be seriously injured or killed.

Caution: When you test to see if the power is off at the service panel, make sure the floor is dry. Stand on a rubber mat or wooden board and do not touch any metal object.

Use a voltmeter to establish whether current is coming into the service panel. Identify the large terminal lugs to which the main power cables are connected. Grasp the voltmeter probes by their insulated covers and carefully touch the probes to the terminal lugs. If you get a reading on the voltmeter, power is present. Do not proceed with this project until you have stopped the current flow. In some cases, you may have to remove the electric meter to break off all power to the panel.

Procedures

If you can add a new circuit, do the following to install surface-mounted receptacles for home workshop tools.

1. Use a receptacle designated for 240-volt, 30-ampere service. Mount the receptacle where the tool is to be located. An easy way to mount the receptacle to a cinder block basement wall is to nail a wood panel to the wall and screw the receptacle housing to the panel. See Chapter 11 for methods of breaking through and installing the receptacle in the block itself.

2. Determine how much cable you need (see Chapter 9). If your local electrical code permits plastic-sheathed cable, use Type NM No. 10 3-conductor cable. Three-conductor cable possesses two hot conductors, a neutral conductor, and a ground wire. If your local electrical code requires flexible armored cable or conduit, see that it is fitted with two AWG No. 10 Type TW hot conductors, one AWG No. 10 Type TW neutral conductor, and a ground wire. Type TW wire is designed for use in a damp location such as a basement.

3. Connect conductors to the receptacle. Notice that there are three terminals. The two top terminals alongside each other hold the two hot conductors. The third terminal, which is centered between and beneath the other two, is for the neutral conductor.

4. There is no terminal for the ground wire. Connect the ground wire to the

A nipple connects a service panel to the electric meter outside. If you cannot turn off power with interior controls, remove the electric meter to cut off all power to the box.

Labels in figure: Service panel · Grounding lock nut · Conduit · Meter box · Plastic bushing · Nipple

back of the metal receptacle box with a machine screw.

5. Run the cable to the service panel, securing it every four feet to basement joists with clamps or insulated staples. Where the cable runs for a distance along a wall, nail a panel to the wall and secure the cable to the panel. You can also run the cable along the floor where the floor and wall meet. Install a wood baseboard to which the cable can be attached.

6. Check to be sure all power is off in the service panel. See above.

7. Knock out one of the covers on the side, bottom or top of the service panel. Notice the type of clamp that is used to secure other cables to the service box and get a similar type. Insert and secure the cable coming from the new receptacle.

8. To connect the cable to a two-pole 30-amp circuit breaker, loosen the circuit breaker terminal screws and attach a hot conductor to each one.

9. Run the neutral conductor to the ground/neutral bus bar and connect it to an unoccupied terminal.

10. Run the ground wire to the ground/neutral bus bar and connect it to an occupied terminal.

11. Press the new circuit breaker into the panel.

12. If your home is equipped with fuses, see if you can connect the cable to an unoccupied 240-volt pull-out of the fuse box. The 240-volt pull-out should be served by two 30-amp cartridge fuses. Do not attach hot conductors for heavy equipment to two 120-volt fuse box terminal screws.

13. To make connections to a 240-volt pull-out, attach each hot conductor coming from the new home workshop receptacle to the unoccupied terminal screws of the 240-volt pull-out. Then, connect the ground/neutral bus bar. Equip the pull-out with cartridge fuses.

14. Reinstall the service panel cover and turn on power.

GLOSSARY

AC Alternating current. The type of current found in most home electrical systems in the U.S.

AL/CU Receptacles and switches to be used with copper or copper-covered aluminum wire.

AWG American Wire Gauge, a system of sizing wire.

Adjustable bar hanger Support installed between the joists of a ceiling to support a junction box.

Ampacity The number of amps that a wire can safely handle.

Ampere, amperage, amps A unit of measurement that defines the rate of electrical flow. Amperes are measured in terms of the number of electrons flowing through a given point in a conductor in one second when the electrons are under a pressure of one volt and the conductor has a resistance of one ohm. When amps are multiplied by volts, you learn the number of watts available for use (VxA=W). Cables and wires are rated by their amperage—the number of amps they can safely handle.

Appliance information plate Metal plate attached to appliances indicating among other things the number of watts or amps the appliance requires.

Automatic time-delay switch Time delay switch with a pre-set period of delay, such as 45 seconds.

BX cable Cable wrapped in a protective, flexible, metal sheathing. BX contains at least two conductors.

Back-wired receptacles Wires are inserted into openings and secured by clamps rather than being hooked to terminal screws.

Back-wired switch Switch with terminal slots instead of terminal screws.

Baffle An opaque shield that aims light in a desired direction. Coves and valances are the most common types of baffles.

Ballast Holds the current in a fluorescent at a proper level. Otherwise too much current would be available and the light would burn out.

Bare wire In a cable, the wire that has no insulation and is designed to function as a ground wire.

Black wire In a cable, the wire designed to function as a "hot" wire.

CAS Canadian Standards Association. See NEC.

CFM Cubic feet per minute. The amount of air a fan can move.

CO/ALR Switches and receptacles to be used with aluminum wiring.

Cable Two or more wires grouped together within a protective sheathing of plastic or metal.

Cable staples Specially designed staples for holding cable in place along joists.

Canada Electrical Code This organization performs the same function as the NEC in the United States.

Canopy Dish-like structure of a ceiling fixture. The canopy covers the wiring, junction box and ceiling opening.

Canopy Light box suspended from the ceiling.

Cartridge fuse Cylindrical fuses designed to carry higher voltage levels than plug fuses. There are two styles: one with blade contacts and one without. Cartridge fuses are used to protect circuits dedicated to a single major appliance and to protect the house circuits at the service panel.

Chalkline See plumb-and-chalkline.

Channel The metal support base of a fluorescent fixture. The channel holds the starter, ballast and lampholders.

Choke ballast Ballast found in small fluorescents. These ballasts have no transformers, which are required for larger tubes.

Circline fluorescent fixture A circular fluorescent fixture.

Circuit A closed path over which electricity moves from the source of supply, to outlets, and back again to the source of supply or to ground. A house circuit can serve from 375 to 500 square feet, depending upon the amperage of the circuit.

Circuit breaker A protective toggle switch that automatically switches off (trips) the power to a circuit in case of short circuit or overload.

Circuit breaker box See service box.

Circuit map A diagram that indicates (1) the locations of all wall switches, receptacles, and major appliances and (2) designates in some fashion the circuit which feeds the electrical items. Useful for determining the actual load level on a given circuit and tracing circuit problems.

Circumstance The environment in which a cable is located.

Clamp plug Plug on which the line cord is inserted into an opening at the back. Prongs then pierce the insulation to make contact with the wires.

Cleats Small blocks of wood to which other larger pieces are nailed for support.

Cold chisel Concrete chisel used to chip out a hole in a plaster wall.

Collar The finishing locknut of a ceiling fixture.

Common Hot terminal on a three-way switch.

Conductor A wire, metal bar or strip that offers minimum resistance to the flow of electricity.

Combination tool A device that strips insulation from a wire, then cuts the wire at the desired length. The insulation cut is beveled by the blade.

Conduit Metal or plastic tubing designed to enclose electrical wire.

Continuity tester Device designed to test the ability of electricity to flow from a power source to an end point. The barrel of a continuity tester houses a battery. The tester has two wires; at the end of one is an alligator clip, at the end of the other is a probe. When the clip is attached to a device, the battery sends power through the device. If the probe is then grounded to a piece of metal, the circuit is complete and the light should light. Do not use a continuity tester to see if a circuit is on; it will explode in your hands. Use a voltage tester for this task.

Cove A cove baffle is attached to a valance to direct light in a given direction.

Current The flow of electrons through a conductor.

DC Direct current. The type of current supplied by a battery.

Damp location Indoor location that is subject to moderate dampness. Usually the location is below ground level.

Decorative lighting Outdoor lighting used to create mood and space.

Dimmer switch A dimmer switch controls the intensity of the light being controlled. There are two styles, Hi-Lo and rotary.

Double-pole switch This switch has four terminals and controls a single major appliance. The toggle is marked.

Dry location Indoor location in which there is little dampness or wetness. Usually a dry location is above ground level.

Dry niche Housing for pool lighting that is so designed that the water level must be lowered to change the lamp.

Duct Metal channel, usually round, through which air is exhausted.

Duplex receptacle Receptacle holding two outlets.

EMT Electrical metal tubing, sometimes called thin-wall conduit.

Elbow connector Right angle pieces used in raceway and conduit runs.

Electrician's knife Knife having a curved blade that locks into position. The shape of the blade simplifies the task of stripping insulation from cables and wires.

End-of-the-run wiring Junction box that is at the final position in a circuit. Only one cable enters a junction box at the end of the run.

End-wired switch Switch with its terminals on the top and the bottom of the switch housing.

Energy efficiency rating (EER) The amount of energy consumed by a given appliance. The higher the EER, the more efficient it is.

Faceplate The decorative plate installed over a switch or receptacle. The plate also covers the wall opening and thus protects the wiring.

Feed wire See Incoming wire.

Filament A thin, fine wire in an incandescent light.

Fishtape Stiff metal strip used to draw wires and cables through walls, raceway and conduit.

Flanged box Ceiling junction box nailed to a joist in an open ceiling.

Fluorescent Tube in which light is generated by passing electricity through mercury and argon gasses.

Four-way switch One of three switches that governs an outlet or fixture. The other two switches are three-way switches. A four-way switch has four terminal screws. The toggle is unmarked.

Front-wired switch Switch with terminal screws facing the front of the switch.

Functional light Outdoor lighting used to highlight walks, steps, gates and other features. Its primary purpose is that of safety.

Fuse A safety device designed to protect house circuits. Built into the fuse is a metal wire that melts or disintegrates in case of a short circuit or an overload. There are plug fuses, which come in as standard, Type S or time-delay styles. There are also cartridge fuses.

Fuse box See Service box.

GR Terminal screw for a ground wire.

Ganging Method of joining two individual junction boxes.

General lighting Lighting designed to illuminate an entire room.

Green wire In a cable, the wire designed to function as a ground wire.

Ground fault circuit interrupter Special device designed to compare the amount of current entering a receptacle on the hot wire with the amount leaving on the white wire. If there is a discrepancy of less than 1/40 of a second, the device breaks the circuit. The device is required in bathrooms and outdoor areas, which are subject to dampness.

Ground wire Wires designed to carry voltage to earth in case of a short circuit. The ground wire is essential to the safety of your house wiring system and of its users.

Ground-wired receptacle Receptacle having a fifth screw, colored green, that functions as a ground terminal. Both outlets have three openings, one for a ground prong.

Harp Metal arch used to support a lampshade.

Heating cables Special electrical cables installed on a roof to melt away accumulated snow and ice.

Hickey (electrical) Bracket-shaped adapter that screws to a threaded stud; a threaded nipple screws into the other end and is secured by a locknut. A hickey is required to support a ceiling fixture weighing more than ten pounds.

Hickey (plumbing) Tool used to bend

conduit. A hickey has a long handle and a curved head. Conduit is inserted into the head and bent by pushing the handle downward.

Horsepower   Designation of power requirements often used for electrical tools such as a power drill or electric saw. One horsepower equals about 1000 watts.

Hot wire   The "live" power-carrying wire in your electrical system.

Housing   The structure that encases the workings of a fixture, switch, receptacle or appliance.

Incandescent light   Light created by passing electric current through a thin wire called a filament. The glow of the filament is called incandescence.

Incoming wire   Hot wire that feeds power into a junction box.

Indirect lighting   Light that is bounced off a ceiling into a room to give glare- and shadow-free illumination.

In-socket switch   Switch included in the socket of a lamp.

Internal clamp   Internal saddle clamp. This device screws into the inside of a junction box to hold cable in place in a U-shaped knockout. Two loops are built in to hold BX cable; remove the loops to hold Romex in place. Clamp the cable, not the wires.

Joists   Joists are the horizontal wood beams mounted 16 inches apart, center to center, in attics and basement. Ceilings and flooring are nailed to joists.

Jumper wires   Short lengths of single conductor wire that are used to complete circuit connections.

Junction   Metal box inside which all standard wire splices and wiring connections must be made.

Kilowatt   A kilowatt (KW) equals 1000 watts.

Kilowatt hour   A kilowatt hour equals one thousand watts used in one hour. A KWH is the measure of the amount of electricity used in your home over a given period of time.

Knockouts   Specially perforated pieces in a junction box. Remove knockouts with a nailset and a hammer.

LB fitting   A right-angle connector used to bring cable through an exterior wall and into a home.

Local building codes   Regulations set at the community level to set minimum standards for all phases of construction. All projects must conform to local codes, which vary from community to community.

Local lighting   Lighting focussed on a specific area to illuminate work done there.

Locking switch   Switch that must be unlocked before it can be turned on.

Locknut   Metal nut used to secure a metal piece such as a switch in position.

Lumen   Amount of illumination given off by a light.

Luminous ceiling   Set of fluorescent tubes installed above translucent panels to provide ample overall light for most tasks.

Malibu light   Low voltage lights designed to light a swimming pool surround.

Manual time-delay switch   Time-delay switch in which the delay period is individually set, in some cases for as long as an hour.

Masonry anchors   Expandable shields used to secure screws in masonry walls.

Mounting slots   Allow you to adjust the position of a switch or receptacle so it is straight in relation to a wall.

Mounting strap   Metal structure built into a switch or receptacle. The strap has slots at the top and the bottom. Screws pass through the slots to attach the switch or receptacle to the junction box. Also specially installed metal strip designed to fit over a ceiling junction box to help support a ceiling fixture.

NM cable   Cable for use only in dry locations.

NMC cable   Used in damp and in dry locations, but not in wet locations.

National Electrical Code   Body of regulations spelling out safe, functional electrical procedures. Local codes can add to but not detract from NEC regulations.

Needlenosed pliers   Pliers having long jaws that narrow down to very small ends. Used for shaping wires into hooks to attach to terminals.

Neutral bus bar   Common connection between the neutral wire coming from the electric company, the neutral and ground wires of the house wiring and the ground wire that protects the service box through a connection to a cold water pipe.

Neutral wire   One of the conductors in electrical cable. The neutral wire carries "dead," or return, current and is an essential part of your electrical system. Together with the hot wires of the system, the neutral wire completes the electrical circuit.

Offset bar hanger   Bar hanger especially designed for insertion in a plaster ceiling. The hanger is nailed to the bottom of ceiling joists.

Ohm, omage   See Resistance.

Overload   Too great a demand for power made upon a circuit. This stems from the number of lights and appliances operated on the circuit. Over-extending a circuit can lead to overloads. The result of the overload is heat, which if unchecked, can cause a fire.

Pilot light switch   A light on the switch indicates when the light or outlet being controlled is on.

Plaster and lath   Wall covering of plaster installed over a "webbing" of wood strips or metal lath.

Plaster ears   Adjustable ears that are

part of a receptacle's mounting strap. The ears enable you to recess the box to allow for a flush finished installation.

Plate holes Access holes cut in the wall and the ceiling by the top plate, the 2x4 that is at the top of the studs.

Plug fuse A device containing a small wire that melts or disintegrates due to an overheated circuit. The overheating can be caused by an overload or a short circuit.

Plumb-and-chalkline Device for marking straight lines perpendicular to ceiling and floor.

Polarized plugs Plug having one prong that is larger than the other. This safety feature enhances the protection from shock.

Polarized receptacle Outlet having prong openings that accepts polarized plugs.

Programmable thermostat Thermostat that maintains a home's temperature between preset high and low temperatures.

Quiet switches Most common type of household switch. A quiet switch is quieter than older switches, but it still makes noise.

Rabbet Groove cut into a board. A frame or diffuser slides into the rabbet.

Raceway Surface wiring that adds outlets, switches and fixtures without necessitating extensive structural work.

Rapid-start fluorescent Lamp in which the starter and ballast are all in the same structure.

Recoded wire White wire to which has been attached black tape or paint. The recoding indicates that the wire now carries power.

Rectifier Device designed to protect relays in a low-voltage remote control system.

Red wire In a cable, the wire designed to be a "hot" wire.

Reflector An incandescent bulb coated on the inside to direct light in a given direction. It comes in two styles, spot and flood.

Relay Electronically powered switch that turns lights and outlets off and on in a remote-control low voltage system.

Resistance Measured in ohms, this is an indication of how much a conductor impedes the flow of electrical current, or electrical flow. The degree of a conductor's resistance depends upon its length, its diameter and its makeup. Increased resistance slows electrical flow; decreased resistance speeds electrical flow.

Rocker arm switch Switch operated by a rocker arm rather than a toggle.

Romex Plastic-sheathed cable containing at least two conductors.

Roof cap Finishing piece for a run of ductwork.

Rotary dimmer switch A rotary dimmer switch provides a range of light intensity.

Service box Metal box holding the fuses, circuit breakers, neutral bus bar and other major elements of the house wiring system.

Service entrance The point at which electricity provided by your local utility enters your house wiring system.

Service panel See Service box.

Setscrew Screw used to hold a wire in position.

Short circuit A short circuit occurs when a bare wire touches another bare wire carrying electricity or touches the metal case of an appliance. The rate of electrical flow increases very rapidly.

Side brackets Extra supports installed on either side of a junction box in gypsum wallboard.

Side-wired receptacles Most common style receptacle. Four terminal screws are mounted on the receptacle. On one side are two brass-colored ones; on the other side are two silver-colored screws.

Side-wired switch Switch with terminal screws on the sides of the housing.

Silent switch Switch in which the toggle shifts a mercury bulb to create the circuit. This switch makes no noise.

Sill plate The 2x4 that is nailed across the bottom of the wall studs.

Single conductor wire Wire purchased individually rather than in cable. Single conductor wire is used to create jumper wires.

Single-pole switch Switch having only two terminals. This switch is the only control governing an outlet or fixture.

Snap switch Older type of switch that has a strong spring and knife-blade contacts. This switch is quite loud.

Soffit Underside of the overhang above cabinets.

Solid wire A single wire usually encased in insulation. Most house wiring is of solid wire.

Spacer plate Special plate designed to increase the depth of a junction box to make room for wires and splices. Used for installation of such devices as raceway and GFI's.

Spackling compound Dry powder which, when mixed with water, is used to repair holes in plaster and drywall constructions.

Standard fuse Screw-in plug that has a base shaped like a light bulb's.

Standard plug Plug on which the line cord is attached to screw terminals.

Stranded wire A single wire made up of many smaller strands of wire. Mainly found in lamp and appliance cord.

Stud locator Magnetic instrument used to locate studs and joists. As the locator passes over the nails of a framing member, the needle indicator tells its position.

Starter A switch in a fluorescent light. The starter closes the circuit only when the amount of power required to light the light is present.

Surround lighting Exterior lighting installed around a pool to add safety for nighttime swimming.

Switch Device that creates or interrupts a circuit to a lighting fixture, appliance or outlet.

Switch loop Installation in which a ceiling fixture is installed between a power source and a switch. The power bypasses through the fixture junction box to the switch. The switch then sends power to the fixture itself.

TW wire Type of wire most often used in home circuits, raceway and exterior conduit.

Template Cardboard pattern used for drawing in the position of a junction box.

Terminals Points where wires are attached to a fixture, switch or receptacle. These are either screws or slots.

Threaded nipple Threaded metal cylinder that attaches to a threaded stud by means of a reducing nut.

Threaded stud Threaded metal cylinder that screws into a mounting strap to anchor a ceiling fixture.

Three-way switch Switch having three terminal screws. Two three-way switches govern a given outlet or fixture. The toggle is unmarked.

Time-clock switch Switch combined with a clock. A time-clock switch turns lights on and off at pre-set times.

Time-delay fuse Fuse designed to allow for a momentary power surge as an appliance such as an air conditioner cycles on or off. If the surge lasts too long, the thick solder plug of a time-delay switch melts through to open the circuit and protect the house wiring.

Time-delay switch Switch that remains on for a period of time after it has been switched off.

Timer switch See Time-clock switch.

Track lighting Set of lights installed in a metal groove attached to a ceiling or soffit.

Transformer Device designed to step down the voltage in a circuit from the normal 120 volts to a lower level. Low voltage exterior lights require only 12 volts; a remote control relay system requires 24 volts.

Traveler terminal Transfers electricity from one three-way switch to another.

Two-part clamp Device for holding cable in a round-knockout in a junction box. The larger part slips over the cable; it is then slid into the box. The second piece is a locknut that secures the cable from inside the box.

Type S fuse A fuse having two parts, the fuse body and a screw-in adapter that remains in the service box. Threading on the adapter and the fuse body vary by amperage; thus you can only install the correct size fuse in a given adapter.

UF cable Used in wet, outdoor locations.

Underwriter's knot Special knot designed for holding wires in position on a plug or a lamp. The knot is sturdy and slip-free.

Underwriters' Laboratories Independent non-profit organization that acts as a watchdog over electrical equipment. The UL label is granted only to equipment that meets preset, minimum standards.

Valance A single board attached to a wall, a cabinet or a ceiling to direct light in a given direction.

Volt, voltage Unit of measurement expressing the amount of pressure (electromotive force) that starts electric current moving and keeps it moving. One volt equals the amount of pressure required to move one ampere through a wire that possesses a resistance of one ohm. Volts, when multiplied by amps will give you the wattage available in a circuit (VxA=W).

Voltage tester Device used to test whether the power is off at a receptacle, switch or fixture. The tester has two probes connected to a light. The probes touch two wires, terminals or plug openings. If the bulb lights, power is present.

Wallboard anchors Expandable shields used to secure screws in wallboard.

Wall cap Finishing piece for a run of ductwork.

Wattage rating Listing of the power requirements of a given appliance or light.

Watts, wattage The amount of power that is available in a circuit, or the amount of power a given fixture or appliance requires to work. To find the number of watts, multiply volts times amps (W=VxA).

Wet location Area in which cable is liable to be saturated with water. The location is usually outdoors, beneath the ground.

Wet niche Waterproof housing that is sealed so that the light can be changed underwater.

White wire Wire designed to function as a neutral wire.

Wire A single strand or several strands of conductive material encased in protective insulation.

Wire cutter A device for cutting a blunt edge on a wire or cable.

Wire nut A cover over a wire splice. The nut is made of plastic. The inside is threaded metal.

Wire stripper Device designed to remove the insulation from a wire without damaging the wire itself.

Zip cord Line cord designed with a thin section between the insulating coverings of the wires. The cord easily splits down the middle.

Metric Conversions

LUMBER

Sizes: Metric cross-sections are so close to their nearest Imperial sizes, as noted below, that for most purposes they may be considered equivalents.

Lengths: Metric lengths are based on a 300mm module which is slightly shorter in length than an Imperial foot. It will therefore be important to check your requirements accurately to the nearest inch and consult the table below to find the metric length required.

Areas: The metric area is a square metre. Use the following conversion factors when converting from Imperial data: 100 sq. feet = 9.290 sq. metres.

METRIC SIZES SHOWN BESIDE NEAREST IMPERIAL EQUIVALENT

mm	Inches	mm	Inches
16 x 75	⅝ x 3	44 x 150	1¾ x 6
16 x 100	⅝ x 4	44 x 175	1¾ x 7
16 x 125	⅝ x 5	44 x 200	1¾ x 8
16 x 150	⅝ x 6	44 x 225	1¾ x 9
19 x 75	¾ x 3	44 x 250	1¾ x 10
19 x 100	¾ x 4	44 x 300	1¾ x 12
19 x 125	¾ x 5	50 x 75	2 x 3
19 x 150	¾ x 6	50 x 100	2 x 4
22 x 75	⅞ x 3	50 x 125	2 x 5
22 x 100	⅞ x 4	50 x 150	2 x 6
22 x 125	⅞ x 5	50 x 175	2 x 7
22 x 150	⅞ x 6	50 x 200	2 x 8
25 x 75	1 x 3	50 x 225	2 x 9
25 x 100	1 x 4	50 x 250	2 x 10
25 x 125	1 x 5	50 x 300	2 x 12
25 x 150	1 x 6	63 x 100	2½ x 4
25 x 175	1 x 7	63 x 125	2½ x 5
25 x 200	1 x 8	63 x 150	2½ x 6
25 x 225	1 x 9	63 x 175	2½ x 7
25 x 250	1 x 10	63 x 200	2½ x 8
25 x 300	1 x 12	63 x 225	2½ x 9
32 x 75	1¼ x 3	75 x 100	3 x 4
32 x 100	1¼ x 4	75 x 125	3 x 5
32 x 125	1¼ x 5	75 x 150	3 x 6
32 x 150	1¼ x 6	75 x 175	3 x 7
32 x 175	1¼ x 7	75 x 200	3 x 8
32 x 200	1¼ x 8	75 x 225	3 x 9
32 x 225	1¼ x 9	75 x 250	3 x 10
32 x 250	1¼ x 10	75 x 300	3 x 12
32 x 300	1¼ x 12	100 x 100	4 x 4
38 x 75	1½ x 3	100 x 150	4 x 6
38 x 100	1½ x 4	100 x 200	4 x 8
38 x 125	1½ x 5	100 x 250	4 x 10
38 x 150	1½ x 6	100 x 300	4 x 12
38 x 175	1½ x 7	150 x 150	6 x 6
38 x 200	1½ x 8	150 x 200	6 x 8
38 x 225	1½ x 9	150 x 300	6 x 12
44 x 75	1¾ x 3	200 x 200	8 x 8
44 x 100	1¾ x 4	250 x 250	10 x 10
44 x 125	1¾ x 5	300 x 300	12 x 12

METRIC LENGTHS

Lengths Metres	Equiv. Ft. & Inches
1.8m	5' 10⅞"
2.1m	6' 10⅝"
2.4m	7' 10½"
2.7m	8' 10¼"
3.0m	9' 10⅛"
3.3m	10' 9⅞"
3.6m	11' 9¾"
3.9m	12' 9½"
4.2m	13' 9⅜"
4.5m	14' 9⅓"
4.8m	15' 9"
5.1m	16' 8¾"
5.4m	17' 8⅝"
5.7m	18' 8⅜"
6.0m	19' 8¼"
6.3m	20' 8"
6.6m	21' 7⅞"
6.9m	22' 7⅝"
7.2m	23' 7½"
7.5m	24' 7¼"
7.8m	25' 7⅛"

All the dimensions are based on 1 inch = 25 mm.

NOMINAL SIZE (This is what you order.)	ACTUAL SIZE (This is what you get.)
Inches	Inches
1 x 1	¾ x ¾
1 x 2	¾ x 1½
1 x 3	¾ x 2½
1 x 4	¾ x 3½
1 x 6	¾ x 5½
1 x 8	¾ x 7¼
1 x 10	¾ x 9¼
1 x 12	¾ x 11¼
2 x 2	1¾ x 1¾
2 x 3	1½ x 2½
2 x 4	1½ x 3½
2 x 6	1½ x 5½
2 x 8	1½ x 7¼
2 x 10	1½ x 9¼
2 x 12	1½ x 11¼

PIPE FITTINGS

Only fittings for use with copper pipe are affected by metrication: metric compression fittings are interchangeable with Imperial in some sizes, but require adaptors in others.

INTERCHANGEABLE SIZES		SIZES REQUIRING ADAPTORS	
mm	Inches	mm	Inches
12	3/8	22	3/4
15	1/2	35	1 1/4
28	1	42	1 1/2
54	2		

Metric capillary (soldered) fittings are not directly interchangeable with imperial sizes but adaptors are available. Pipe fittings which use screwed threads to make the joint remain unchanged. The British Standard Pipe (BSP) thread form has now been accepted internationally and its dimensions will not physically change. These screwed fittings are commonly used for joining iron or steel pipes, for connections on taps, basin and bath waste outlets and on boilers, radiators, pumps etc. Fittings for use with lead pipe are joined by soldering and for this purpose the metric and inch sizes are interchangeable.

(Information courtesy Metrication Board, Millbank Tower, Millbank, London SW1P 4QU)

WOOD SCREWS

SCREW GAUGE NO.	NOMINAL DIAMETER		LENGTH	
	Inch	mm	Inch	mm
0	0.060	1.52	3/16	4.8
1	0.070	1.78	1/4	6.4
2	0.082	2.08	5/16	7.9
3	0.094	2.39	3/8	9.5
4	0.0108	2.74	7/16	11.1
5	0.122	3.10	1/2	12.7
6	0.136	3.45	5/8	15.9
7	0.150	3.81	3/4	19.1
8	0.164	4.17	7/8	22.2
9	0.178	4.52	1	25.4
10	0.192	4.88	1 1/4	31.8
12	0.220	5.59	1 1/2	38.1
14	0.248	6.30	1 3/4	44.5
16	0.276	7.01	2	50.8
18	0.304	7.72	2 1/4	57.2
20	0.332	8.43	2 1/2	63.5
24	0.388	9.86	2 3/4	69.9
28	0.444	11.28	3	76.2
32	0.5	12.7	3 1/4	82.6
			3 1/2	88.9
			4	101.6
			4 1/2	114.3
			5	127.0
			6	152.4

Dimensions taken from BS1210; metric conversions are approximate.

BRICKS AND BLOCKS

Bricks

Standard metric brick measures 215 mm x 65 mm x 112.5. Metric brick can be used with older, standard brick by increasing the mortaring in the joints. The sizes are substantially the same, the metric brick being slightly smaller (3.6 mm less in length, 1.8 mm in width, and 1.2 mm in depth).

Concrete Block

Standard sizes

390 x 90 mm
390 x 190 mm
440 x 190 mm
440 x 215 mm
440 x 290 mm

Repair block for replacement of block in old installations is available in these sizes:
448 x 219 (including mortar joints)
397 x 194 (including mortar joints)

Index

CONTRIBUTORS
ADDRESSES
PICTURE CREDITS

We wish to extend our thanks to the individuals, associations, and manufacturers who graciously provided information and photographs for this book. Specific credit for individual photos is given below, with the names and addresses of the contributors.

Allmilo Corporation c/o Haynes-Williams Inc. 261 Madison Avenue, New York, New York 10016   51 upper right, 91 right

American Hardboard Association Box 2245, Morris Township, New Jersey 07960   113

American Olean Tile 2583 Cannon Avenue, Lansdale, Pennsylvania 19446   94 lower

Broan Manufacturing Co., Inc. 926 State Street, Hartford, Wisconsin 53207   116

Craig Buchanan, photographer 490 2nd Street, Room 207, San Francisco, California 94107   115

Monte Burch Humansville, Missouri 65674   77 center left

California Redwood Association 1 Lombard Street, San Francisco, California 94111   86 upper right, 87

Jane Cary 16 E. 61st Street, New York, New York 10028   114

General Electric, Lamp Division, Appliance Park, Louisville, Kentucky 40225   100, 101, 102, 109

General Electric, Wiring Device Department 95 Hathaway Street, Providence, Rhode Island 02940   122, 124, 125

Leviton Manufacturing Co., Inc. 59-25 Little Neck Parkway, Little Neck, New York 11352   103

Richard P. Nunn, Media Marks Productions Falls Church Inn, 6633 Arlington Boulevard, Falls Church, Virginia 22045   64 lower right, 66 center and lower right, 69 left, 79 center and right

David Ulrich and Neal DeLeo, Ulrich, Inc. 100 Chestnut Street, Ridgewood, New Jersey 07450   82 upper, 83 lower left and right, 84 lower, 85, 86 center, 87 center

U.S. School of Professional Paperhangers 16 Chaplin, Rutland, Vermont 05701   84 upper

Western Wood Products Association Yeon Building, Portland, Oregon 97204   83 upper left

Tom Yee 30 West 26th St., New York, New York 10010   86 upper left

Extracts from 1981 National Electrical Code

Reprinted by permission from NFPA 70-1981, National Electrical Code, copyright© National Fire Protection Association, Quincy, MA 92269. This reprinted material is not the complete and official position of the NFPA on the referenced subject which is represented only by the standard in its entirety.

National Electrical Code® and NEC® are registered trademarks of the National Fire Protection Association, Inc., Quincy, Massachusetts, for a triennial electrical publication. The terms, *National Electrical Code or NEC*, as used herein mean the triennial publication constituting the *National Electrical Code* and are used with permission of the National Fire Protection Association, Inc.

ARTICLE 200—USE AND IDENTIFICATION OF GROUNDED CONDUCTORS

200-1. Scope. This article provides requirements for: (1) identification of terminals; (2) grounded conductors in premises wiring systems; and (3) identification of grounded conductors.

See Article 100 for definitions of "Grounded Conductor" and "Grounding Conductor."

200-2. General. All premises wiring systems shall have a grounded conductor that is identified in accordance with Section 200-6.

Exception: Circuits and systems exempted or prohibited by Sections 210-10, 215-7, 250-3, 250-5, 250-7, 503-13, and 517-104.

The grounded conductor, when insulated, shall have insulation: (1) which is suitable, other than color, for any ungrounded conductor of the same circuit on circuits of less than 1000 volts, or (2) rated not less than 600 volts for solidly grounded neutral systems of 1 kV and over as described in Section 250-152(a).

200-3. Connection to Grounded System. Premises wiring shall not be electrically connected to a supply system unless the latter contains, for any grounded conductor of the interior system, a corresponding conductor which is grounded.

For the purpose of this section, "electrically connected" shall mean connection capable of carrying current as distinguished from connection through electromagnetic induction.

200-6. Means of Identifying Grounded Conductors.
(a) Sizes No. 6 or Smaller. An insulated gounded conductor of No. 6 or smaller shall be identified by a continuous white or natural gray outer finish along its entire length.

Exception No. 1: The grounded conductor of a mineral-insulated, metal-sheathed cable shall be identified at the time of installation by distinctive marking at its terminations.

Exception No. 2: Where the conditions of maintenance and supervision assure that only qualified persons will service the installation, grounded conductors in multiconductor cables shall be permitted to be permanently identified at their terminations at the time of installation by a distinctive white marking or other equally effective means.

(b) Sizes Larger than No. 6. An insulated grounded conductor larger than No. 6 shall be identified either by a continuous white or natural gray outer finish along its entire length or at the time of installation by a distinctive white marking at its terminations.

Exception: Where the conditions of maintenance and supervision assure that only qualified persons will service the installation, grounded conductors in multiconductor cables shall be permitted to be permanently identified at their terminations at the time of installation by a distinctive white marking or other equally effective means.

(c) Flexible Cords. An insulated conductor intended for use as a grounded conductor, where contained within a flexible cord, shall be identified by a white or natural gray outer finish or by methods permitted by Section 400-22.

200-7. Use of White or Natural Gray Color. A continuous white or natural gray covering on a conductor or a termination marking of white or natural gray color shall be used only for the grounded conductor.

Exception No. 1: An insulated conductor with a white or natural gray finish shall be permitted as an ungrounded conductor where permanently reidentified to indicate its use, by painting or other effective means at its termination, and at each outlet where the conductor is visible and accessible.

Exception No. 2: A cable containing an insulated conductor with a white or natural gray outer finish shall be permitted for single-pole, 3-way, or 4-way switch loops where the white or natural gray conductor is used for the supply to the switch, but not as a return conductor from the switch to the switched outlet. In these applications, reidentification of the white or natural gray conductor shall not be required.

Exception No. 3: A flexible cord for connecting an appliance having one conductor identified with a white or natural gray outer finish, or by any other means permitted by Section 400-22, shall be permitted whether or not the outlet to which it is connected is supplied by a circuit having a grounded conductor.

Exception No. 4: A white or natural gray conductor of circuits of less than 50 volts shall be required to be grounded only as required by Section 250-5(a).

200-9. Means of Identification of Terminals.
The identification of terminals to which a grounded conductor is to be connected shall be substantially white in color. The identification of other terminals shall be of a readily distinguishable different color.

Exception: Where the conditions of maintenance and supervision assure that only qualified persons will service the installations, terminals for grounded conductors shall be permitted to be permanently identified at the time of installation by a distinctive white marking or other equally effective means.

200-10. Identification of Terminals.
(a) Device Terminals. All devices provided with terminals for the attachment of conductors and intended for connection to more than one side of the circuit shall have terminals properly marked for identification.

Exception No. 1: Where the electrical connection of a terminal intended to be connected to the grounded conductor is clearly evident.

Exception No. 2: Single-pole devices to which only one side of the line is connected.

Exception No. 3: The terminals of lighting and appliance branch-circuit panelboards.

Exception No. 4: Devices having a normal current rating of over 30 amperes other than polarized attachment plugs and polarized receptacles for attachment plugs as required in (b) below.

(b) Receptacles, Plugs, and Connectors. Receptacles, polarized attachment plugs and cord connectors for plugs and polarized plugs shall have the terminal intended for connection to the grounded (white) conductor identified.

Identification shall be by a metal or metal coating substantially white in color or the word "white" located adjacent to the identified terminal.

If the terminal is not visible, the conductor entrance hole for the connection shall be colored white or marked with the word "white."

The terminal for the connection of the equipment grounding conductor shall be identified by: (1) a green-colored, not readily removable terminal screw with a hexagonal head; (2) a green-colored, hexagonal, not readily removable terminal nut; or (3) a green-colored pressure wire connector. If the terminal for the grounding conductor is not visible, the conductor entrance hole shall be marked with the word "green" or otherwise identified by a distinctive green color.

Exception: Terminal identification shall not be required for 2-wire nonpolarized attachment plugs.

(c) Screw Shells. For devices with screw shells, the terminal for the grounded conductor shall be the one connected to the screw shell.

(d) Screw-Shell Devices with Leads. For screw-shell devices with attached leads, the conductor attached to the screw shell shall have a white or natural gray finish. The outer finish of the other conductor shall be of a solid color that will not be confused with the white or natural gray finish used to identify the grounded conductor.

(e) Appliances. Appliances that have a single-pole switch or a single-pole overcurrent device in the line or any line-connected screw-shell lampholders, and that are to be connected (1) by permanent wiring methods or (2) by field-installed attachment plugs and cords with three or more wires (including the equipment grounding conductor) shall have means to identify the terminal for the grounded circuit conductor (if any).

200-11. Polarity of Connections.
No grounded conductor shall be attached to any terminal or lead so as to reverse designated polarity.

ARTICLE 210—BRANCH CIRCUITS

A. General Provisions

210-1. Scope.
The provisions of this article apply to branch circuits supplying lighting or appliance loads or combinations of both. Where motors or motor-operated appliances are connected to any branch circuit that also supplies lighting or other appliance loads, the provisions of both this article and Article 430 shall apply. Article 430 applies where a branch circuit supplies motor loads only.

Exception: See Section 668-3(c), Exceptions No. 1 and No. 4 for electrolytic cells.

210-3. Classifications.
Branch circuits recognized by this article shall be classified in accordance with the maximum permitted ampere rating or setting of the overcurrent device. The classification for other than individual branch circuits shall be: 15, 20, 30, 40, and 50 amperes. Where conductors of higher ampacity are used for any reason, the ampere rating or setting of the specified overcurrent device shall determine the circuit classification.

210-4. Multiwire Branch Circuits.
Branch circuits recognized by this article shall be permitted as multiwire circuits. Multiwire branch circuits shall supply only line to neutral load.

Exception No. 1: A multiwire branch circuit that supplies only one utilization equipment.

Exception No. 2: Where all ungrounded conductors of the multiwire branch circuit are opened simultaneously by the branch-circuit overcurrent device.

All conductors shall originate from the same panelboard.

In dwelling units a multiwire branch circuit supplying more than one receptacle on the same yoke shall be provided with a means to disconnect simultaneously all ungrounded conductors at the panelboard where the branch circuit originated.

210-5. Color Code for Branch Circuits.
(a) Grounded Conductor. The grounded conductor of a branch circuit shall be identified by a continuous white or natural gray color. Where conductors of different systems are installed in the same raceway, box, auxiliary gutter, or other types of enclosures, one system neutral, if required, shall have an outer covering of white or natural gray. Each other system neutral, if required, shall have an outer covering of white with

an identifiable colored stripe (not green) running along the insulation or other and different means of identification.

Exception No. 1: The grounded conductors of mineral-insulated, metal-sheathed cable shall be identified by distinctive marking at the terminals during the process of installation.

Exception No. 2: As permitted in Exception No. 2 of Section 200-6(a) and the Exception to Section 200-6(b).

(b) Equipment Grounding Conductor. The equipment grounding conductor of a branch circuit shall be identified by a continuous green color or a continuous green color with one or more yellow stripes unless it is bare.

Exception No. 1: As permitted in Section 250-57(b), Exceptions No. 1 and 3 and Section 310-12(b), Exceptions No. 1 and 2.

Exception No. 2: The use of conductor insulation having a continuous green color or a continuous green color with one or more yellow stripes shall be permitted for internal wiring of equipment if such wiring does not serve as the lead wires for connection to branch-circuit conductors.

210-6. Maximum Voltage.

(a) Voltage to Ground. Branch circuits supplying lampholders, fixtures, or standard receptacles rated 15 amperes or less shall not exceed 150 volts to ground.

(c) Voltage Between Conductors.

(1) The voltage shall not exceed 150 volts between conductors on branch circuits supplying screw-shell lampholder(s), receptacle(s), or appliance(s) in dwelling unit(s) and guest rooms in hotels, motels, and similar occupancies.

Exception No. 1: Permanently connected appliances.

Exception No. 2: Cord- and plug-connected loads of more than 1380 watts or ¼ horsepower or greater rating.

See Article 100 for definition of Receptacle.

(2) The voltage shall not exceed 150 volts between conductors on branch circuits supplying one or more medium-base, screw-shell lampholders in occupancies other than those specified in (c) (1).

See Exception No. 1 to (a) above for 300-volt limitation for mogul-base, screw-shell lampholders under specific conditions in industrial establishments.

210-7. Receptacles and Cord Connectors.

(a) Grounding Type. Receptacles installed on 15- and 20-ampere branch circuits shall be of the grounding type. Grounding-type receptacles shall be installed only on circuits of the voltage class and current for which they are rated, except as provided in Tables 210-21(b) (2) and (b) (3).

Exception No. 1: Grounding-type receptacles of the type that reject nongrounding-type attachment plugs or which are of the locking type shall be permitted for specific purposes or in special locations. Receptacles required in Sections 517-10(a)(3) and 517-101(c) shall be considered as meeting the requirements of this section.

Exception No. 2: Nongrounding-type receptacles installed in accordance with Section 210-7(d). Exception.

(b) To Be Grounded. Receptacles and cord connectors having grounding contacts shall have those contacts effectively grounded.

Exception: Receptacles mounted on portable and vehicle-mounted generators in accordance with Section 250-6.

(c) Methods of Grounding. The grounding contacts of receptacles and cord connectors shall be grounded by connection to the equipment grounding conductor of the circuit supplying the receptacle or cord connector.

For installation requirements for the reduction of electrical noise, see Section 250-74, Exception No. 4.

The branch circuit or branch-circuit raceway shall include or provide a grounding conductor to which the grounding contacts of the receptacle or cord connector shall be connected.

Section 250-91(b) describes acceptable grounding means.

For extensions of existing branch circuits, see Section 250-50.

(d) Replacements. Grounding-type receptacles shall be used as replacements for existing nongrounding types and shall be connected to a grounding conductor installed in accordance with (c) above.

Exception: Where a grounding means does not exist in the receptacle enclosure a nongrounding type of receptacle shall be used.

(e) Cord-and Plug-Connected Equipment. The installation of grounding-type receptacles shall not be used as a requirement that all cord- and plug-connected equipment be of the grounded type.

See Section 250-45 for type of cord-and plug-connected equipment to be grounded.

(f) Noninterchangeable Types. Receptacles connected to circuits having different voltages, frequencies, or types of current (ac or dc) on the same premises shall be of such design that the attachment plugs used on these circuits are not interchangeable.

210-8. Ground-Fault Protection for Personnel.

(a) Dwelling Units. **(1)** All 125-volt, single-phase, 15- and 20-ampere receptacles installed in bathrooms shall have ground-fault circuit-interrupter protection for personnel.

(2) All 125-volt, single-phase, 15- or 20-ampere receptacles installed in garages shall have ground-fault circuit-interrupter protection for personnel.

Exception No. 1 to (a)(2): Receptacles which are not readily accessible.

Exception No. 2 to (a)(2): Receptacles for appliances occupying dedicated space which are cord- and plug-connected in accordance with Section 400-7(a)(6), (a)(7), or (a)(8).

Receptacles installed under Exceptions to Section 210-8(a)(2) shall not be considered as meeting the requirements of Section 210-52(f).

(3) All 125-volt, single-phase, 15- and 20-ampere receptacles installed outdoors where there is direct grade level access to the dwelling unit and to the receptacles shall have ground-fault circuit-interrupter protection for personnel.

Bathroom: A bathroom is an area including a basin with one or more of the following: a toilet, a tub, or a shower.

Such ground-fault circuit-interrupter protection may be provided for other circuits, locations, and occupancies, and, where used, will provide additional protection against line-to-ground shock hazard.

See Section 215-9 for feeder protection.

210-10. Ungrounded Conductors Tapped from Grounded Systems.

Two-wire dc circuits and ac circuits of two or more ungrounded conductors shall be permitted to be tapped from the ungrounded conductors of circuits having a grounded neutral conductor. Switching devices in each tapped circuit shall have a pole in each ungrounded conductor. All poles of multi-pole switching devices shall manually switch together where such switching devices also serve as a disconnecting means as required by Section 422-21(b) for an appliance; Section 424-20 for a fixed electric space heating unit; Section 426-21 for electric de-icing and snow-melting equipment; Section 430-85 for a motor controller; and Section 430-103 for a motor.

B. Branch-Circuit Ratings

210-19. Conductors—Minimum Ampacity and Size.

(a) General. Branch-circuit conductors shall have an ampacity of not less than the rating of the branch circuit and not less than the maximum load to be served. Cable assemblies with the neutral conductor smaller than the ungrounded conductors shall be so marked.

See Tables 310-16 through 310-19 for ampacity ratings of conductors.

See Part B of Article 430 for minimum rating of motor branch-circuit conductors.

Conductors for branch circuits as defined in Article 100, sized to prevent a voltage drop exceeding 3 percent at the farthest outlet of power, heating, and lighting loads, or combinations of such loads and where the maximum total voltage drop on both feeders and branch circuits to the farthest outlet does not exceed 5 percent, will provide reasonable efficiency of operation. See Section 215-2 for voltage drop on feeder conductors.

(b) Household Ranges and Cooking Appliances. Branch-circuit conductors supplying household ranges, wall-mounted ovens, counter-mounted cooking units, and other household cooking appliances shall have an ampacity not less than the rating of the branch circuit and not less than the maximum load to be served. For ranges of 8¾ kW or more rating, the minimum branch-circuit rating shall be 40 amperes.

Exception No. 1: The neutral conductor of a 3-wire branch circuit supplying a household electric range, a wall-mounted oven, or a counter-mounted cooking unit shall be permitted to be smaller than the ungrounded conductors where the maximum demand of a range of 8¾ kW or more rating has been computed according to Column A of Table 220-19, but shall have an ampacity of not less than 70 percent of the ampacity of the ungrounded conductors and shall not be smaller than No. 10.

Exception No. 2: Tap conductors supplying electric ranges, wall-mounted electric ovens, and counter-mounted electric cooking units from a 50-ampere branch circuit shall have an ampacity of not less than 20 and shall be sufficient for the load to be served. The taps shall be no longer than necessary for servicing the appliance.

(c) Other Loads. Branch-circuit conductors supplying loads other than cooking appliances as covered in (b) above and as listed in Section 210-2 shall have an ampacity sufficient for the loads served and shall not be smaller than No. 14.

Exception No. 1: Tap conductors for such loads shall have

an ampacity not less than 15 for circuits rated less than 40 amperes and not less than 20 for circuits rated at 40 or 50 amperes and only where these tap conductors supply any of the following loads:

a. Individual lampholders or fixtures with taps extending not longer than 18 inches (457 mm) beyond any portion of the lampholder or fixture.

b. A fixture having tap conductors as provided in Section 410-67.

c. Individual outlets with taps not over 18 inches (457 mm) long.

d. Infrared lamp industrial heating appliances.

e. Nonheating leads of de-icing and snow-melting cables and mats.

Exception No. 2: Fixture wires and cords as permitted in Section 240-4.

210-20. Overcurrent Protection.

(a) General. Branch-circuit conductors and equipment shall be protected by overcurrent protective devices having a rating or setting (1) not exceeding that specified in Section 240-3 for conductors; (2) not exceeding that specified in the applicable articles referenced in Section 240-2 for equipment; and (3) as provided for outlet devices in Section 210-21.

Exception: Tap conductors, fixture wire, and cords as permitted in Section 210-19(c) shall be considered as being protected by the circuit overcurrent device.

See Section 240-1 for the purpose of overcurrent protection and Sections 210-22 and 220-2 for continuous loads.

210-21. Outlet Devices.

Outlet devices shall have an ampere rating not less than the load to be served and shall comply with (a) and (b) below.

(a) Lampholders. Where connected to a branch circuit having a rating in excess of 20 amperes, lampholders shall be of the heavy-duty type. A heavy-duty lampholder shall have a rating of not less than 660 watts if of the admedium type and not less than 750 watts if of any other type.

(b) Receptacles.

(1) A single receptacle installed on an individual branch circuit shall have an ampere rating of not less than that of the branch circuit.

See definition of Receptacle in Article 100.

(2) Where connected to a branch circuit supplying two or more receptacles or outlets, a receptacle shall not supply a total cord- and plug-connected load in excess of the maximum specified in Table 210-21(b) (2).

(3) Where connected to a branch circuit supplying two or more receptacles or outlets, receptacle ratings shall conform to the values listed in Table 210-21(b) (3).

(4) It shall be acceptable to base the ampere rating of a range receptacle on a single range demand load specified in Table 220-19.

210-22. Maximum Loads.

The total load shall not exceed the rating of the branch circuit, and it shall not exceed the maximum loads specified in (a) through (c) below under the conditions specified therein.

(a) Motor-Operated and Combination Loads. Where a

circuit supplies only motor-operated loads, Article 430 shall apply. Where a circuit supplies only air-conditioning and/or refrigerating equipment, Article 440 shall apply. For circuits supplying loads consisting of motor-operated utilization equipment that is fastened in place and that has a motor larger than ⅛ horsepower in combination with other loads, the total computed load shall be based on 125 percent of the largest motor load plus the sum of the other loads.

Table 210-21(b) (2)
Maximum Cord- and Plug-Connected Load to Receptacle

Circuit Rating Amperes	Receptacle Rating Amperes	Maximum Load Amperes
15 or 20	15	12
20	20	16
30	30	24

Table 210-21(b)(3)
Receptacle Ratings for Various Size Circuits

Circuit Rating Amperes	Receptacle Rating Amperes
15	Not over 15
20	15 or 20
30	30
40	40 or 50
50	50

(b) Inductive Lighting Loads. For circuits supplying lighting units having ballasts, transformers, or autotransformers, the computed load shall be based on the total ampere ratings of such units and not on the total watts of the lamps.

(c) Other Loads. Continuous loads, such as store lighting and similar loads, shall not exceed 80 percent of the rating of the branch circuit.

Exception No. 1: Motor loads having demand factors computed in accordance with Article 430.

Exception No. 2: Circuits that have been derated in accordance with Note 8 to Tables 310-16 through 310-19.

Exception No. 3: Circuits supplied by an assembly together with its overcurrent devices that is listed for continuous operation at 100 percent of its rating.

It shall be acceptable to apply demand factors for range loads in accordance with Table 220-19, including Note 4.

210-23. Permissible Loads. In no case shall the load exceed the branch-circuit ampere rating. It shall be acceptable for an individual branch circuit to supply any load for which it is rated. A branch circuit supplying two or more outlets shall supply only the loads specified according to its size in (a) through (c) below and summarized in Section 210-24 and Table 210-24.

(a) 15- and 20-Ampere Branch Circuits. A 15- or 20-ampere branch circuit shall be permitted to supply lighting units, appliances, or a combination of both. The rating of any one cord- and plug-connected appliance shall not exceed 80 percent of the branch-circuit ampere rating. The total rating of appliances fastened in place shall not exceed 50 percent of the branch-circuit ampere rating where lighting units, cord- and plug-connected appliances not fastened in place, or both, are also supplied.

Exception: The small appliance branch circuits required in a dwelling unit(s) by Section 220-3(b) shall supply only the receptacle outlets specified in that section.

(b) 30-Ampere Branch Circuits. A 30-ampere branch circuit shall be permitted to supply fixed lighting units with heavy-duty lampholders in other than dwelling unit(s) or appliances in any occupancy. A rating of any one cord- and plug-connected appliance shall not exceed 80 percent of the branch-circuit ampere rating.

(c) 40- and 50-Ampere Branch circuits. A 40- or 50-ampere branch circuit shall be permitted to supply fixed lighting units with heavy-duty lampholders or infrared heating units in other than dwelling units or cooking appliances that are fastened in place in any occupancy.

210-24. Branch-Circuit Requirements—Summary. The requirements for circuits having two or more outlets, other than the receptacle circuits of Section 220-3(b) as specifically provided for above, are summarized in Table 210-24.

Table 210-24
Summary of Branch-Circuit Requirements
(Type FEP, FEPB, RUW, SA, T, TW, RH, RUH, RHW, RHH, THHN, THW, THWN, and XHHW conductors in raceway or cable.)

CIRCUIT RATING CONDUCTORS	15 Amp	20 Amp	30 Amp	40 Amp	50 Amp
(Min. Size)					
Circuits Wires*	14	12	10	8	6
Taps	14	14	14	12	12
Fixture Wires and Cords	Refer to Section 240-4				
OVERCURRENT PROTECTION	15 Amp	20 Amp	30 Amp	40 Amp	50 Amp
OUTLET DEVICES:					
Lampholders Permitted	Any Type	Any Type	Heavy Duty	Heavy Duty	Heavy Duty
Receptacle Rating**	15 Max. Amp	15 or 20 Amp	30 Amp	40 or 50 Amp	50 Amp
MAXIMUM LOAD	15 Amp	20 Amp	30 Amp	40 Amp	50 Amp
PERMISSIBLE LOAD	Refer to Section 210-23(a)	Refer to Section 210-23(a)	Refer to Section 210-23(b)	Refer to Section 210-23(c)	Refer to Section 210-23(c)

*These ampacities are for copper conductors where derating is not required. See Tables 310-16 through 310-19.

**For receptacle rating of cord-connected electric-discharge lighting fixtures, see Section 410-30(c).

C. Required Outlets

210-50. General. Receptacle outlets shall be installed as specified in Section 210-52 through 210-62.

(a) Cord Pendants. A cord connector that is supported by a permanently installed cord pendant shall be considered a receptacle outlet.

(b) Cord Connections. A receptacle outlet shall be installed wherever flexible cords with attachment plugs are used. Where flexible cords are permitted to be permanently connected, it shall be permitted to omit receptacles for such cords.

(c) Laundry Outlet. Appliance outlets installed in a dwelling unit for specific appliances, such as laundry equipment, shall be installed within 6 feet (1.83 m) of the intended location of the appliance.

210-52. Dwelling Unit Receptacle Outlets.

(a) General Provisions. In every kitchen, family room, dining room, dining room, living room, parlor, library, den, sun room, bedroom, recreation room, or similar rooms of dwelling units, receptacle outlets shall be installed so that no point along the floor line in any wall space is more than 6 feet (1.83 m), measured horizontally, from an outlet in that space, including any wall space 2 feet (610 mm) or more in width and the wall space occupied by sliding panels in exterior walls. The wall space afforded by fixed room dividers, such as free-standing bar-type counters, shall be included in the 6-foot (1.83-m) measurement.

As used in this section a "wall space" shall be considered a wall unbroken along the floor line by doorways, fireplaces, and similar openings. Each wall space 2 or more feet (610 mm or more) wide shall be treated individually and separately from other wall spaces within the room. A wall space shall be permitted to include two or more walls of a room (around corners) where unbroken at the floor line.

The purpose of this requirement is to minimize the use of cords across the doorways, fireplaces, and similar openings.

Receptacle outlets shall, insofar as practicable, be spaced equal distances apart. Receptacle outlets in floors shall not be counted as part of the required number of receptacle outlets unless located close to the wall.

The receptacle outlets required by this section shall be in addition to any receptacle that is part of any lighting fixture or appliance, located within cabinets or cupboards, or located over 5½ feet (1.68 m) above the floor.

Exception: Permanently installed electric baseboard heaters equipped with factory-installed receptacle outlets or outlets provided as a separate assembly by the manufacturer shall be permitted as the required outlet or outlets for the wall space utilized by such permanently installed heaters. Such receptacle outlets shall not be connected to the heater circuits.

(b) Counter Tops. In kitchen and dining areas of dwelling units a receptacle outlet shall be installed at each counter space wider than 12 inches (305 mm). Counter top spaces separated by range tops, refrigerators, or sinks shall be considered as separate counter top spaces. Receptacles rendered inaccessible by appliances fastened in place or appliances occupying dedicated space shall not be considered as these required outlets.

(c) Bathrooms. In dwelling units at least one wall receptacle outlet shall be installed in the bathroom adjacent to the basin location. See Section 210-8(a)(1).

(d) Outdoor Outlets. For one- and two-family dwellings at lease one receptacle outlet shall be installed outdoors. See Section 210-8(a)(3).

(e) Laundry Areas. In dwelling units at least one receptacle outlet shall be installed for the laundry.

(f) Basements and Garages. For a one-family dwelling at least one receptacle outlet in addition to any provided for laundry equipment shall be installed in each basement and in each attached garage. See Section 210-8(a)(2).

210-70. Lighting Outlets Required.
Lighting outlets shall be installed where specified in (a) and (b) below.

(a) Dwelling Unit(s). At least one wall switch-controlled lighting outlet shall be installed in every habitable room; in bathrooms, hallways, stairways, and attached garages; and at

outdoor entrances.

A vehicle door in an attached garage is not considered as an outdoor entrance.

At least one lighting outlet shall be installed in an attic, underfloor space, utility room and basement only where these spaces are used for storage or containing equipment requiring servicing.

Exception No. 1: In habitable rooms, other than kitchens, one or more receptacles controlled by a wall switch shall be permitted in lieu of lighting outlets.

Exception No. 2: In hallways, stairways, and at outdoor entrances remote, central, or automatic control of lighting shall be permitted.

ARTICLE 300—WIRING METHODS

300-4. Protection Against Physical Damage.
Where subject to physical damage, conductors shall be adequately protected.

(a) Cables Through Wood Framing Members.

(1) Bored Holes. In both exposed and concealed locations, where a cable or raceway-type wiring method is installed through bored holes in joists, rafters, or similar structural wood members, holes shall be bored at the approximate center of the face of the member. Holes in studs for cable-type wiring methods shall be bored so that the edge of the hole is not less than 1¼ inches (31.8 mm) from the nearest edge of the stud or shall be protected from nails and screws by either a steel plate or bushing at least 1/16 inch (1.59 mm) thick and of appropriate length and width installed to cover the area through which nails or screws might penetrate the installed cable.

(2) Notches in Wood. Where there is no objection because of weakening the building structure, in both exposed and concealed locations, cables shall be permitted to be laid in notches in wood studs, joists, rafters, or other wood members where the cable at those points is protected against nails or screws by a steel plate at least 1/16 inch (1.59 mm) thick installed before the building finish is applied.

(b) Cables Through Metal Framing Members. In both exposed and concealed locations where nonmetallic-sheathed cables pass through either factory or field punched, cut or drilled slots or holes in metal members, the cable shall be protected by bushings or grommets securely fastened in the opening. Where nails or screws are likely to penetrate the cable, a steel sleeve, steel plate or steel clip not less than 1/16 inch (1.59 mm) in wall thickness shall be used to protect the nonmetallic cable.

300-5. Underground Installations.

(a) Minimum Cover Requirements. Direct buried cable or conduit or other raceways shall be installed to meet the minimum cover requirements of Table 300-5.

Exception No. 1: The minimum cover requirements shall be permitted to be reduced by 6 inches (152 mm) for installations where a 2-inch (50.8-mm) thick concrete pad or equivalent in physical protection is placed in the trench over the underground installation.

Exception No. 2: The minimum cover requirements shall not apply to conduits or other raceways which are located under a building or exterior concrete slab not less than 4 inches (102 mm) in thickness and extending not less than 6 inches (152 mm) beyond the underground installation.

Exception No. 3: Areas subject to heavy vehicular traffic, such as thoroughfares, shall have a minimum cover of 24 inches (610 mm).

Table 300-5
Minimum Cover Requirements, 0 to 600 Volts, Nominal

(Cover is defined as the distance between the top surface of direct buried cable, conduit, or other raceways and the finished grade.)

Wiring Method	Minimum Burial (Inches)
Direct Buried Cables	24
Rigid Metal Conduit	6
Intermediate Metal Conduit	6
Rigid Nonmetallic Conduit	
Approved for Direct Burial without Concrete Encasement	18
Other Approved Raceways*	18

For SI units: one inch = 25.4 millimeters.

*Note: Raceways approved for burial only when concrete encased shall require a concrete envelope not less than 2 inches (50.8 mm) thick.

Exception No. 4: Residential branch circuits rated 300 volts or less and provided with overcurrent protection of not more than 30 amperes shall be permitted with a cover requirement of 12 inches (305 mm).

Exception No. 5: Lesser depths are permitted where cables and conductors rise for terminations or splices or where access is otherwise required.

Exception No. 6: In airport runways, including adjacent defined areas where trespass is prohibited, cable shall be permitted to be buried not less than 18 inches (457 mm) deep and without raceways, concrete encasement or equivalent.

Exception No. 7: Raceways installed in solid rock shall be permitted to be buried at a lesser depth when covered by 2 inches (50.8 mm) or more of concrete over the installation and extending down to the rock surface.

Exception No. 8: Circuits for the control of irrigation and landscape lighting systems which are limited to not more than 30 volts and are installed with Type UF or other approved cable shall be permitted with a minimum cover of 6 inches (152 mm).

(b) Grounding. Metallic shielding, sheath, or metallic conduit shall be effectively grounded at terminations and meet the requirements of Section 250-51.

(c) Underground Cables Under Buildings. Underground cable installed under a building shall be in a raceway that is extended beyond the outside walls of the building.

(d) Protection from Damage. Conductors emerging from the ground shall be protected by enclosures or raceways extending from below grade to a point 8 feet (2.44 m) above finished grade.

Conductors entering a building shall be protected to the point of entrance.

Where subject to physical damage, the conductors shall be installed in rigid metal conduit, intermediate metal conduit, Schedule 80 rigid nonmetallic conduit, or equivalent.

(e) Splices and Taps. Underground cables in trenches shall be permitted to be spliced or tapped without the use of splice boxes. The splices or taps shall be made by methods and with material identified for the purpose.

(f) Backfill. Backfill containing large rock, paving materials, cinders, large or sharply angular substance, or corrosive material shall not be placed in an excavation where materials may damage raceways, cables, or other substructures or prevent adequate compaction of fill or contribute to corrosion of raceways, cables or other substructures.

Where necessary to prevent physical damage to the raceway or cable, protection shall be provided in the form of granular or selected material, suitable running boards, suitable sleeves, or other approved means.

(g) Raceway Seals. Conduits or raceways through which moisture may contact energized live parts shall be sealed or plugged at either or both ends.

(h) Bushing. A bushing shall be used at the end of a conduit which terminates underground where cables leave the conduit as a direct burial wiring method. A seal incorporating the physical protection characteristics of a bushing shall be permitted to be used in lieu of a bushing.

(i) Single Conductors. All conductors of the same circuit including the grounding conductor where required shall be installed in the same raceway or shall be installed in close proximity in the same trench.

300-6. Protection Against Corrosion. Metal raceways, cable armor, boxes, cable sheathing, cabinets, elbows, couplings, fittings, supports, and support hardware shall be of materials suitable for the environment in which they are to be installed.

(a) General. Ferrous raceways, cable armor, boxes, cable sheathing, cabinets, metal elbows, couplings, fittings, supports, and support hardware shall be suitably protected against corrosion inside and outside (except threads at joints) by a coating of approved corrosion-resistant material such as zinc, cadmium, or enamel. Where protected from corrosion solely by enamel, they shall not be used out-of-doors or in wet locations as described in (c) below. When boxes or cabinets have an approved system of organic coatings and are marked "Raintight," "Rainproof" or "Outdoor Type," they shall be permitted out-of-doors.

(b) In Concrete or in Direct Contact with the Earth. Ferrous or nonferrous metal raceways, cable armor, boxes, cable sheathing, cabinets, elbows, couplings, fittings, supports, and support hardware shall be permitted to be installed in concrete or in direct contact with the earth, or in areas subject to severe corrosive influences when made of material judged suitable for the condition, or when provided with corrosion protection approved for the condition.

(c) Indoor Wet Locations. In portions of dairies, laundries, canneries, and other indoor wet locations, and in locations where walls are frequently washed or where there are surfaces of absorbent materials, such as damp paper or wood, the entire wiring system, including all boxes, fittings, conduits, and cable used therewith, shall be mounted so that there is at least ¼-inch (6.35-mm) air space between it and the wall or supporting surface.

In general, areas where acids and alkali chemicals are handled and stored may present such corrosive conditions, particularly when wet or damp. Severe corrosive conditions may also be present in portions of meat-packing plants, tanneries, glue houses, and some stables; installations immediately adjacent to a seashore and swimming pool areas; areas where chemical de-icers are used; and storage cellars or rooms for hides, casings, fertilizer, salt, and bulk chemicals.

300-10. Electrical Continuity of Metal Raceways and Enclosures. Metal raceways, cable armor, and other metal enclosures for conductors shall be metallically joined together into a continuous electric conductor, and shall be so connected to all boxes, fittings, and cabinets as to provide effective electrical continuity. Raceways and cable assemblies shall be mechanically secured to boxes, fittings, cabinets, and other enclosures, except as provided for nonmetallic boxes in Section 370-7(c).

300-11. Secured in Place. Raceways, cable assemblies, boxes, cabinets, and fittings shall be securely fastened in place, unless otherwise provided for specific purposes elsewhere in this Code.

See Article 318 for cable trays.

300-12. Mechanical Continuity—Raceways and Cables. Metal or nonmetallic raceways, cable armors, and cable sheaths shall be continuous between cabinets, boxes, fittings, or other enclosures or outlets.

300-13. Mechanical and Electrical Continuity—Conductors.

(a) General. Conductors shall be continuous between outlets, devices, etc., and there shall be no splice or tap within a raceway itself.

Exception No. 1: As provided in Section 374-8 for auxiliary gutters.

Exception No. 2: As provided in Section 362-6 for wireways.

Exception No. 3: As provided in Section 300-15(a), Exception No. 1 for boxes or fittings.

Exception No. 4: As provided in Section 352-7 for metal surface raceways.

(b) Device Removal. In multiwire circuits the continuity of a grounded conductor shall not be dependent upon device connections, such as lampholders, receptacles, etc., where the removal of such devices would interrupt the continuity.

300-14. Length of Free Conductors at Outlets and Switch Points. At least 6 inches (152 mm) of free conductor shall be left at each outlet and switch point for splices or the connection of fixtures or devices.

Exception: Conductors that are not spliced or terminated at the outlet or switch point.

300-15. Boxes or Fittings—Where Required.

(a) Box or Fitting. A box or fitting shall be installed at each conductor splice connection point, outlet, switch point, junction point, or pull point for the connection of conduit, electrical metallic tubing, surface raceway, or other raceways.

Exception No. 1: A box or fitting shall not be required for a conductor splice connection in surface raceways, wireways, header-ducts, multi-outlet assemblies, auxiliary gutters, cable trays, and conduit bodies having removable covers which are accessible after installation.

Exception No. 2: As permitted in Section 410-31 where a fixture is used as a raceway.

(b) Box Only. A box shall be installed at each conductor splice connection point, outlet, switch point, junction point, or pull point for the connection of Type AC cable, Type MC cable, mineral-insulated, metal-sheathed cable, nonmetallic-sheathed cable, or other cables, at the connection point between any such cable system and a raceway system and at each outlet and switch point for concealed knob-and-tube wiring.

Exception No. 1: As permitted by Section 336-11 for insulated outlet devices supplied by nonmetallic-sheathed cable.

Exception No. 2: As permitted by Section 410-62 for rosettes.

Exception No. 3: Where accessible fittings are used for straight-through splices in mineral-insulated, metal-sheathed cable.

Exception No. 4: Where cables enter or exit from conduit or tubing which is used to provide cable support or protection against physical damage.

Exception No. 5: A device having brackets that securely fasten the device to a structural member in walls or ceilings of conventional on-site frame construction for use with nonmetallic-sheathed cable shall be permitted without a separate box.

See Sections 336-5, Exception No. 2; 545-10; 550-8(j); and 551-14(e), Exception No. 1.

Exception No. 6: Where metallic manufactured wiring systems are used.

300-16. Raceway or Cable to Open or Concealed Wiring.

(a) Box or Fitting. A box or terminal fitting having a separately bushed hole for each conductor shall be used wherever a change is made from conduit, electrical metallic tubing, nonmetallic-sheathed cable, Type AC cable, Type MC cable, or mineral-insulated, metal-sheathed cable and surface raceway wiring to open wiring or to concealed knob-and-tube wiring. A fitting used for this purpose shall contain no taps or splices and shall not be used at fixture outlets.

(b) Bushing. A bushing shall be permitted in lieu of a box or terminal fitting at the end of a conduit or electrical metallic tubing where the raceway terminates behind an open (unenclosed) switchboard or at an unenclosed control and similar equipment. The bushing shall be of the insulating type for other than lead-sheathed conductors.

300-17. Number and Size of Conductors in Raceway. The number and size of conductors in any raceway shall not be more than will permit dissipation of the heat and ready installation or withdrawal of the conductors without damage to the conductors or to their insulation.

See the following sections of this Code: conduit, 345-7 and 346-6; electrical metallic tubing, 348-6; rigid nonmetallic conduit, 347-11; electrical nonmetallic tubing, 331-6; flexible metallic tubing, 349-12; flexible metal conduit, 350-3; liquidtight flexible metal conduit, 351-6; liquidtight nonmetallic flexible conduit, 351-25; surface raceways, 352-4 and 352-25; underfloor raceways, 354-5; cellular metal floor raceways, 356-5; cellular concrete floor raceways, 358-9; wireways, 362-5; auxiliary gutters, 374-5; fixture wire, 402-7; theaters, 520-5; signs,

600-21(d); elevators, 620-33; sound recording, 640-3 and 640-4; Class 1, Class 2, and Class 3 circuits, Article 725; and fire protective signaling circuits, Article 760.

300-18. Inserting Conductors in Raceways.

(a) Installation. Raceways shall first be installed as a complete raceway system without conductors.

Exception: Exposed raceways having a removable cover or capping.

(b) Pull Wires. Pull wires, if to be used, shall not be installed until the raceway system is in place.

(c) Lubricants. Cleaning agents or materials used as lubricants that have a deleterious effect on conductor coverings shall not be used.

300-19. Supporting Conductors in Vertical Raceways.

(a) Spacing Intervals—Maximum. Conductors in vertical raceways shall be supported. One cable support shall be provided at the top of the vertical raceway or as close to the top as practical, plus a support for each additional interval of spacing as specified in Table 300-19(a).

Exception No. 1: If the total vertical riser is less than 25 percent of the spacing specified in Table 300-19(a), no cable support shall be required.

Exception No. 2: Steel wire armor cable shall be supported at the top of the riser with a cable support that clamps the steel wire armor. A safety device shall be permitted at the lower end of the riser to hold the cable in the event there is slippage of the cable in the wire armored cable support. Additional wedge-type supports shall be permitted to relieve the strain on the equipment terminals caused by expansion of the cable under load.

Table 300-19(a). Spacings for Conductor Supports

Conductors		Aluminum or Copper-Clad Aluminum	Copper
No. 18	thru No. 8 .... Not greater than	100 feet	100 feet
No. 6	thru 0 .... Not greater than	200 feet	100 feet
No. 00	thru No. 0000 ...... Not greater than	180 feet	80 feet
211,601 CM thru 350,000 CM	. Not greater than	135 feet	60 feet
350,001 CM thru 500,000 CM	. Not greater than	120 feet	50 feet
500,001 CM thru 750,000 CM	. Not greater than	95 feet	40 feet
Above 750,000 CM	.... Not greater than	85 feet	35 feet

For SI units: one foot = 0.3048 meter.

(b) Support Methods. One of the following methods of support shall be used:

(1) By clamping devices constructed of or employing insulating wedges inserted in the ends of the conduits. Where clamping of insulation does not adequately support the cable, the conductor also shall be clamped.

(2) By inserting boxes at the required intervals in which insulating supports are installed and secured in a satisfactory manner to withstand the weight of the conductors attached thereto, the boxes being provided with covers.

(3) In junction boxes, by deflecting the cables not less than 90 degrees and carrying them horizontally to a distance not less than twice the diameter of the cable, the cables being carried on two or more insulating supports, and additionally secured thereto by tie wires if desired. When this method is used, cables shall be supported at intervals not greater than 20

percent of those mentioned in the preceding tabulation.

(4) By a method of equal effectiveness.

300-20. Induced Currents in Metal Enclosures or Metal Raceways.

(a) Conductors Grouped Together. Where conductors carrying alternating current are installed in metal enclosures or metal raceways, they shall be so arranged as to avoid heating the surrounding metal by induction. To accomplish this, all phase conductors and, where used, the neutral and all equipment grounding conductors shall be grouped together.

Exception No. 1: permitted in Section 250-50, Exception for equipment grounding connections.

Exception No. 2: As permitted in Section 427-47 for skin effect heating.

(b) Individual Conductors. When a single conductor of a circuit passes through metal with magnetic properties the inductive effect shall be minimized by: (1) cutting slots in the metal between the individual holes through which the individual conductors pass, or (2) passing all the conductors in the circuit through an insulating wall sufficiently large for all of the conductors of the circuit.

Exception: In the case of circuits supplying vacuum or electric-discharge lighting systems or signs, or X-ray apparatus, the currents carried by the conductors are so small that the inductive heating effect can be ignored where these conductors are placed in metal enclosures or pass through metal.

Because aluminum is not a magnetic metal, there will be no heating due to hysteresis; however, induced currents will be present. They will not be of sufficient magnitude to require grouping of conductors or special treatment in passing conductors through aluminum wall sections.

300-21. Spread of Fire or Products of Combustion. Electrical installations in hollow spaces, vertical shafts, and ventilation or air-handling ducts shall be so made that the possible spread of fire or products of combustion will not be substantially increased. Openings around electrical penetrations through fire resistance rated walls, partitions, floors, or ceilings shall be firestopped using approved methods.

300-22. Wiring in Ducts, Plenums, and Other Air-Handling Spaces. The provisions of this section apply to the installation and uses of electric wiring and equipment in ducts, plenums, and other air-handling spaces.

See Article 424, Part F for Electric Duct Heaters.

(a) Ducts for Dust, Loose Stock, or Vapor Removal. No wiring systems of any type shall be installed in ducts used to transport dust, loose stock, or flammable vapors. No wiring system of any type shall be installed in any duct, or shaft containing only such ducts, used for vapor removal or for ventilation of commercial-type cooking equipment.

(b) Ducts or Plenums Used for Environmental Air. Only wiring methods consisting of mineral-insulated, metal-sheathed cable, Type MC cable employing a smooth or corrugated impervious metal sheath without an overall nonmetallic covering, electrical metallic tubing, flexible metallic tubing, intermediate metal conduit, or rigid metal conduit shall be installed in ducts or plenums used for environmental air. Flexible metal conduit and liquidtight flexible metal conduit shall be permitted, in lengths not to exceed 4 feet (1.22 m), to connect physically adjustable equipment and devices permitted to be in these ducts and plenum chambers. The connectors used with flexible metal conduit shall effectively close any openings in the connection. Equipment and devices shall be permitted within such ducts or plenum chambers only if necessary for their direct action upon, or sensing of, the contained air. Where equipment or devices are installed and illumination is necessary to facilitate maintenance and repair, enclosed gasketed-type fixtures shall be permitted.

The above applies to ducts and plenums specifically fabricated to transport environmental air.

305-3. Grounding. All grounding shall conform with Article 250.

305-5. Guarding. For temporary wiring over 600 volts, nominal, suitable fencing, barriers, or other effective means shall be provided to prevent access of other than authorized and qualified personnel.

ARTICLE 310—CONDUCTORS FOR GENERAL WIRING

310-1. Scope. This article covers general requirements for conductors and their type designations, insulations, markings, mechanical strengths, ampacity ratings, and uses. These requirements do not apply to conductors that form an integral part of equipment, such as motors, motor controllers, and similar equipment, or to conductors specifically provided for elsewhere in this Code.

For flexible cords and cables, see Article 400. For fixture wires, see Article 402.

310-2. Conductors.

(a) **Insulated.** Conductors shall be insulated.

Exception: Where covered or bare conductors are specifically permitted elsewhere in this Code.

See Section 250-152 for insulation of neutral conductors of a solidly grounded high-voltage system.

(b) **Conductor Material.** Conductors in this article shall be of aluminum, copper-clad aluminum, or copper unless otherwise specified.

310-3. Stranded Conductors. Where installed in raceways, conductors of size No. 8 and larger shall be stranded.

Exception No. 1: When used as busbars or in mineral-insulated, metal-sheathed cable.

Exception No. 2: Bonding conductors as required in Sections 680-20(b)(1) and 680-22(b).

310-4. Conductors in Parallel. Aluminum, copper-clad aluminum, or copper conductors of size 1/0 and larger, comprising each phase or neutral, shall be permitted to be connected in parallel (electrically joined at both ends to form a single conductor) only if all of the following conditions are met: all of the parallel conductors shall be of the same length, of the same conductor material, same circular-mil area, same insulation type, and terminated in the same manner. Where run in sep-

arate raceways or cables, the raceways or cables shall have the same physical characteristics.

Exception No. 1: As permitted in Section 620-12(a)(1), Exception.

Exception No. 2:Conductors in sizes smaller than No. 1/0 AWG shall be permitted to be run in parallel to supply control power to indicating instruments, contactors, relays, solenoids, and similar control devices provided: (a) they are contained within the same raceway or cable; (b) the ampacity of each individual conductor is sufficient to carry the entire load current shared by the parallel conductors; and (c) the overcurrent protection is such that the ampacity of each individual conductor will not be exceeded if one or more of the parallel conductors become inadvertently disconnected.

When metallic equipment grounding conductors are used with conductors in parallel, they shall comply with the requirements of this section except that they shall be sized as per Section 250-95.

When conductors are used in parallel, space in enclosures shall be given consideration (see Articles 370 and 373).

Conductors installed in parallel shall be subject to ampacity reduction factors as required in Note 8 to Tables 310-16 through 310-19.

310-5. Minimum Size of Conductors. The minimum size of conductors shall be as given in Table 310-5.

Exception No. 1: For flexible cords as permitted by Section 400-12.

Exception No. 2: For fixture wire as permitted by Section 410-24.

Exception No. 3: For fractional horsepower motors as permitted by Section 430-22.

Exception No. 4: For cranes and hoists as permitted by Section 610-14.

Exception No. 5: For elevator control and signaling circuits as permitted by Section 620-12.

Exception No. 6: For Class 1, Class 2, and Class 3 circuits as permitted by Sections 725-16, 725-37, and 725-40.

Exception No. 7: For fire protective signaling circuits as permitted by Sections 760-16, 760-27, and 760-30.

Exception No. 8: For 2001-5000 volt for Types AVA, AVB, and AVL cables, the minimum conductor size is No. 14 AWG copper or No. 12 AWG aluminum or copper-clad aluminum.

Exception No. 9: For Type V cables, the minimum conductor sizes are: No. 12 AWG for 2000-volt rating, No. 10 AWG for 3000-volt rating, and No. 8 AWG for 4000-volt rating.

Exception No. 10: For motor control circuits as permitted by Section 430-72.

Table 310-5

Voltage Rating of Conductor—Volts	Minimum Conductor Size—AWG
Up to 2000	14 Copper 12 Aluminum or Copper-Clad Aluminum
2001 to 5000	8
5001 to 8000	6
8001 to 15000	2 100% Insulation Level* 1 133%Insulation Level*
15001 to 28000	1
28001 to 35000	1/0

*See Table 310-34, Definitions.

310-8. Wet Locations.

(a) Insulated Conductors. Insulated conductors used in wet locations shall be (1) lead-covered; (2) Types RHW, RUW, TW, THW, THWN, XHHW; or (3) of a type listed for use in wet locations.

(b) Cables. Cables of one or more conductors used in wet locations shall be of a type listed for use in wet locations.

Conductors used for direct burial applications shall be of a type listed for such use.

310-9. Corrosive Conditions. Conductors exposed to oils, greases, vapors, gases, fumes, liquids, or other substances having a deleterious effect upon the conductor or insulation shall be of a type suitable for the application.

310-10. Temperature Limitation of Conductors. No conductor shall be used in such a manner that its operating temperature will exceed that designated for the type of insulated conductor involved. In no case shall conductors be associated together in such a way with respect to type of circuit, the wiring method employed, or the number of conductors that the limiting temperature of any conductor is exceeded.

The temperature rating of a conductor (see Tables 310-13 and 310-31) is the maximum temperature, at any location along its length, that the conductor can withstand over a prolonged time period without serious degradation. Tables 310-16 through 310-19 and 310-39 through 310-54, the correction factors at the bottom of these tables, and the notes to the tables provide guidance for coordinating conductor sizes, types, allowable load currents, ambient temperatures, and number of associated conductors.

The principal determinants of operating temperature are:

1. Ambient temperature. Ambient temperature may vary along the conductor length as well as from time to time.

2. Heat generated internally in the conductor as the result of load current flow.

3. The rate at which generated heat dissipates into the ambient medium. Thermal insulation which covers or surrounds conductors will affect the rate of heat dissipation.

4. Adjacent load-carrying conductors. Adjacent conductors have the dual effect of raising the ambient temperature and impeding heat dissipation.

310-11. Marking.

(a) Required Information. All conductors and cables shall be marked to indicate the following information, using the applicable method described in (b) below.

(1) The maximum rated voltage for which the conductor was listed.

(2) The proper type letter or letters for the type of wire or cable as specified elsewhere in this article, in Tables 310-13 and 310-31, and in Articles 336, 337, 338, 339, 340, and Section 725-40(b)(3).

(3) The manufacturer's name, trademark, or other distinctive marking by which the organization responsible for the product can be readily identified.

(4) The AWG size or circular-mil area.

(b) Method of Marking.

(1) Surface Marking. The following conductors and cables shall be durably marked on the surface at intervals not exceeding 24 inches (610 mm):

(a) Single- and multiconductor rubber- and thermoplastic- insulated wire and cable.

(b) Nonmetallic-sheathed cable.

(c) Service-entrance cable.

(d) Underground feeder and branch-circuit cable.

(e) Tray cable.

(f) Irrigation cable.

(g) Power-limited tray cable

(2) Marker Tape. Metal-covered multiconductor cables shall employ a marker tape located within the cable and running for its complete length.

Exception No. 1: Mineral-insulated, metal-sheathed cable.

Exception No. 2: Type AC cable.

Exception No. 3: the information required in Section 310-11(a)(1), (2), and (4) above shall be permitted to be durably marked on the outer nonmetallic covering of Type MC or Type PLTC cables at intervals not exceeding 24 inches (610 mm).

Exception No. 4: The information required in Section 310-11(a) shall be permitted to be durably marked on a nonmetallic covering under the metallic sheath of Type PLTC cable at intervals not exceeding 24 inches (610 mm).

Included in the group of metal-covered cables are: Type AC cable (Article 333), Type MC cable (Article 334) and lead-sheathed cable.

(3) Tag Marking. The following conductors and cables shall be marked by means of a printed tag attached to the coil, reel, or carton:

(a) Mineral-insulated, metal-sheathed cable.

(b) Switchboard wires.

(c) Metal-covered, single-conductor cables.

(d) Conductors having outer surface of asbestos.

(e) Type AC cable.

(4) Optional Marking of Wire Size. For the following multiconductor cables, the information required in (a) (4) above shall be permitted to be marked on the surface of the individual insulated conductors:

(a) Type MC cable.

(b) Tray cable.

(c) Irrigation cable.

(d) Power-limited tray cable.

(c) Suffixes to Designate Number of Conductors. A type letter or letters used alone shall indicate a single insulated conductor. The following letter suffixes shall indicate the following:

D—for two insulated conductors laid parallel within an outer nonmetallic covering.

M—for an assembly of two or more insulated conductors twisted spirally within an outer nonmetallic covering.

310-12. Conductor identification.

(a) Grounded conductors. Insulated conductors of No. 6 or smaller, intended for use as grounded conductors of circuits, shall have an outer identification of a white or natural gray color. Multiconductor flat cable No. 4 or larger shall be permitted to employ an external ridge on the grounded conductor.

Exception No. 1: Multiconductor varnished-cloth-insulated cables.

Exception No. 2: Fixture wires as outlined in Article 402.

Exception No. 3: Mineral-insulated, metal-sheathed cable.

Exception No. 4: A conductor identified as required by Section 210-5(a) for branch circuits.

Exception No. 5: Where the conditions of maintenance and supervision assure that only qualified persons will service the installation, grounded conductors in multiconductor cables shall be permitted to be permanently identified at their terminations at the time of installation by a distinctive white marking or other equally effective means.

For aerial cable the identification shall be as above, or by means of a ridge so located on the exterior of the cable as to identify it.

Wires having their outer covering finished to show a white or natural gray color by having colored trace threads in the braid, identifying the source of manufacture, shall be considered as meeting the provision of this section.

For identification requirements for conductors larger than No. 6, see Section 200-6.

(b) Equipment Grounding conductors. Bare, covered or insulated grounding conductors shall be permitted. Individually covered or insulated grounding conductors shall have a continuous outer finish that is either green, or green with one or more yellow stripes.

Exception No. 1: An insulated conductor larger than No. 6 shall, at the time of installation, be permitted to be permanently identified as a grounding conductor at each end and at every point where the conductor is accessible. Identification shall be accomplished by one of the following means.

a. Stripping the insulation from the entire exposed length;

b. Coloring the exposed insulation green; or

c. Marking the exposed insulation with green colored tape or green colored adhesive labels.

Exception No. 2: Where the conditions of maintenance and supervision assure that only qualified persons will service the installation, an insulated conductor in a multiconductor cable shall, at the time of installation, be permitted to be permanently identified as a grounding conductor at each end and at every point where the conductor is accessible by one of the following means:

a. Stripping the insulation from the entire exposed length;

b. Coloring the exposed insulation green; or

c. Marking the exposed insulation with green tape or green colored adhesive labels.

(c) Ungrounded Conductors. Conductors which are intended for use as ungrounded conductors, whether used as single conductors or in multiconductor cables, shall be finished to be clearly distinguishable from grounded and grounding conductors. Ungrounded conductors shall be distinguished by colors other than white, natural gray, or green; or by a combination of color plus distinguished marking. Distinguishing markings shall also be in a color other than white, natural gray, or green and shall consist of a stripe or stripes or a regularly spaced series of identical marks. Distinguishing markings shall not conflict in any manner with the surface markings required by Section 310-11(b)(1).

310-13. Conductor Constructions and Applications. Insulated conductors shall comply with the applicable provisions of one or more of the following: Tables 310-13, 310-31, 310-32, 310-33, 310-34, 310-35, 310-36, and 310-37.

These conductors shall be permitted for use in any of the wiring methods recognized in Chapter 3 and as specified in their respective tables.

Thermoplastic insulation may stiffen at temperatures colder than minus 10°C (plus 14°F), requiring care be exercised during installation at such temperatures. Thermoplastic insulation may also be deformed at normal temperatures where subjected to pressure, requiring care be exercised during installation and at points of support.

310-14. Aluminum Conductor Material. Solid aluminum conductors No. 8, 10, and 12 AWG shall be made of an aluminum alloy conductor material.

310-15. Ampacity.

(a) Applications covered by Tables. Ampacities for conductors rated 0-2000 volts shall be a specified in Tables 310-16 through 310-19 and their accompanying notes. The ampacity for Types V, AVA, AVB, and AVL conductors rated 2001-5000 volts shall be the same as for those conductor types rated 0-2000 volts. The ampacities for solid dielectric insulated conductors rated 2001 to 35000 volts shall be as specified in Tables 310-39 through 310-54 and their accompanying notes.

ARTICLE 410—LIGHTING FIXTURES, LAMPHOLDERS, LAMPS, RECEPTACLES, AND ROSETTES

A. General

410-1. Scope. This article covers lighting fixtures, lampholders, pendants, receptacles, and rosettes, incandescent filament lamps, arc lamps, electric-discharge lamps, the wiring and equipment forming part of such lamps, fixtures and lighting installations which shall conform to the provisions of this article.

Exception: As otherwise provided in this Code.

410-2. Application to Other Articles. Equipment for use in hazardous (classified) locations shall conform to Articles 500 through 517.

410-3. Live Parts. Fixtures, lampholders, lamps, rosettes, and receptacles shall have no live parts normally exposed to contact. Exposed accessible terminals in lampholders, receptacles, and switches shall not be installed in metal fixture canopies or in open bases of portable table or floor lamps.

Exception: Cleat-type lampholders, receptacles, and rosettes located at least 8 feet (2.44 m) above the floor shall be permitted to have exposed contacts.

B. Fixture Locations

410-4. Fixtures in Specific Locations.

(a) Wet and Damp Locations. Fixtures installed in wet or damp locations shall be so constructed or installed that water cannot enter or accumulate in wireways, lampholders, or other electrical parts. All fixtures installed in wet locations shall be marked, "Suitable for Wet Locations." All fixtures installed in damp locations shall be marked, "Suitable for Wet Locations" or "Suitable for Damp Locations."

Installations underground or in concrete slabs or masonry in direct contact with the earth, and locations subject to saturation with water or other liquids, such as locations exposed to weather and unprotected, vehicle washing areas, and like locations, shall be considered to be wet locations with respect to the above requirement.

Interior locations protected from weather but subject to moderate degrees of moisture, such as some basements, some barns, some cold-storage warehouses and the like, the partially protected locations under canopies, marquees, roofed open porches, and the like, shall be considered to be damp locations with respect to the above requirements.

See Article 680 for lighting fixtures in swimming pools, fountains, and similar installations.

(b) Corrosive Locations. Fixtures installed in corrosive locations shall be of a type approved for such locations.

See Section 210-7 for receptacles in fixtures.

410-5. Fixtures Near Combustible Material.
Fixtures shall be so constructed, or installed, or equipped with shades or guards that combustible material will not be subjected to temperatures in excess of 90°C (194°F).

410-6. Fixtures Over Combustible Material.
Lampholders installed over highly combustible material shall be of the unswitched type. Unless an individual switch is provided for each fixture, lampholders shall be located at least 8 feet (2.44 m) above the floor, or shall be so located or guarded that the lamps cannot be readily removed or damaged.

410-7. Fixtures in Show Windows.
Externally wired fixtures shall not be used in a show window.

Exception: Fixtures of the chain-supported type may be externally wired.

410-8. Fixtures in Clothes Closets.
(a) Location. A fixture in a clothes closet shall be permitted to be installed:

(1) On the wall above the closet door, provided the clearance between the fixture and a storage area where combustible material may be stored within the closet is not less than 18 inches (457 mm), or

(2) On the ceiling over an area which is unobstructed to the floor, maintaining an 18-inch (457-mm) clearance horizontally between the fixture and a storage area where combustible material may be stored within the closet.

A flush recessed fixture with a solid lens or a ceiling-mounted fluorescent fixture shall be permitted to be installed provided there is a 6-inch (152-mm) clearance, horizontally, between the fixture and the storage area.

(b) Pendants. Pendants shall not be installed in clothes closets.

410-9. Space for Cove Lighting.
Coves shall have adequate space and shall be so located that lamps and equipment can be properly installed and maintained.

D. Fixture Supports

410-15. Supports—General.
Fixtures, lampholders, rosettes, and receptacles shall be securely supported. A fixture that weighs more than 6 pounds (2.72 kg) or exceeds 16 inches (406 mm) in any dimension shall not be supported by the screw shell of a lampholder.

410-16. Means of Support.
(a) Outlet Boxes. Where the outlet box or fitting will provide adequate support, a fixture shall be attached thereto or be supported as required by Section 370-13 for boxes. A fixture that weighs more than 50 pounds (22.7 kg) shall be supported independently of the outlet box.

(b) Inspection. Fixtures shall be so installed that the connections between the fixture conductors and the circuit conductors can be inspected without requiring the disconnection of any part of the wiring.

Exception: Fixtures connected by attachment plugs and receptacles.

(c) Suspended Ceilings. Framing members of suspended ceiling systems used to support fixtures shall be securely fastened to each other and shall be securely attached to the building structure at appropriate intervals. Fixtures so supported shall be securely fastened to the ceiling framing member by mechanical means, such as bolts, screws, or rivets. Clips identified for use with the type of ceiling framing member(s) and fixture(s) shall also be permitted.

(d) Fixture Studs. Fixture studs that are not a part of outlet boxes, hickeys, tripods, and crowfeet shall be made of steel, malleable iron, or other approved material.

(e) Insulating joints. Insulating joints that are not designed to be mounted with screws or bolts shall have an exterior metal casing, insulated from both screw connections.

(f) Raceway Fittings. Raceway fittings used to support lighting fixtures shall be suitable to support the fixture(s).

(g) Busways. Fixtures shall be permitted to be connected to busways in accordance with Section 364-12.

E. Grounding

410-17. General.
Fixtures and lighting equipment shall be grounded as provided in Part E of this article.

410-18. Exposed Fixture Parts.
(a) With Exposed Conductive Parts. The exposed conductive parts of lighting fixtures and equipment directly wired or attached to outlets supplied by a wiring method which provides an equipment ground shall be grounded.

(b) Made of Insulating Material. Fixtures directly wired or attached to outlets supplied by a wiring method which does not provide a ready means for grounding shall be made of insulating material and shall have no exposed conductive parts.

410-19. Equipment Over 150 Volts to Ground.
(a) Metal Fixtures, Transformers, and Transformer Enclosures. Metal fixtures, transformers, and transformer enclosures on circuits operating at over 150 volts to ground shall be grounded.

(b) Other Exposed Metal Parts. Other exposed metal parts shall be grounded or insulated from ground and other conducting surfaces and inaccessible to unqualified persons.

Exception: Lamp tie wires, mounting screws, clips, and decorative bands on glass lamps spaced not less than 1½ inches (38 mm) from lamp terminals shall not be required to be grounded.

410-20. Equipment Grounding Conductor Attachment. Fixtures with exposed metal parts shall be provided with a means for connecting an equipment grounding conductor for such fixtures.

Exception: This requirement shall become effective April 1, 1982.

410-21. Methods of Grounding. Equipment shall be considered grounded where mechanically connected in a permanent and effective manner to metal raceway, the armor of armored cable, mineral-insulated, metal-sheathed cable, and the continuous sheath of Type MC cable, the grounding conductor in nonmetallic-sheathed cable, or to a separate grounding conductor sized in accordance with Table 250-95, provided that the raceway, armor, or grounding conductor is grounded in a manner specified in Article 250.

F. Wiring of Fixtures

410-22. Fixture Wiring—General. Wiring on or within fixtures shall be neatly arranged and shall not be exposed to physical damage. Excess wiring shall be avoided. Conductors shall be so arranged that they shall not be subjected to temperatures above those for which they are rated.

410-23. Polarization of Fixtures. Fixtures shall be so wired that the screw shells of lampholders will be connected to the same fixture or circuit conductor or terminal. The identified grounded conductor, where connected to a screw-shell lampholder, shall be connected to the screw shell.

410-24. Conductors.

(a) Insulation. Fixtures shall be wired with conductors having insulation suitable for the environmental conditions, current, voltage, and temperature to which the conductors will be subjected.

(b) Conductor Size. Fixture conductors shall not be smaller than No. 18.

For ampacity of fixture wire, see Table 402-5.

For maximum operating temperature and voltage limitation of fixture wires, see Section 402-3.

410-28. Protection of Conductors and Insulation.

(a) Properly Secured. Conductors shall be secured in a manner that will not tend to cut or abrade the insulation.

(b) Protection Through Metal. Conductor insulation shall be protected from abrasion where it passes through metal.

(c) Fixture Stems. Splices and taps shall not be located within fixture arms or stems.

(d) Splices and Taps. No unnecessary splices or taps shall be made within or on a fixture.

For approved means of making connections, see Section 110-14.

(e) Stranding. Stranded conductors shall be used for wiring on fixture chains and on other movable or flexible parts.

(f) Tension. Conductors shall be so arranged that the weight of the fixture or movable parts will not put a tension on the conductors.

L. Receptacles, Cord Connectors, and Attachment Plugs (Caps)

410-56. Rating and Type.

(a) Receptacles. Receptacles installed for the attachment of portable cords shall be rated at not less than 15 amperes, 125 volts, or 15 amperes, 250 volts, and shall be of a type not suitable for use as lampholders.

Exception: The use of receptacles of 10-ampere, 250-volt rating used in nonresidential occupancies for the supply of equipment other than portable hand tools, portable handlamps, and extension cords shall be permitted.

(b) Faceplates. Metal faceplates shall be of ferrous metal not less than 0.030 inch (762 micrometers) in thickness or of nonferrous metal not less than 0.040 inch (1 mm) in thickness. Metal faceplates shall be grounded. Faceplates of insulating material shall be noncombustible and not less than 0.10 inch (2.54 mm) in thickness but shall be permitted to be less than 0.10 inch (2.54 mm) in thickness if formed or reinforced to provide adequate mechanical strength.

(c) Position of Receptacle Faces. After installation, receptacle faces shall be flush with or project from faceplates of insulating material and shall project a minimum of 0.015 inch (381 micrometers) from metal faceplates. Faceplates shall be installed so as to completely cover the opening and seat against the mounting surface. Boxes shall be installed in accordance with Section 370-10.

(d) Attachment Plugs. All 15- and 20-ampere attachment plugs and connectors shall be so constructed that there are no exposed current-carrying parts except the prongs, blades, or pins. The cover for wire terminations shall be a part, which is essential for the operation of an attachment plug or connector (dead-front construction).

(e) Attachment Plug Ejector Mechanisms. Attachment plug ejector mechanisms shall not adversely affect engagement of the blades of the attachment plug with the contacts of the receptacle.

(f) Noninterchangeability. Receptacles, cord connectors, and attachment plugs shall be constructed so that the receptacle or cord connectors will not accept an attachment plug with a different voltage or current rating than that for which the device is intended. Nongrounding-type receptacles and connectors shall not accept grounding-type attachment plugs.

Exception: A 20-ampere T-slot receptacle or cord connector shall be permitted to accept a 15-ampere attachment plug of the same voltage rating.

(g) Conductors. Receptacles rated 20 amperes or less directly connected to aluminum conductors shall be marked CO/ALR.

410-57. Receptacles in Damp or Wet Locations.

(a) Damp Locations. A receptacle installed outdoors in a location protected from the weather or in other damp locations shall have an enclosure for the receptacle that is weatherproof when the receptacle is covered (attachment plug cap not inserted and receptacle covers closed).

An installation suitable for wet locations shall also be considered suitable for damp locations.

A receptacle shall be considered to be in a location protected from the weather where located under roofed open porches, canopies, marquees, and the like, and will not be subjected to a beating rain or water run-off.

(b) Wet Locations. A receptacle installed outdoors where exposed to weather or in other wet locations shall be in a weatherproof enclosure, the integrity of which is not affected when the receptacle is in use (attachment plug cap inserted).

Exception: An enclosure that is weatherproof only when a self-closing receptacle cover is closed shall be permitted to be used for a receptacle installed outdoors where the receptacle is not to be used with other than portable tools or other portable equipment not left connected to the outlet indefinitely.

(c) Protection for Floor Receptacles. Standpipes of floor receptacles shall allow floor-cleaning equipment to be operated without damage to receptacles.

(d) Flush Mounting with Faceplate. The enclosure for a receptacle installed in an outlet box flush-mounted on a wall surface shall be made weatherproof by means of a weatherproof faceplate assembly that provides a watertight connection between the plate and the wall surface.

(e) Installation. A receptacle outlet installed outdoors shall be located so that water accumulation is not likely to touch the outlet cover or plate.

410-58. Grounding-type Receptacles, Adapters, Cord Connectors, and Attachment Plugs.

(a) Grounding Poles. Grounding-type receptacles, cord connectors, and attachment plugs shall be provided with one fixed grounding pole in addition to the circuit poles.

Exception: The grounding contacting pole of grounding-type attachment plugs on the power supply cords of portable handheld, hand-guided, or hand-supported tools or appliances shall be permitted to be of the movable self-restoring type on circuits operating at not over 150 volts between any two conductors nor over 150 volts between any conductor and ground.

(b) Grounding-Pole Identification. Grounding-type receptacles, adapters, cord connections and attachment plugs shall have a means for connection of a grounding conductor to the grounding pole. A terminal for connection to the grounding pole shall be designated by:

(1) A green-colored hexagonal headed or shaped terminal screw or nut, not readily removable; or

(2) A green-colored pressure wire connector body (a wire barrel); or

(3) A similar green-colored connection device in the case of adapters. The grounding terminal of a grounding adapter shall be a green-colored rigid ear, lug, or similar device. The grounding connection shall be so designed that it cannot make contact with current-carrying parts of the receptacle, adapter, or attachment plug. The adapter shall be polarized.

(4) If the terminal for the equipment grounding conductor is not visible, the conductor entrance hole shall be marked with the word "Green" or otherwise identified by a distinctive green color.

(c) Grounding Terminal Use. A grounding terminal or grounding-type device shall not be used for purposes other than grounding.

(d) Grounding-Pole Requirements. Grounding-type attachment plugs and mating cord connectors and receptacles shall be so designed that the grounding connection is made before the current-carrying connections. Grounding-type devices shall be designed so grounding poles of attachment plugs cannot be brought into contact with current-carrying parts of receptacles or cord connectors.

(e) Use. Grounding-type attachment plugs shall be used only where an equipment ground is to be provided.

N. Special Provisions for Flush and Recessed Fixtures

410-64. General. Fixtures installed in recessed cavities in walls or ceilings shall comply with Sections 410-65 through 410-72.

410-65. Temperature.

(a) Combustible Material. Fixtures shall be so installed that adjacent combustible material will not be subjected to temperatures in excess of 90°C (194°F).

(b) Fire-Resistant Construction. Where a fixture is recessed in fire-resistant material in a building of fire-resistant construction, a temperature higher than 90°C (194°F), but not higher than 150°C (302°F), shall be considered acceptable if the fixture is plainly marked that it is approved for that service.

(c) Recessed Incandescent Fixtures. Incandescent fixture shall have thermal protection and shall so be identified as thermally protected.

Exception No. 1: Recessed incandescent fixtures identified for use and installed in poured concrete.

Exception No. 2: Recessed incandescent fixtures identified as suitable for installation in cavities where the thermal insulation will be in direct contact with the fixture.

The requirements of Section 410-65(c) shall become effective April 1, 1982.

410-66. Clearance. Recessed portions of enclosures, other than at points of support, shall be spaced at least ½ inch (12.7 mm) from combustible material. Thermal insulation shall not be installed within 3 inches (76 mm) of the recessed fixture enclosure, wiring compartment, or ballast and shall not be so installed above the fixture as to entrap heat and prevent the free circulation of air unless the fixture is otherwise identified for installation within thermal insulation.

410-67. Wiring.

(a) General. Conductors having insulation suitable for the temperature encountered shall be used.

(b) Circuit Conductors. Branch-circuit conductors having an insulation suitable for the temperature encountered shall be permitted to terminate in the fixture.

(c) Tap Conductors. Tap conductors of a type suitable for the temperature encountered shall be permitted to run from the fixture terminal connection to an outlet box placed at least

1 foot (305 mm) from the fixture. Such tap conductors shall be in a suitable metal raceway of at least 4 feet (1.22 m) but not more than 6 feet (1.83 m) in length.

P. Construction of Flush and Recessed Fixtures

410-68. Temperature. Fixtures shall be so constructed that adjacent combustible material will not be subject to temperatures in excess of 90°C (194°F).

410-69. Enclosure. Sheet metal enclosures shall be protected against corrosion and shall not be less than No. 22 MSG.

Exception: Where a wireway cover is within the No. 22 MSG enclosure, it shall be permitted to be of No. 24 MSG metal.

410-70. Lamp Wattage Marking. Incandescent lamp fixtures shall be marked to indicate the maximum allowable wattage of lamps. The markings shall be permanently installed, in letters at least ¼ inch (6.35 mm) high, and shall be located where visible during relamping.

410-71. Solder Prohibited. No solder shall be used in the construction of a fixture box.

410-72. Lampholders. Lampholders of the screw-shell type shall be of porcelain or other suitable insulating materials. Where used, cements shall be of the high-heat type.

Q. Special Provisions for Electric-Discharge Lighting Systems of 1000 Volts or Less

410-76. Fixture Mounting.
(a) **Exposed Ballasts.** Fixtures having exposed ballasts or transformers shall be so installed that such ballasts or transformers will not be in contact with combustible material.
(b) **Combustible Low-Density Cellulose Fiberboard.** Where a surface-mounted fixture containing a ballast is to be installed on combustible low-density cellulose fiberboard, it shall be approved for this condition or shall be spaced not less than 1½ inches (38 mm) from the surface of the fiberboard. Where such fixtures are partially or wholly recessed, the provisions of Sections 410-64 through 410-72 shall apply.

Combustible low-density cellulose fiberboard includes sheets, panels, and tiles that have a density of 20 pounds per cubic foot (320.36 kg/cu m) or less, and that are formed of bonded plant fiber material but does not include solid or laminated wood, nor fiberboard that has a density in excess of 20 pounds per cubic foot (320.36 kg/cu m) or is a material that has been integrally treated with fire-retarding chemicals to the degree that the flame spread in any plane of the material will not exceed 25, determined in accordance with tests for surface burning characteristics of building materials. See Method of Test for Surface Burning Characteristics of Building Materials, ANSI A2.5-1977.

410-77. Equipment Not Integral with Fixture.
(a) **Metal Cabinets.** Auxiliary equipment, including reactors, capacitors, resistors, and similar equipment, where not installed as part of a lighting fixture assembly, shall be enclosed in accessible, permanently installed metal cabinets.
(b) **Separate Mounting.** Separately mounted ballasts that are intended for direct connection to a wiring system shall not be required to be separately enclosed.

410-78. Autotransformers. An autotransformer which is used to raise the voltage to more than 300 volts, as part of a ballast for supplying lighting units, shall be supplied only by a grounded system.

410-79. Switches. Snap switches shall comply with Section 380-14.